D0507678

Also in the *Globalizing Sport Studies* series:

Global Media Sport

Flows, Forms and Futures

David Rowe

BLOOMSBURY ACADEMIC

First published in 2011 by

Bloomsbury Academic
an imprint of Bloomsbury Publishing Plc
50 Bedford Square, London WC1B 3DP, UK
and
175 Fifth Avenue, New York, NY 10010, USA

CIP records for this book are available from the British Library and the
Library of Congress

ISBN 978-1-84966-070-9 (hardback)
ISBN 978-1-84966-675-6 (ebook)

This book is produced using paper that is made from wood grown in managed,
sustainable forests. It is natural, renewable and recyclable. The logging and
manufacturing processes conform to the Environmental regulations of
the country of origin.

Printed and bound in Great Britain by the MPG Books Group, Bodmin, Cornwall

Cover design: Burge Agency

www.bloomsburyacademic.com

To Kenneth Charles Rowe (1920–2004)
and Margaret Jean Rowe

Contents

Globalizing Sport Studies
Series Editor's Preface

There is now a considerable amount of expertise nationally and internationally in the social scientific and cultural analysis of sport in relation to the economy and society more generally. Contemporary research topics, such as sport and social justice, science and technology and sport, global social movements and sport, sports mega-events, sports participation and engagement and the role of sport in social development, suggest that sport and social relations need to be understood in non-Western developing economies, as well as European, North American and other advanced capitalist societies. The current high global visibility of sport makes this an excellent time to launch a major new book series that takes sport seriously, and makes this research accessible to a wide readership.

The series *Globalizing Sport Studies* is thus in line with a massive growth of academic expertise, research output and public interest in sport worldwide. At the same time it seeks to use the latest developments in technology and the economics of publishing to reflect the most innovative research into sport in society currently underway in the world. The series is multi-disciplinary, although primarily based on the social sciences and cultural studies approaches to sport.

The broad aims of the series are to: *act* as a knowledge hub for social scientific and cultural studies research in sport, including, but not exclusively, anthropological, economic, geographic, historical, political science and sociological studies; *contribute* to the expanding field of research on sport in society in the United Kingdom and internationally by focussing on sport at regional, national and international levels; *create* a series for both senior and more junior researchers that will become synonymous with cutting edge research, scholarly opportunities and academic development; *promote* innovative discipline-based, multi-, inter- and trans-disciplinary theoretical and methodological approaches to researching sport in society; *provide* an English language outlet for high quality non-English writing on sport in society; *publish* broad overviews, original empirical research studies and classic studies from non-English sources; and thus attempt to *realise* the potential for *globalizing* sport studies through open content licensing with 'Creative Commons'.

The relationship between the mass media and sport has always been an important one, and the media have helped to construct what is meant by sport. In the early part of the nineteenth century 'sport' was a word restricted to describing field sport (hunting, shooting and fishing) and what later became known as 'cruel' sports, such as bull and bear baiting and cock fighting. At the end of the nineteenth century the newly forming modern press assisted in boundary marking and boundary shifting of what was defined as sport, and even what a champion was. During the twentieth century commercial leisure expanded in many ways, but the mass media, especially television, has been a central factor and formulator of sporting culture from the mid-1950s onward. The philosophical question – 'what is, and what is not, sport?' – has been decided pragmatically by what appears in the sport sections of newspapers or in radio or television broadcasts.

Whilst a good case can be made for maintaining a distinction between the mass mediated form of spectacular sport and sport as a form of cultural life outside of its purely symbolic representation, in the past twenty years there has been an enormous increase in the amount of sport on television and covered in the press, radio and other forms of media throughout developing economies as well as the advanced capitalist economies. In these circumstances it becomes necessary to think about media sport as a global and globalizing phenomenon.

It is with great delight therefore that I write this preface to David Rowe's book on *Global Media Sport*. It is a very engagingly written and accomplished work that covers a lot of ground and makes many insightful analytical observations along the way. This is a book that is exceptionally rich in detail and provides a careful examination of many of the issues relating to media and globalisation that many other writers overlook – such as the economics of media sport, contestation over sports content, and the growth of (new) media sport audiences in light of the impact of new media technologies. The book is full of excellent, and at times humorous, contemporary examples that follow how sports change. This is a sociological and scholarly piece of work that at the same time will be attractive to a broad audience.

John Horne, Preston and Edinburgh 2011

Acknowledgements

Of all the difficult tasks in writing a book, none is more searching than selecting for mention those people and organizations that have contributed most to it. I thank first my estimable academic colleagues at the Centre for Cultural Research (soon to be members of a shiny new Institute for Culture and Society), which since 2006 has been a most hospitable and highly stimulating place to work – a rare combination. In particular, I acknowledge Founding Director Ien Ang's extraordinary institution-building capacity and her persuasiveness in getting me on the bus. Amongst the team of splendid research support staff, Maree O'Neill and Reena Dobson kept me afloat with unstinting support and eventide humour, especially during my action-packed, three-year term as director, while Tulika Dubey has combined calming efficiency with handy *vox pops* on Indian cricket sentiment. The research assistants who devoted their skills and talent to different aspects of this work – Callum Gilmour, Kylie Brass, Stephanie Alice Baker and Vibha Bhattarai Upadhyay – were valuable collaborators and way more than hired hands.

The Australian Research Council funded two Discovery grants that were crucial to the book: 'Handling the "Battering Ram": Rupert Murdoch, News Corporation and the Global Contest for Dominance in Sports Television' (DP0556973) and 'Struggling for Possession: The Control and Use of Online Media Sport' (DP0877777, with Brett Hutchins).

I also thank the amiably encouraging Series Editor John Horne for pitching the idea, and Emily Salz for helping to realize it, as well as the anonymous readers for constructive suggestions aimed at improving the final book. Only too painfully aware of its limitations, I resort to that classical sociological defence as articulated by Monty Python: 'It's a fair cop, but society is to blame'. Among those who contributed in diverse, unimpeachable ways to my professional and personal sustainability I mention this time, on this page: Alina Bernstein, Andy Billings, Raymond Boyle, Brett Hutchins, Geoff Lawrence, Jim McKay, Toby Miller, Luo Qing, Andy Ruddock, Jay Scherer, Larry Wenner and Garry Whannel. Sounding board and psyche repair duties were performed with distinction by Deborah Stevenson. There are many others who have, lamentably, gone unacknowledged here. Daniel and Madeleine Rowe were, as ever, deserving of completely objective parental pride, and the Rowes, Henders and Hurleys of the United Kingdom (with the lovely addition of Francesca) kept authorial feet on the ground as only families can.

Rowe, D (2011). Global Media sport Flows, forms and futures. London: Bloomsbury Academic. "Then page number"

1

Arrivals Hall Message

Global media, global sport

Touching the World of Screens

Towards the end of the last century, the faintly glimpsed idea of global media sport began to take shape. Of course, the media had, following the development of satellite technology in the era following the 1964 Tokyo Olympics (Tagsold 2009), been carrying real-time moving images of sport around the world for some time. But *global* carried other connotations when discussing media and sport that went far beyond the idea of the merely *international*. A global media sport suggests such qualities as omnipresence, inescapability and universal accessibility and, consequently, the substantial erosion of the particularities and peculiarities of the local. As satellite transmission became routine and, in particular, the *fin de siècle* Internet matured as a multidirectional, multimedia vector of sport, the possibility of global media sport emerged. It is important to say possibility rather than reality here, in resisting the tendency among many Western commentators to forget that broadcasting, telephony and computing still remain unavailable to the domestic dwellings and other inhabited spaces of billions of this planet's citizens (*Sociological Inquiry* 2010). Nonetheless, for many other people, not all of whom are Western or affluent, the cultural forms and experiences surrounding media sport have become so familiar that engagement with them are now demanded as of right (Scherer and Whitson 2009).

Thus, free-to-air television viewing of major media sports events like the Olympic Games and the World Cup of Association Football is now widely regarded as a sign of membership of the 'human family' (Scherer and Rowe 2012). Their respective governing bodies, the International Olympic Committee (IOC) and the Fédération Internationale de Football Association (FIFA), both emphasize the importance of taking a global role on behalf of both sports participants and spectators. In FIFA's (2010a) mission statement there is a pledge to '[d]evelop the game, touch the world, build a better future' in using the sport of football as a tool of social progress across the globe:

> We see it as our mission to contribute towards building a better future for the world by using the power and popularity of football. This mission gives meaning and direction to each and every activity that FIFA is involved in – football being an integrated part of our society …

> Touch the world. Take world-class football action and passion at all levels to every corner of the planet through our 208 member associations. The broad

range of competitions shows the many faces of football, spearheaded by the FIFA World Cup™.

There is, it will be noted, some irony in the placement of such edifying sentiments alongside the legally enforceable trademark protection of the competition name and in the light of some of the critical literature on FIFA's structure and operations (e.g. Jennings 2006; Sugden and Tomlinson 1999a, 2003). Nonetheless, it is a clear indication of global ambition and scope in taking the action to every corner of planet earth – and by a body with more member associations than the United Nations – through both physical practice and media representation.

Similarly, the IOC stakes a grand claim for its global reach. Section 49(1) of the current Olympic Charter (which came into force on 11 February 2010), 'Media Coverage of the Olympic Games', declares that '[t]he IOC takes all necessary steps in order to ensure the fullest coverage by the different media and the widest possible audience in the world for the Olympic Games' (IOC 2010: 96). However, the IOC's enthusiastic patrolling of its lucrative broadcast (and other media) rights, and tight control over media representation of the Olympics, may be clearly in conflict with the 'fullest coverage' as indicated by the following law and bye-laws of its Charter:

> 2. All decisions concerning the coverage of the Olympic Games by the media rest within the competence of the IOC.

Bye-law to Rule 49

> 1 It is an objective of the Olympic Movement that, through its contents, the media coverage of the Olympic Games should spread and promote the principles and values of Olympism.
>
> 2 The IOC Executive Board establishes all technical regulations and requirements regarding media coverage of the Olympic Games in an IOC Media Guide, which forms an integral part of the Host City Contract. The contents of the IOC Media Guide, and all other instructions of the IOC Executive Board, are binding for any and all persons involved in media coverage of the Olympic Games.
>
> 3 Only those persons accredited as media may act as journalists, reporters or in any other media capacity. Under no circumstances, throughout the duration of the Olympic Games, may any athlete, coach, official, press attaché or any other accredited participant act as a journalist or in any other media capacity. (IOC 2010: 96–7)

Claiming absolute 'competence' over Olympic media matters, including enforcing a binding contract and guide, and determining who can be accredited as a journalist are practices of questionable consistency with the 'principles and values of Olympism' and are in various ways at odds with the maximization of media coverage across the globe. But, as with FIFA (another keen seller of massive broadcast and other media rights), it is important that the IOC signals its commitment to broad access to coverage of its major sports events. Here it can be seen how the globalization of sport through the media creates dynamic tensions between rights and rewards, informal pleasures and organized production. The passage of sport under modernity from village green (Elias and Dunning 1986) to global village (Giulianotti and Robertson 2007; Maguire 1999) has not only involved the mutation of sport but also profoundly affected the societies and cultures that have housed and received it.

As it has become more global, media sport has become both increasingly familiar and more difficult to grasp. Acknowledgements of spectacular global media sport audiences, while rather breathlessly announced, have become almost routine. Media research companies and sports organizations are quick to inform the world of the latest records in TV sport viewing. For example, soon after the end of the Beijing Olympics, Neilsen (2008) declared,

> The 2008 Beijing Olympics set many world records, with the latest being the Most Watched Games ever. According to latest intelligence from The Nielsen Company, the Beijing Olympic Games attracted the cumulative eyeballs of 4.7 billion viewers over the 17 days from August 8 to August 24, 'out-viewing' the 3.9 billion who followed the Athens 2004 Games by 21 percent, and the 3.6 billion who tuned in to the Sydney Games in 2000 by 31 percent, or 1.1 billion additional viewers.

> The 4.7 billion viewers who accessed television coverage of the Beijing Olympics officially translates into approximately 70 percent of the world's population, or more than two in every three people globally.

In the competition for the biggest television sport audience both in terms of earlier World Cups and other sports events, FIFA subsequently estimated after South Africa 2010 that 'around 700 million people watched the final live. If that is correct, the match would beat out the estimated 600 million that caught the opening ceremony at the 2008 Beijing Olympics and would be on par, or slightly above, the 700 million that watched the World Cup final four years ago' (Reuters 2010). But broadcast television is now only a part (albeit still a – probably the – pivotal one) of the media sport landscape, and FIFA (2010b) has also emphasized this:

> Multimedia platforms proved central to fans' enjoyment of the 2010 FIFA World Cup™ as FIFA – through its web and Twitter feeds – successfully delivered a range of complementary digital experiences to football enthusiasts around the world.

> In addition to the many millions of fans watching the matches on TV, over 220,000 people followed FIFA's official tweets on Twitter, while members of the five million-strong FIFA.com Club swapped 120 million virtual stickers and made over one million comments on the website as they debated the finer points of the tournament.

> With its wide variety of content and interactivity over the course of the tournament's 31 days, FIFA.com attracted over 250 million visits – approximately 150 million unique users, triggering seven billion page views: 410 million of those page views were recorded in a single day. When England and the USA played

simultaneously, FIFA.com technicians reported a throughput of 1,000,000 hits per second at the height of the activity.

The level of demand for FIFA's online content has surpassed FIFA's expectations. FIFA.com welcomed three times more unique users than in 2006, serving pages to 150 million people over the course of the 2010 FIFA World Cup™. FIFA exceeded forecasts for page impressions by 1.5 billion. The 2010 FIFA World Cup South Africa™ has witnessed a new level of digital engagement from fans across the globe.

Thus, simple 'eyeball on TV screen' count is now complemented by new, rather esoteric measures of global media attention, such as 'unique views' and 'page impressions'. It is indicative of the growth of the 'media sports cultural complex', a concept that I have developed previously (Rowe 2004a) to describe the profound, systematic and dynamic integration of media and sport over the past century. This sociocultural formation, like sport itself, first emerged in Western societies and spread across the world as imperialism, colonialism, trade, capitalist expansion and cultural diffusion fostered international sporting competition, media communication and sport industry development. In the twenty-first century, globalization of media sport is supplanting the predominantly uni-directional process of internationalization and Western cultural exportation that preceded it, creating complex flows of sports, competitions, teams, athletes, genres, images, fan communities, audience formations and mediated messages (Rowe and Gilmour 2009). As media sport has globalized, it occupies increasing sociocultural space not only in the sphere of physical activity and popular entertainment but also in the domains of intercultural relations, politics and diplomacy. It is, therefore, a phenomenon that demands critical analytical attention that goes well beyond the rather banal shibboleths in common currency, such as 'sport is now a business', 'the media have taken over sport' or 'sport is a vehicle for greater understanding between nations'. Global media sport, it should be acknowledged, is paradoxically both prone and resistant to grand summations of its arrival and nature.

I have also in other places (solely and with co-authors) addressed in greater detail the phenomenon of global media sport as it is related, in turn, to three major sociocultural processes: 'globalization', 'mediatization' and 'sportification' (Miller et al. 2001; Rowe 2004a, 2011a). In this book I will try to avoid replaying or unnecessarily elaborating on them – academic books on media sport should not resemble many of the sport texts that they are meant to analyse. Instead, I will seek to tease out various dimensions of them in the ensuing chapters, describing and analysing their flows, forms and futures in a manner intended to allow readers to match and build on their interests and orientations in the interdisciplinary field of the social sciences and humanities. This is, therefore, a research-driven work that sets out to foster more informed, reflexive research and scholarship. The simultaneously enduring and evanescent phenomenon of global media sport can be approached as if it is predictable and known (or even the now infamous 'unknown unknowns' – Horne 2007) or as so ever-changing and fragmented as to be permanently elusive. Certainly, there are apparent continuities and discontinuities, the strategic balance of which can be difficult to discern. My aim here is to demonstrate their coexistence in a manner that tries to avoid both complacency and exaggeration, but also *a priori* judgment and *post hoc* rationalization.

To put it very briefly at this point, a book with the primary title *Global Media Sport* connects an adjective with two nouns. 'Global' expresses both reach and circumstance, whereby spaces, jurisdictions, institutions, protocols and practices have intermeshed in a variety of ways (Anheier and Isar 2010). 'Media' refer to means of communication, the vehicles through which sociocultural phenomena are symbolically 'carried' across space, time and the barriers of historical and social circumstance (Curran 2010). 'Sport' here is the constellation of structures, practices, values and sentiments that passes in and through the global by means of the media (Bernstein and Blain 2003). But these are not stable entities that interact in predictable ways as just so many collisions and points of contact. What we understand by the global cannot be neatly distinguished from the vectors (including media) and cultural constituents (sport) that comprise it, any more than media and sport can be insulated from the globalizing processes that are constantly working on them, both voluntarily and as disruptive forces to be, with variable degrees of success, resisted or countered (Miller *et al.* 2001). These complex relationships lead us to the subtitle, which seeks to capture the 'flows' across global media sport terrains, the 'forms' that are manifest and in a constant state of reconfiguration and renewal, and the 'futures' that many try to predict and prepare for but which are so difficult to anticipate (e.g. few if any media sport futurists 'picked' the impact of social networking on sport communication (Hutchins 2011)) and which rely on highly contested histories and projections (Whannel 2008).

An additional difficulty, as in all social science, is that the analyst is both inside and outside what is being analysed and so is affected by the global media sport that they would like, magisterially, to appraise from afar. By way of illustrative anecdote, I cite the case of a conversation with the proprietor of isolated holiday cabins prior to the Sydney 2000 Olympics. Each could have been booked several times over, I was informed, as her customers sought refuge from the Games in a place that received no television, radio, fixed or mobile telephone communication. Others had decided to leave the country for the duration. To be required to go to such lengths to avoid mega media sports events strikingly demonstrates how difficult it is to hide from them – while many more people will enthusiastically immerse themselves in media sport coverage or be routinely exposed to it as a 'natural' part of their life world. This book, then, is dedicated to the task of unravelling some of the mysteries and exposing several unwarranted certainties about a global media sports cultural complex that is increasingly taking on the appearance of now being forever with us – and, for those born into it, perhaps as having always been so. In so doing, it exposes the preposterous nature of the claim to command the field of global media sport. It is impossible to do justice to its sprawling canvas, wild complexity and ever-changing terrain. I have concentrated mainly on areas that I know to some degree (with all attendant limitations), rather than touching on lightly acquainted subjects before passing through as if engaged in some virtual sport tourism simulation of a visit to World Expo, acquiring the passport stamp of each pavilion while barely pausing to absorb the surroundings. There is, then, no claim to comprehensiveness here, but it is hoped that *Global Media Sport: Flows, Forms and Futures* will offer something for readers and researchers to bounce off, filling in the gaps, highlighting counter-examples, challenging perspectives and conclusions. Its impulse is dialogical rather than categorical, intending to open up an interdisciplinary space that will suggest new avenues of inquiry. But, to use one of many available sporting metaphors, how can pole and grid positions be determined among contending analytical starters?

Unfolding *Global Media Sport*

Deciding where to start in analysing global media sport does not so much demand a search for origins as a point of entry into an object that won't stay still, a little analogous to getting onto a moving carousel. An orthodox Marxist approach or, indeed, one dedicated to the celebration of a capitalist ethic, would begin with its economics – its material production and consumption. To begin by addressing 'filthy lucre' isn't very romantic, but the world of sport is given over enough already to romantic mythology without any unnecessary encouragement. More importantly, it is argued in this book that for all the many pleasures surrounding sport and the sociable uses to which it can be put – attractions to which this author is by no means immune – it is undeniable that the organized, competitive physical play that in the nineteenth century became what we call sport (Elias and Dunning 1986) was given enormous impetus by material forces beyond any potential intrinsic popular appeal. The ready compatibility of sport with the emerging leisure, media and advertising industries (Horne 2006) saw, eventually, a flood of capital into sport and a powerful platform of visibility that conferred very considerable developmental advantages on it (Clarke and Critcher 1985), not least through sport's key role in globalization.

As noted above, the media sport spectacle is so compelling for many – and in other respects unavoidable by all – that its economic substructure is incompletely understood by many sports fans and even some critical sports theorists. There is a common complaint that 'sport is now just a business' but widespread uncertainty as to who or what actually owns and controls it. International sports organizations, individual clubs, media and communications corporations, sponsors and advertisers, investment companies, entrepreneurs, national governments and fan groups can all claim some economic (as well as affective) stake in sport. The development of the global media sports cultural complex has made the economics of sport more complicated and difficult to isolate from other areas of industrial and financial activity. For this reason, it is useful to start with the 'economic base', not because it is argued that sport is primarily economic accumulation 'dressed up' as culture but because it is impossible to consider its global development in mediated form without acknowledging the direct and indirect impingement of economic forces that accelerated its global cultural availability. In Chapter 2, 'Markets in Movement: Economic Dimensions of the Media Sport Spectacle', then, I seek to provide the political economic underpinning of the book by critically analysing the material dynamics of a contemporary sport terrain in which capital is generated, exchanged and transformed in diverse, multidimensional ways, enriching some but exploiting many others. Global media sport is shown to be a significant 'player' in current processes and debates surrounding such key economic issues as the commodification of physical culture, the circulation of labour and the distribution of wealth.

It is apparent in addressing the economics of global media sport that despite frequent (though disputed) claims that television in general, and as a consequence broadcast television sport in particular, is in terminal decline given the growth of non-broadcast digital technologies such as the Internet and mobile telephony (Katz and Scannell 2009), television remains unquestionably the most important sport medium in the second decade of the twenty-first century. Having for over half a century underwritten sport's economy and established its global audience, there is as yet no convincing sign that, judging by both the massive audience figures cited above and the escalating broadcast rights fees that key sports can command (Klayman 2008), television is being marginalized in sport. Broadcast television is, though, sharing the audio-visual coverage of sport with new(er) media with which it is becoming increasingly integrated rather than alienated (Hutchins and Rowe 2009a, 2012). Chapter 3 'Television: Wider Screens, Narrower Visions?', then, addresses the condition of sports television, in particular contestation over sports content and audience access. It examines the relationship between sports television as a national cultural resource and as an internationally traded commodity, and also questions its role as a dominant twentieth-century technology that both distributes and seeks to ration premium sports content on a regional/national basis in a post-millennial era of global, networked, digital, mobile media communication. The implications of these changes for rights of cultural (as opposed to more traditionally conceived political or economic) citizenship (Miller 2006) pertaining to media sport are interrogated, alongside a critical appraisal of the sport TV viewing experiences of audiences in different *milieux* across the globe.

Having pondered – though displayed some scepticism towards – the imminent end of the hegemony of sports television in the previous chapter, Chapter 4, 'Digital Media, Networking and Executive Fandom', considers in greater detail the new, converged media technologies that facilitate both the globalization of sport and the transformation of media sport reception and audience relations. Here there is a focus on the consequences of a move from the one-to-many, single medium framework of sport reception traditionally offered by television to the many-to-many possibilities of Internet-enabled sport viewing 'participation'. This chapter considers the positive possibilities and pitfalls of a post-broadcast era of media sport, including the significance of a 'digital divide' that may exacerbate existing inequalities of cultural citizenship regarding access to media sport that were already extant in a predominantly analogue broadcast environment and became more so as subscription television displaced free-to-air broadcasting in many national sports contexts. The emergence of information and communication technology-facilitated active global fandom is discussed here, using the recent example of MyFootballClub (MYFC 2011), which claims to be the 'world's first and only web-community owned football club'. In so doing, the relationship of media sport audiences and fan bases to new forms of space and place is considered, and its implications for contemporary sport reassessed.

After appraising the contemporary position of television, new media technologies and modes of what I call 'executive' fandom in global sport, the discussion turns to the exchange of media sport texts and affiliations in different directions across the globe. Chapter 5, 'From West to East – and Back Again', is concerned with the ways in which media sport has 'broken out' of nations in some respects and become a regular part of everyday media consumption in new territories. The first cases examined present a fairly traditional export model of media sport from West to East in the form of English Premier League Football and American basketball, and the response from the 'receiving' context in those sports. The focus then turns to countervailing trends through linked case studies of Indian Premier League cricket and the dominant role of India in world cricket and also the staging of global mega media sports events like the 2008 Beijing Olympics and the 2010 World Cup of association football in South Africa. In these instances, current power within media sport is both reproduced and challenged. The chapter concludes with an assessment of the 'balance of power' in the global media sports cultural complex, seeking to establish the extent to which Western and Northern hemispheric media sport power has been strengthened, maintained, challenged or eroded in the face of developments in the global East and South.

The book then engages in a closer analysis of the sociocultural and political implications of these developments. In Chapter 6, 'Tactical Manoeuvres, Public Relations Disasters and the Global Sport Scandal', the globalization of media sport described and analysed in the previous chapters is shown to resonate far beyond the sporting sphere *per se*. Sport, it is demonstrated, is routinely harnessed as a popular political force, both in the interests of international cooperation and friendship and in the fostering of nationalism and, on occasions, national chauvinism and xenophobia. It has been used as a vehicle for international relations (as, famously, in the case of the US Nixon administration's 'ping-pong diplomacy' in the early 1970s) and as a means of signalling arrival on the global 'stage' (as occurred with the 1988 Seoul and 2008 Beijing Olympics). But the global media sports cultural complex can be unpredictable and confound well-laid plans of those who seek to use it to their advantage. For example, global media coverage of Tibet protests against China during the torch relay in the lead up to the 2008 Beijing Olympics demonstrates how nation state aspirations can go awry. Regarding a commercial corporation, the persistent use of various media to criticize Nike's (and its subcontractors') treatment of its Asian workers in leisurewear factories can turn slogans such as 'Just Do It' on their head. For sport celebrities who have become their own corporations, such as Tiger Woods, global visibility can turn quickly from celebration to notoriety through off-field misconduct, while on-field transgressions (e.g. Zinedine Zidane's head butt of Marco Materazzi during the 2006 World Cup Final) can precipitate global debates about the politics of 'race' (*New Formations* 2007). It is argued that such volatile incidents highlight the ways in which media sport can operate as an instant vehicle for global political discourse of a particularly intense and sometimes deeply resonant kind.

Global Media Sport: Flows, Forms and Futures then concludes with 'Departure Lounge Note: Convulsions, Continuities and Campaigns' (Chapter 7) in reflecting on the condition of the contemporary global media sports cultural complex and attempting to discern its principal trends and developments. This discussion makes a case for a more sophisticated analytical understanding of globalizing and localizing forces in sport that takes appropriate account of its histories, political economic processes and sociocultural dynamics. It then briefly canvasses sites of intervention in the global cultural politics of media sport in the defence and promotion of existing and emerging rights of cultural citizenship.

It is important to emphasize continually matters of power and equality because there is a danger that, as noted earlier, global media sport can seem to be so familiar through omnipresence, and remorseless in its development, as to encourage blasé responses to it. By this I mean that, in the affluent West and increasingly in the burgeoning Asia-Pacific region, citizens have become increasingly accustomed to sport as a compulsorily installed feature of the cultural furniture. This does not mean that it is universally approved of, but its presence is mainly treated with a combination of enthusiasm and resignation. As a result, it becomes harder to problematize global media sport in any thoroughgoing, critically reflective and socially interventionist way. Ironically, therefore, one of the most rapidly changing aspects of contemporary global culture can be treated as immoveable and dismissed with the comfortingly passive response that 'it was ever thus'. But it is important to deconstruct rather than parrot such shibboleths. The idea that the global is a single, irreversible, consistent process is disempowering, just as the notion that there is a single entity going under the rubric of 'the media' that acts in a predictable, preordained way is profoundly misleading and deters legitimate demands for improvement and reform. The familiar suggestion that there is a single set of physical practices called sport handed down in an unbroken line from the Ancient Greeks misunderstands how historically contingent and mutable physical culture can be and certainly fails to recognize the arbitrariness of sporting classification and the structural processes that privilege some sporting forms at the expense of others. Such 'distinctions' (Bourdieu 1978, 1984) are not merely questions of and for sport – they range across the social spectrum and up and down its hierarchies, deeply intertwined with matters of power and the social as they apply to class, gender, 'race', ethnicity, sexuality, age, the body and so on. Global media sport, then, both in terms of individual constituent parts and elements in constant interplay, can never be, whatever the heuristic temptations, taken for granted as a unitary, predictable phenomenon. In the following pages it is hoped that this voyage around the global media sports cultural complex, and search for passages between its continental masses, will provide not just some useful maps but also a companionate guide to a subject that, by turns, exhilarates and infuriates.

The metaphors of space and mobility deployed above chime with the subject of the book in a range of ways. Sports contests are always 'emplaced' but where they are held and in what kinds of spatial context are subjects of constant contestation: cities and nations bid for mega events; sports stadia are embroiled in competition over land use; sport is used as a justification for urban redevelopment and so on (*International Journal of Cultural Policy* 2008). Radiating outwards from the stadium, circuit or course – the spaces in which sporting motion takes place – are those in which sport is organized and administered, and the domiciles of local fans. But, as will be argued throughout, the relationship between sport and the local is becoming more attenuated and complex. The athletes who comprise sport's most conspicuous and valuable labour market are drawn, often for short periods, from distant places, as, increasingly, are their employers and sponsors. In some sports they are almost perpetually 'on the road' – the tennis year approved by the Association of Tennis Professionals (ATP), for example, is now substantially free of the restrictions of the Northern hemisphere winter, as lucrative tournaments in the southern hemisphere encourage players to play for eleven months per year – with obvious consequences for 'wear and tear' on their bodies and minds (Associated Press 2010). For most people involved with sport, though, the most important space is anywhere in front of a screen, with the 'immaterial' signs of sports (visual, aural, textual) conveyed with greater facility and rapidity across the globe. Those sport screens are still dominated by broadcast television, but the restrictions imposed on viewer mobility imposed by signals and aerials, and then by desktop computers, are themselves becoming outmoded (Johnson *et al*. 2011). Such diverse twenty-first-century mobilities disturb and reconfigure established relationships between places, people, objects and organizational units (Urry 2003, 2007), proposing new 'senses of sport' that render problematic many of its received wisdoms and routine.

In addressing the elusive subject of immobilities and mobilities in media sport, I have avoided a conventional summary and review of globalization theory in this work. This task has been performed elsewhere (e.g. Miller *et al*. 2001; Rowe 2003), and it is preferred to set aside this task in favour of a more direct engagement with the book's primary objects of analysis – sport and media. Thus, for example, the analytical relationships between globalization and cultural imperialism, or globalization and mediatization, are intended to emerge out of specific encounters with the field of global sport. This approach is as much about what the study of sport reveals about globalization and mediatization as the reverse, although to seek to isolate them conceptually and empirically in a quest for causality would be a denial of their interdependence. It would also point to a rather well-worn path of 'glossing' the main positions and work that constitute the globalization canon. As Ramaswami Harindranath (2006: 8) has argued in a work that questions this approach,

Academic publication on the subject of globalization has become a veritable publishing industry, with particular names associated with specific debates – Giddens, Beck, Robertson, Castells, Harvey, Jameson – to name only the best known, whose contributions have, through subsequent interventions by other academics and through discussions in classrooms, formed a canon of literature on the subject.

Harindranath, in presenting non-Western perspectives on 'global cultures', determines to 'bring to the table voices, both academic and cultural, from outside the canon, as well as concerns and anxieties that normally fall outside the purview of the received wisdom on globalization' (Harindranath 2006: 8). While several of these canonical names can be found in this book, it is plausible to argue that a canon of literature on the subject of sport, media and globalization also now exists, that there is something of a 'received wisdom' and, perhaps, that this author is part of it, certainly within the Anglophone world. It is, though, hoped that what follows is not a defence or elaboration of this canon but an invitation, in the familiar language of sports commentary, to take it on, take it apart and take it to a new level.

2

Markets in Movement

Economic dimensions of the media sport spectacle

Showing the money, tracking the beneficiaries

Some snatches of dialogue in a small number of films enter popular consciousness and speech as catchphrases. In the 1983 film *Sudden Impact*, for example, Clint Eastwood's character (Harry Callahan) entreats an armed robber to 'go ahead, make my day', and it was not long before it was inserted into many and varied everyday conversations. The sports film genre has supplied its fair share of catchphrases, including *Knute Rockne* and *All American* (1940), with its famous call to 'win just one for the Gipper' (a reference to a gridiron player George Gipp, played in the film by the future US President Ronald Reagan, for whom it became a political slogan and nickname). The expostulation 'show me the money!' in the 1996 film about an eponymous sports agent, *Jerry Maguire*, is distinguished by both its frequent use in the media and in casual talk, and by its applicability to the economics of global media sport. That the agent (played by Tom Cruise) is made repeatedly to shout the demand, down the telephone and at ever increasing volume, by African American footballer Rod Tidwell (played by Cuba Gooding Jr), is a negation in popular film of the romantic notion that sport is played for its own sake (Rowe 1998). It is also, as will be argued below, something of an inversion of the wider structures of racialized exploitation that characterize much of the sports world. The money in global media sport is both highly visible and concentrated in a few hands. It is spread around the globe but tends to 'stick' in familiar places and rapidly to disappear in others. In the following discussion, I will revisit the history of the political economy of sport, also working outwards inductively from some instructive cases that throw light on how it has become progressively commercial, mediated and global.

In so doing, it is important not to reduce sport as culture to sport as capital accumulation, as if a grasp of the latter is sufficient to understand sport as a sociocultural institution and cultural form. The history of sport is characterized by continuing conflict over commoditization just as it is in other areas of popular culture, such as rock music, which both emerged under capitalism and retained elements of its formative ethos critiquing it (Frith 1978). Questions of community, authenticity and resistance consistently come to the fore across popular culture (Fiske 1989), with ambivalence about cultural capitalism symptomatic of the resilient strain of romanticization that jars with commercial exploitation when it is too starkly exposed. Contemporary sport contains what Raymond Williams (1977) describes as 'dominant', 'residual' and 'emergent' elements within cultural forms that can be said in this context to correspond roughly with commercial capitalist, pre-modern communitarian and postmodern pragmatic values. The various combinations and collisions of these components within the global cultural economy of sport ensure that, when combined with specificities of history and place, there are highly variable, coexistent patterns and trajectories. These first developed, like capitalism itself, in the seemingly unpropitious setting of, first, English village life and, later, in its new urban environments.

Origins of the global media sport economy

This is a familiar story but one that needs to be retold – with brevity and perhaps in unseemly haste – because, in the swirl of frequent changes, it is easy to lose analytical bearings. The competitive physical play that became sport was, in its origins, highly localized, disorganized, intermittent and mainly amateur – what is typically called folk culture. As it mutated into the institution of sport in modernity under industrialization, urbanization and capitalism, all of these formative characteristics changed with it (Clarke and Critcher 1985). In moving across the centuries from the village green to the cathedral stadium, sport was not entirely deracinated but became much less anchored to place and so both multi-local and diffuse. Sports contests, initially based on communal propinquity, expanded in geographical scope with the advent of regional tournaments, travelling teams and touring circuits. As cities developed neighbourhoods and suburbs engaged in sports contests, and then cities played each other, first in their own countries and then across national borders. Nations themselves became sporting entities and competed with each other in 'home and away' sports events. The more that sports contests, participants and spectators became mobile, the higher the costs of attending them (Holt 1989). Transportation, accommodation and hospitality all demanded expenditure and planned provision, and the 'performers' began to demand the coverage of their expenses and appropriate remuneration for their efforts. In other words, an exchange economy based on capital began to emerge that contrasted with older relations of reciprocity and informal support. This innovation required the spaces of sport to themselves change, with the enclosure of playing areas and, increasingly, purpose-built stadia, enabling entry charges to watch increasingly elite sports contests between individuals and teams from widely dispersed places (Bale 1993). Within and immediately around those spaces of sport various forms of commerce could be conducted, including gambling and the provision of food and drink. Many of these sites had and still retain a strong sense of place or came to develop one (Vertinsky and Bale 2004), although later relocations to so-called green field sites to accommodate motor vehicle access and standardized stadium designs (including artificial grass) have in many cases militated against distinctive spatial identities (Inglis 2000).

This initial moving of athletes, sports administrators and spectators around a country was integral to the process of making sport global. It created the incipient sports industry that emerged as part of the wider embrace of leisure time as an opportunity to spend some of the discretionary wage surplus that, in turn, fed back into the creation of the goods and services that constituted the labour of others (Tomlinson 1999, 2005, Part III). But taking people to event space is only a limited means of diminishing the importance of locality in sport. Of much greater import is taking the event to the people who weren't (or usually couldn't be) there when something unique happened in time and space. Witnessing actual events from a short distance means either being a local or a visitor (or even what later became known as a sports tourist – Hinch and Higham 2004; Weed and Bull 2004). But viewing from a distance came to mean more than holding a pair of binoculars with the advent of the television set. Sport could never become truly global – socially, culturally or economically – by relying on people movement. Taking people to sport is important in providing a sense of occasion and a lively event atmosphere, but it is time-consuming and comparatively inefficient. Turning images and sounds of sport into vibrant and artfully packaged communicative texts, whose reach is limited not by geography but by technology and consumption capability, is a very different proposition. Hence, as noted earlier, mediatization (used here in Nick Couldry's (2008: 377) formulation as the 'transformation of many disparate social and cultural processes into forms or formats suitable for media representation') has been essential to the evolution of global media sport.

In the first instance, the media were crucial as a means of sports reportage. Telegraph-relayed sport results could provide spare details of 'shots heard round the world', but news print could offer elaborate technical accounts of sports action and substantial observational descriptions of what it felt like to be there for those who weren't (Boyle and Haynes 2009; Rowe 2004a). Indeed, even diversions from the field of play to take in the crowd atmosphere or the surrounding natural and built environments could bear pleasurable, even educational witness to what had not been seen. These were attractive lures, especially for (in the first instance, mainly male) aficionados of sport, to buy newspapers and magazines from street corner vendors or, more conveniently, to subscribe to them. Specialist sports magazines and newspapers, increasingly enlivened by dramatic sports photography, and sports sections in newspapers that also enhanced typeface with action images, helped install sport across the everyday cultural spectrum, rather than confining it to a weekend pursuit. Later, radio broadcasts gave real-time sport event descriptions with 'actuality' sounds (which, if they could not be delivered because of technological limitations, were sometimes simulated). Radio, unlike magazines and newspapers, is limited by spectrum availability, and as likely to be dominated by public ownership (as in much of Europe) as by commercial control (such as in the United States). But, irrespective of the type of broadcast system or of broadcaster philosophy, sport's circulation through audio and print media enhanced both its cultural availability and commercial value/potential. When television supplemented and then dominated other media with live and recorded audio-visual coverage of actual sports events, its economic potential was plain for all, literally, to see (Weber 1996). When, later still, all types of text could be carried by the Internet and on mobile phones and other devices, mediated sport could be largely set free of the constraints of place (Hutchins and Rowe 2009a) and begin to realize its often-proclaimed, but still 'under construction', global status.

Transcending the local, though, could create nothing more than an untidy clash of practices if not accompanied by rationalization of sports organization and governance. The chaos of early forms of sport, with its lax rules and loose enforcement, was no more a solid foundation for a new industry than other primitive modes of production, practice and accumulation. Sport needed to be 'disciplined' if it were not to become unintelligible and ungovernable in each new context. Thus, as sport became less local, it also became more ordered so as to be transferable and exchangeable. In a manner analogous to the development of markets and currencies across the late nineteenth and early twentieth centuries, sports produced evermore elaborate codes, rules and even laws overseen by national and then transnational governing bodies and monitored and measured in increasingly minute aspects of performance to produce sporting records that could be compared across space and time. Allen Guttmann (1978: 16) has influentially, in adapting and applying the sociology of Max Weber, outlined this move from 'ritual to record' with seven abstract defining characteristics of modern sport: 'secularism, equality of opportunity to compete and in the conditions of competition, specialization of roles, rationalization, bureaucratic organization, quantification, [and] the quest for records'. Two examples of these characteristics are especially important for sport's economic development. 'Rationalization' of sport can, in economic terms, be regarded as equivalent to product standardization and differentiation – that is, a range of sports can be readily practised and displayed as recognizable, traceable components of the sports market. Without agreement, say, on the numbers of players, how scoring is calculated, which parts of the body can be used and in which ways, the dimensions and materials of sporting implements, how long the contest should be and so on, there could be no competitive sports event and so nothing, in a strictly sporting sense, to sell. This does not mean that rationalization has always, everywhere been a direct response to economic imperatives, but that it is a precondition of a modern sport and so a developed sports economy.

For example, Guttmann notes of the 'invention of basketball' in the late nineteenth century that it emerged as an indoor winter sport for young people in the decidedly non-commercial environment of the Young Men's Christian Association (YMCA) in the north-east of the United States, an organization imbued with the principles of 'healthy spirit, healthy mind, healthy body' that provided an important moral rationale (Hargreaves 1986) for both compulsory sport in schools and voluntary physical activities in organizational contexts such as the YMCA, although the anticipated fitness and self-denial could also be connected (with a view to Guttmann's aforementioned intellectual debt to Max Weber) to desirable characteristics of industrial workers and so linked to *The Protestant Ethic and the Spirit of Capitalism* (Weber 2003). What followed was what Guttmann (1978: 41) calls 'amazingly rapid ludic diffusion' and the 'triumph of ludic rationality', as after James Naismith had produced the game 'prototype' in 1891, it spread and developed such universal rules as five-player teams and those concerning the return of balls that had gone out of bounds. Although some rule variations (such as length of quarters) could be, and still remain, variable according to level of competition (e.g. national and international), there are only ever four quarters and there is never any confusion as to which rules apply in any given context. On the basis of this rationalization, basketball was able to become a global force in sport, being played at the Olympic Games, having its own World Championships and producing a league, the United States' National Basketball Association (NBA), which is amongst the most recognizable sports brands in the world (see Chapter 5), as well as one of the most renowned leagues in women's sport, the Women's National Basketball Association (WNBA) (Grundy and Shackelford 2005). Not only did basketball become a prominent global sport for men and women, it also spawned a 'female appropriate' (though now also played by men) variant in the nineteenth century that became especially popular among girls and women in the so-called Commonwealth countries – netball (Treagus 2005). In the late twentieth century, due both to extraordinary sporting ability and high pressure, and innovative sponsorship by the Nike sports good company, basketball also produced in Michael Jordan one of the most recognizable people in the world (Andrews 1996).

The second defining characteristic of modern sport to be foregrounded (following Guttmann) in this section is 'quantification'. Unlike most other fields of culture, such as the visual arts or literature, quantification of performance or quality is not just a phenomenon that follows qualitative (predominantly aesthetic judgements), but it is integral to the cultural form itself. Winning the United Kingdom's Turner prize for contemporary art or the Nobel or Man Booker prizes for literature is, although important in aesthetic fields (Street 2005), not the result of direct physical, real-time contestation under agreed rules by artists and writers but the outcome of a process of nomination and then voting by a panel of judges. In the case of sport, however, each encounter is expected to provide a quantifiably substantiated result, without which it would not be deemed to be a sport. Of course, there is considerable variation between sport where scoring is based on judgements of style (such as gymnastics and ice skating) and observable accomplishments such as balls crossing lines/boundaries or entering nets (as with, in various permutations, rugby, gridiron, association football, baseball, basketball, cricket and hockey). But whatever the method by which the ultimate result is calculated, sports contests occur in real time before large numbers of spectators under codified rules administered by co-present officials with the responsibility of authorizing a score in precise numerical terms. Thus, as Guttmann (1978: 47) puts it,

> The Polynesians of Tikopia scored their dart game with a complicated system and similar systems existed for calculating points in many ancient ball games, but modern sports are characterized by the almost inevitable tendency to transform *every* athletic feat into one that can be quantified and measured. The accumulation of statistics on every conceivable aspect of the game is a hallmark of football, baseball, basketball, hockey, and of track and field sports too, where the accuracy of quantification has, thanks to an increasingly precise technology, reached a degree that makes the stopwatch seem positively primitive.

This emphasis on quantification provided sport with diverse, minute means of performative measurement that could also, by means of physiological measurement, training procedures, trends and records, give to sport a performative history and, following the standardization of procedures and rules mentioned previously, portability across territories. This trend was conducive to the maturation of a global sports economy whereby, for example, the expert labour power of champion footballers, basketballers and baseball players could be transferred between elite clubs and cheaper athletic labour sourced from the economic periphery in central America, Africa and parts of the Asia-Pacific, under what has been called 'the new international division of cultural labour' (Miller *et al.* 2001). As sport was increasingly permeated by the spirit of capitalism, the measures of athletic performance progressively intermeshed with other significant and economically crucial calculations, such as spectator numbers at sport contests, television viewer ratings, broadcast rights fees, sponsorship agreements and endorsement contracts.

Stock markets, batting averages and an underground economy

The sporting 'obsession' with performance numbers clearly echoes that involving shares, currency values and interest rates. The business sections of newspapers, magazines and websites carry copious data on share values, price movements, dividend yields, price-earnings ratios, currency exchange rates and so on (my personal favourite being Earnings before Interest, Taxes, Depreciation and Amortization (EBITDA)). Their equivalents in sport carry league tables and collated statistics of teams involving points from games, goal differences and leading scorers, and there is a proliferation of such measures as gross production average (GPA – 1.8 times on-base percentage plus slugging percentage, divided by four) in baseball, player efficiency rating in basketball and strike and run rates in cricket. Michael J. Schell's (1999: 5) sophisticated statistical quest to establish (United States) baseball's all-time best hitters is symptomatic of the fetishization of sporting statistics that echoes that of business analysts:

> There are many different baseball statistics. Batting average and slugging average both combine singles, doubles, triples, home runs, and outs into single measures. Batting average is computed by totalling the different kinds of hits and dividing by the number of at bats, while slugging average totals the number of bases that you reach on the hits before being divided by the total number of at bats. However, both of them ignore factors like the walk average, numbers of RBIs and less well-measured things like hit-and-run or clutch hitting ability. There are other ballplayer abilities as well, such as run scoring, base stealing, and fielding.

In addition to such arcane performative measures in sport (to which baseball is historically attached) consistent connections between share market activity as a predictive practice and betting on the outcomes of sports events are evident, with sports-betting companies providing a welter of statistical odds not just on event outcomes but also regarding so-called spot betting that breaks sport contests down into their component parts and enables gambling on a range of outcomes within individual events. Thus, acquiring insider information and/or corruptly manipulating outcomes are ways of generating illicit gains from sport that undermine its foundational competitive uncertainty and arise directly from its reliance on intricate quantification. New communications technologies that transcend national boundaries make regulation of such practices more difficult than when gambling on sport was mainly restricted to national contexts using paper-based transactions through a restricted number of high-street betting outlets.

A story from cricket, 'broken' in 2010 by the now-defunct British newspaper *News of the World*, is an illustration of the globalization of a legal and illegal sport gambling economy. In a classic tabloid 'sting', representatives of the newspaper allegedly gave £150,000 to a 'go between' who indicated, with perfect accuracy, when three front-foot 'no-balls' were to be bowled by Pakistan in a test match with England at Lords in London (BBC 2010c). Such collusion would enable insiders betting on these specific mini-outcomes (in this case, a bowler 'accidentally' overstepping a line monitored by umpires) to make a considerable profit on the bet, with communication technologies and betting opportunities enabling (alleged at the time of writing) illegal transactions of this kind to occur in any time zone – and, indeed, to overcome restrictions imposed by individual nation states:

> Gambling is illegal in cricket-mad Pakistan and highly restricted in India. But that doesn't stop criminal gangs setting up illegal markets eager to exploit the recent explosion in satellite television coverage of live cricket from around the world. So people in Mumbai and Lahore find it as easy to bet on English one-day matches as they do on domestic fixtures. Somewhere in the world there is always likely to be a match on which to bet. (BBC 2010d)

An important point that can also be made here is that illegality and impropriety is a significant feature of the global media sport economy (Hill 2010). There is an understandable tendency among the promoters of sport to concentrate only on its favourable side – such as large, passionate audiences consuming a range of legitimately produced goods and services – rather than its undesirable and/or illegitimate features. In these terms also, the growth of global media sport is only ever represented as desirable, with, seemingly, nobody losing and everyone benefiting from a 'bigger pie'. For example, the deleterious environmental consequences of the global motor-racing circuit or of the building of water-, fertilizer- and chemical-intensive resort golf courses in sensitive habitats (and also sometimes with negative social ramifications by displacing the people who live in and around them) (Miller *et al.* 2001) disappear from view in 'boosterist' rhetoric. In the case of illegal activity, the globalization of sport can be said to go hand in hand with the globalization of crime. This is not to argue that globalization is inherently undesirable but to demand scrutiny of the blithe assumptions constantly circulated by 'sportsbiz' advocates concerning commercial sport diffusion and its beneficial, readily governable effects. As Chris Rojek (2010: 156) argues with regard to contemporary leisure,

> The evolution of a global economy in leisure, media and entertainment produces leaky policing. For the police force in a given territory face not only the threat of domestic supply chains of illegal leisure commodities re-defining themselves, but new sources of production and exchange in territories beyond their jurisdiction. Arguably, from the moment of the industrial revolution it was ever so. But the digital order and air transport network enhance the flexibility and contribute to the semi-transparency of illegal leisure and recreation channels of supply. In the era of the internet there is no credible system for police to monitor and detect illegal activity.

Sport is not, of course, uniquely subject to quantification. Production, exchange and consumption of various kinds can be converted into numbers, especially under the 'digital order' that depends, ultimately, on compulsive building on the binary division of the values of 0 and 1. But a key characteristic of modern sport, to return to Guttmann, is that sport is not just available for quantification but that it cannot exist as a cultural formation without it. Sports practices of necessity produce statistics not as bi-products of accounting but as inscriptions on all its visible features, without which it would not be recognizable as sport. Keeping the score and measuring performance is, then, integral to the conduct of the business of sport.

It is no coincidence, then, that the sport and business sections, described above as resembling each other in terms of their fixation on numerical performance, regularly appear next to each other in broadcast news, newspaper supplements and on news-oriented websites. Furthermore, the discourses of sport and business have substantially permeated each other. As I have previously argued (e.g. Rowe 2004a), sport has supplied commerce (as well as politics) with a vibrant everyday language that represents often abstract, complicated economic phenomena in easily decodable ways. Debates about business regulation, for example, are regularly discussed in terms of the need for 'level-playing fields' and 'hurdles', or takeovers as 'slam dunks', and ill-fated share purchase positions as 'own goals'. It is rather less common to see sports events described in terms of 'leveraged buyouts' or 'collateralized debt obligations'. What sport has taken from commerce is not so much language as rhythm. As it moved out from the local and was progressively rationalized and quantified, sport came to mimic the continuous process production associated with industrial manufacturing. Sports contests were originally rather irregular, sporadically occurring on certain days of the year or taking place at considerable intervals when motivation and resources merited. The new framework of sport demanded a more regular flow of 'product' – just as the media that covered it emerged as a space that needed to be filled on a daily basis with content irrespective of actual degrees of 'newsworthiness'. The sports calendar became busier and, while still guided by its seasons (which first followed and then increasingly straddled those of the earthly calendar), could transcend them as athletes and teams criss-crossed the hemispheres for scheduled events, as both carbon and satellite footprints extended across the globe.

Exhausted markets, new horizons and sport celebrity labour power

This 'mass production' and global circulation of sport created a problem that was very familiar in more traditional spheres of commodity exchange. Once a market for sport had been developed, it needed to be of a size and consistency of activity that would assure expansion and profitability, including a ceaseless search for new sporting labour and consumer markets (Miller, Rowe and Lawrence 2010). Production downtimes are to be avoided where possible and preferably limited to routine maintenance and, if strictly necessary, scheduled holiday shutdowns. But the more that is produced, the less 'special' the product becomes. If standardization produced economies of scale and lowered marginal cost, it also created an increased familiarity that needed to be countered by constant novelty – or at least its appearance through functional and stylistic innovations. At any one time the production of goods and services in various markets and market segments, especially for discretionary leisure and entertainment items, is in transition, with an establishment phase demanding high levels of standardization, consolidation requiring broad acquaintance and use, and then diversification to prevent boredom, exhaustion and redundancy. Here, advertising, marketing and promotion are especially important, as in the absence of major technological advances or other product innovations, old products can be 'badged' in ways that make them look and feel radically new and improved, or novel uses and applications proposed for familiar goods and services. So, for example, just as chemically similar shampoos are promoted as 'green' or contain a familiar substance with a different name, or cars and computers can be identical 'under the bonnet' but have rather different looking chassis and casings, each season launch of a major sport proposes both continuity and innovation. Similarly, an item of technology like a computer that was first sold as an educational or work-oriented device can become used for leisure purposes such as sport gaming, and mobile phones sold on the basis of enhancing personal security can become an essential tool of social networking and live sport viewing.

As noted earlier, the practice of sport was initially local, seasonally dependent and intermittent, a break in the routines of rural and then early urban, industrial life. As sport became established through professionalization and marketization, and proliferated in terms of types, levels and sites, there was not just an increase in demand for it, but it was necessary to maintain and enhance its supply in order to support its growing infrastructure, including dedicated stadia, management, transport, travel and payments to officials and athletes. Under a regime of amateurism, compulsory sporting activity in schools and voluntary sporting participation outside it was extensive, but by definition it was of a non-marketized nature (although, of course, it requires sports clothing and equipment). A genuine, capital growth-oriented sports business needs to find multiple, continuous sites of commodity exchange (Horne 2009), hence the expansion of leagues and competitions occurring on an annual and multi-year basis across many territories and, as is strikingly the case with college sport in the United States, bringing ostensibly amateur institutionalized sport into a commercial orbit that has de-emphasized educational values (Bowen and Levin 2003) and even investing voluntary junior and youth sport with a proto-professionalism that facilitated, for a minority, entry into a sports career and so a deep engagement with its market (Messner 2009). It was in the United States that the full commercial and ultimately global potential of sport was appreciated and activated by adopting its pioneering 'business practices and marketing strategies' and a 'new kind of corporate integration in the media and entertainment industries' involving a combination of transnational expansion and vertical integration (i.e. control of both content and distribution). By this means, sport was woven into the fabric of corporate promotion in a manner that made it increasingly difficult to 'unpick' and isolate from branded entertainment packages (Whitson 1998: 38–9).

The early organization of sport was chaotic in nature, and emergent markets also have a propensity to be so. As a result, modern sport, with its heavy reliance on rule-based quantification and performative hierarchies, required governmental discipline in its scheduling and dedicated circuits in order to prevent undesirable breaks in the production cycle. Thus, as with stock markets and gambling regimes, at any one time somewhere on the globe a major sport is being practised. Tennis players, golfers and other sportspeople organize their schedules by 'following the sun', and elite association footballers have their already crammed and extended competitive seasons supplemented by promotional tours and exhibition matches in developing markets, especially in the Asia-Pacific region and North America. The progressive loss of down time for routine maintenance on the engine of sport – the athletic body – has, as noted above regarding the ATP season, resulted in considerable strain and sometimes catastrophic injury. In the case of the increasingly busy international cricket calendar, in November 2010 the England team travelled to Australia to play five five-day test matches, two Twenty20 and seven one-day games (plus five other games), before returning home for three-day turnaround before departing for the World Cup of cricket hosted by India, Sri Lanka and Bangladesh that would last until early April (BBC 2011). It is unsurprising, then, that the team was afflicted by several player injuries and signs of 'burnout'.

Innovations in sports science and medicine have attempted to manage this risk and 'inefficiency' in the management of sporting labour through technological (including pharmacological) innovations and, crucially, has handsomely rewarded the small number of sport celebrities who have been willing to trade their long-term physical and psychological health for spectacular, often short-term, returns. So, for example, when a footballer or basketballer travels from game to game over considerable distances without proper rest, preparation and acclimatization and suffers injury, or when a champion rugby player is 'given the needle' to deaden the pain of an injury that would otherwise prevent them from playing, they are doing so in the knowledge that many workers in much less glamorous occupations – and in which, without sport, many of them would be working – also get injured 'on the job' and do not receive equivalent compensation. They are also aware that previous generations of amateur, semi-professional and professional sportspeople suffered serious, even career-ending injuries that left them without the necessary resources – educational and occupational – to prosper either in or outside sport. The collective organization of players in originally amateur team sports such as cricket and rugby, and in those that commercialized at an earlier stage of development such as gridiron and basketball, as well as in individual sports like tennis and golf, followed the realization that a considerable capital surplus was being built in sport and that owners and administrators were not in general disposed to share it equitably with them. The 'star' power of mostly male sports figures could be mobilized effectively because it was integral to the heroic myths that have infused and animated sport as a competitive arena where extraordinary physical powers could be recognized as meriting extraordinary esteem and material reward (Whannel 2001). Barry Smart (2005: 196) notes the following:

> As modern professional sport has developed the importance of individual action has not diminished, it has grown, as has the value of charismatic star players. Modern sport organizations continually search for potential stars, for players with charisma, those with an apparent ability to rewrite the record books and set new standards by doing the unheard-of.

It is here that the tightness of the media-sport nexus is most clearly exposed. The lionization of certain sportspeople and teams would be severely limited if they were required to generate their own publicity and to pay like most other commodity producers for their own advertising and promotion. Sport is strikingly well positioned to be its own news – effectively to sell itself *as* news. Continuous sport production articulates the routine and the remarkable – staple quantifiable information about what has occurred, visual and text-based description and depiction, and the extraction of certain people from the common sporting weal – such as a Michael Jordan, Serena Williams, David Beckham or Tiger Woods – who are able, at least temporarily, to cross over into a wider media sphere that is bigger than sport (Andrews 2006; Andrews and Jackson 2001) and which comes to the attention of those with barely a passing interest in it. The media, then, are critical to the global economy of sport and, while not exactly achieving parity of power (in survivalist terms, the media would have greater independent resources than sport in the profoundly unlikely event that their relationship were to be severed), sport has supplied the media with a large number of celebrities who provide compelling content across its full spectrum from news and current affairs to unalloyed entertainment.

Yet, of necessity, not all sportspeople are 'special'. The majority of members of this athletic labour market is far less 'aristocratic', with rewards and risks as unevenly distributed as in all commercial corporate-dominated cultural industries and with a much larger cohort of would-be entrants than those currently making even a minimal living in them (Hesmondhalgh 2007; Rowe 1995; Ryan 1992). Most aspiring sportspeople, like actors and musicians, never 'make it', and most of those who become full-time professionals are, even in the most affluent sports, more proletarian than bourgeois, foot soldier than general, journeyman than leader. The apparently chaotic sporting labour market, in fact, rigorously sorts sports and sportspeople into elites and the rest along lines including gender, race and position regarding the global core and periphery. Indeed, it draws considerable energy from the constant jostling for position and fame that its own celebrity system stimulates. In summary, there is never any shortage of people who want to play in Major League Baseball or the Indian Premier League. Sports academies and training programmes, whether run by the state, educational establishments or private enterprise, mine the globe for athletic talent, seeking to source the cheapest human 'raw materials' for elaborate transformation in the most lucrative markets (Miller *et al.* 2010). Often, as in the case of international football academies, the families of young aspirants in developing nations devote precious scarce resources to the slim chance of breaking through into the tightly sealed world of elite professional sport where highly paid, internationally lauded sport celebrity awaits (Miller *et al.* 2001). For encouragement, they need look no further than the sport and entertainment media.

Media as sport stimuli

The media, as noted earlier, are highly dependent on continuous sport production. In every news market, proprietors and spectators dread the end of major sport competitions and tournaments, worrying as to how they are going to retain audience interest. The answer, just as with sport's stretching of playing seasons and circulation around time zones, has been to maintain coverage of premium sports at a high pitch even when their main competitions have ended. The team sports labour market, in particular, is especially useful in this regard as an area of spectatorship in its own right. Unlike most spheres of work, the recruitment, retention and separation of players take place largely in public and, given that their performativity is minutely and relentlessly scrutinized, and that their affiliation to a particular club is highly significant regarding symbolic identity, there are manifold opportunities for media coverage of player movements. Of course, this coverage need not have any legitimate foundation – much media coverage of potential player movements are classic examples of slow news day gossip and speculation, using unnamed sources to stir up an instant controversy in the certain knowledge that any mention of a sports celebrity, especially in relation to their mobility between sports clubs, is inherently newsworthy for the more obsessive followers of that sport (Boyle 2006). Indeed, such sources often include player agents 'planting' stories about interest from other clubs and even sports (Michael Jordan's unusual and unsuccessful temporary switch from basketball to baseball notwithstanding, cases such as player movements in Australia between rugby union, rugby league, Australian rules and association football are an indicator of an incipient pan-code football labour market for those with transferable skills) during contract negotiations in order to improve their final terms. That sports journalists seem prepared to be used in this way (sometimes in return for a 'scoop') is ethically questionable but does not appear to trouble those for whom the principal imperative is popular attention in a crowded general and sports news market (Boyle, Rowe and Whannel 2010; Rowe 2007a).

It is not even necessary, though, for the airing of player transfer matters to occur in comparative downtimes, such as during the pre-season player draft deliberations in various sports (especially American) that provide structured opportunities for discussion in the sports media. When the action on the field of play is intense, and massive amounts of mediated sports coverage already available, the volatile sports labour market nonetheless receives concentrated, often hysterical attention. For example, when in October 2010 the leading Manchester United footballer Wayne Rooney announced his intention to leave the world's most valuable sports club (according to Forbes business magazine valued at US$1.84 billion (£1.2 billion) ahead of a top ten of the Dallas Cowboys, New York Yankees, Washington Redskins, New England Patriots, Real Madrid, New York Giants, Arsenal, New York Jets and Houston Texans – Callow 2010) by not renewing his contract with it, the result was enormous, global media coverage in the middle of the football season. The following excerpts from a British newspaper commentary of the time effectively capture the melodramatic flavour of contract negotiations conducted through the media (White 2010a):

> Claim, counter-claim, fevered speculation, seething discontent, banners, chanting, internet forums going into meltdown, a nocturnal rattle of the security gates by a bunch of balaclava-clad heavies: what a way to conduct contract negotiations …
>
> The comments were workshopped up in the media as evidence of a gaping rift between player and manager, there was talk of the old disciplinarian, tiring of his former favourite's wayward personal behaviour, dispatching him from the inner circle. He was, so the rumour insisted, being frozen out …
>
> For those who report on the game, there was something teasingly appropriate about such a conclusion. It beautifully articulated the plotline of the modern game. It had everything. Here were United, their prominence largely built on money, latterly suffering from acquisition by foreign raiders, unable to keep possession of their most valuable property. The loss of it to their significantly more endowed rivals down the road [Manchester City, owned by the Abu Dhabi United Group for Development and Investment] was particularly poignant. Ferguson's noisy neighbours were drowning out the waning Old Trafford roar.
>
> As for Rooney, well what did we expect from a modern footballer? Mercenaries all, they were motivated only by finance. It was a drama almost Greek in its certainties. Whatever happens, everyone agreed, he could not now stay at United.

Jim White's article in the sports pages of a conservative broadsheet newspaper vividly reveals the conflicts and contradictions surrounding contemporary sport in which the media, while expressing distaste, are deeply implicated. It highlights the frenzied, multifaceted nature of player/agent and club manoeuvring in the media spotlight. Both sides of the negotiating table used the media, seeking advantage by gaining public support. International capital, celebrity branding, sexual scandal and passionate fandom (tipping over into the threatening graffiti message 'Join City and You're Dead' on a billboard outside a Nike store in Manchester in a strike also against his sponsorship by that company) were all involved, with an opportunistic media simultaneously acting as an instrument for the contending parties. In themselves deriving economic benefit from increased sales and circulation, broadcast ratings and web traffic, the media are commercially compromised by capitalizing on while decrying the process in which they are willing actors. As disturbances such as these reverberate across the global media sports cultural complex, the inner workings of its industrial machinery are exposed.

As noted earlier, there is a danger that such saturation media coverage of sport-related matters can result in over-familiarity and 'exhaustion'. But in economic terms mainstream media corporations thrive, stagnate or decline according to their capacity to mediate content for their audiences. As sport is probably the most efficient and adaptable cultural form yet devised to generate primary and secondary content (i.e. actual broadcast content and then all the discursive content about that content) that can be turned into convertible media currency, the more common calculation is not that familiarity breeds contempt but, as with other areas of news content (the term 'news' being used loosely), that it is perilous to be left behind in a 24-hour news cycle characterized by media 'herd' behaviour. In a chapter originally written in the late 1980s, Robert W. McChesney (2008: 229) notes in relation to US sports television (and the failure of some new leagues in sports, including ice hockey, team tennis, basketball and gridiron) at the time that

> [m]ore than a few analysts have looked at these casualties and predicted that sports, in general, were being overexposed on television and that eventually public sentiment would turn against them. That has yet to happen, at least in the minds of all important advertisers who have subsidized the boom. Not that revenues and profits have increased without upheaval; as with any industry, there have been ups and downs for specific firms and general excesses caused by speculative frenzy. Nevertheless, the general pattern has been upward. In the 1980s several cable networks have been established that have given sports coverage prominence: indeed, they rank among the few cable operations that have had any success. Specifically, ESPN was established to broadcast sports 24 hours a day. Upon its creation, one ESPN executive remarked, 'We believe the appetite for sports in this country is insatiable.'

Over two decades later, there is much more broadcast sport around the world, and it is being substantially supplemented by web-based and mobile platforms. But, as has been discussed above, and is acknowledged by McChesney (2008: 230–1), what counts as sports content in the media far exceeds actual 'live' and recorded sports action, now sprawling across the entire media apparatus and taking on many guises. In a previous work I discussed this phenomenon (prompted by an observation of the journalist Paul Sheehan) as the 'strategic chaos of media sport' (Rowe 2004a: 80–8). In tracing this transition from relatively disorganized folk and proto-professional sport to the increased rationalization of formal amateur and fully professional sport, it is not intended to impose a rigid processual order on a resistant context. Instead, it is suggested that the organizing logic that has powerfully influenced how sport is practised, organized and experienced is responsible for creating the conditions for rapid change and sudden disruption. This is the familiar logic of the commodity – in this case that of sport under hyper-rationalization, mediatization and globalization – that eats itself as part of a capitalist compulsion to be remade and to accelerate its growth.

There are still those who find something shocking about the flourishing of the commodity form in sport. This is because, more than in most forms of popular culture, sport is constitutively attached to the romance of transformative mythology and to a moral order that still finds elements of paying to play and to watch a little repugnant. There is nothing particularly unusual about the regret that sport is no longer an uncommodified expression of folk culture (Rowe 1995). Across the whole sociocultural spectrum, folk life ('the world we have lost', in the memorable phrase of the historian Peter Laslett (1965)) progressively disappeared with modernity. Nostalgic yearnings for simpler, more 'authentic' times are understandable though obviously flawed (it is only necessary to consider such issues as life expectancy, representative democracy, political rights, gender equity and literacy to give pause for anyone not among the contemporary world's most disadvantaged people to hark back to a better life in pre-modernity). But modern sport is residually infused with the ethic of amateurism, which specifically proscribes professionalized labour (except among educators and elements of the administrative strata). Amateur sport has not disappeared, but its place within its institutional hierarchy of ethics and practices has slipped substantially as sport industrialized, to the extent that 'amateur' is often used pejoratively as connoting sporting inferiority (McKay *et al.* 2001). Yet its ethical residue remains whenever 'the love of the game' is celebrated and given primacy, and when distaste is expressed concerning the economic motives of athletes, sports bodies and the many organizations benefiting from the selling of sport in a multitude of ways, from player contracts to media deals to sponsor branding.

Laments for the love of the game

Residual elements of anti-commercialism in sport are related to the justifications of its installation as compulsory in the curriculum of schools after schooling itself became compulsory. Deployed first in British elite, fee-paying, all-male schools attended mainly by boarders to keep the pupils occupied and to discharge energies that could be put to 'unsavoury' uses, sport was also used to encourage school identity and cohesion in contests with rival schools and as a micro-system of preparation for adult living deemed to instil respect for cooperation, leadership, goal-directed cooperation, unselfishness, nobility and bodily competence that could be used in all walks of life including, above all, commanding military combat in the service of Empire (Hargreaves 1986). These values coalesced around the desirable qualities of discipline and mental and corporeal fitness that then spread to government-funded and other less exclusive schools and, despite their close association with masculinity, also found expression in the routines of girls at school. The close, systematic connection to formal pedagogy meant that sport was to some degree set apart from the world of labour and industry and when organized in civil society experienced difficulty in maintaining a boundary between voluntary, unremunerated leisure (amateur sport) and contracted, paid work (professional sport). Graham Scambler

(2005: 36) notes the awkward dilemmas posed after 1850 (as industrialism and capitalism took firm hold) as the '"cult of athleticism" ... epitomized by the concepts of "manliness" and "muscular Christianity" ... spread from the major public schools to a wider, if still privileged, public arena'. In examining the establishment of the English Amateur Athletic Association (AAA), he notes the problems of maintaining the 'amateur/professional dichotomy':

> [It] had very different connotations for the Greeks than it came to have for the gentlemen of Victorian England. It is in fact a dichotomy with a complex history ... In British athletics the first 'amateurs' were spectators, equivalent to late twentieth-century fans. Its usage in relation to sportsmen derived from rowing. Lovesey (1979: 22) writes 'In 1835 *Bell's Life* defined an amateur as anyone who rowed and was not a waterman or otherwise engaged in rowing for a living'. (Scambler 2005: 39)

Scambler quotes Lovesey's observation that by the middle of the century, the division had been drawn more exactingly in relation to social class: 'An amateur was a gentleman' drawn from approved organizations such as universities, and absolutely excluded 'tradesmen, labourers, artisans or working mechanics', while the Amateur Athletic Club (which later became part of the AAA) shifted between lesser (though nonetheless significant) qualifications for amateur status like never having 'taught or assisted in the pursuit of athletic exercises as a means of livelihood' to the qualification that '[a]n amateur is any gentleman...' (Scambler 2005: 39). This aristocratic claiming of the amateur was patently class based but, as in the wider society, folded into the aspirations of the emerging bourgeoisie and lower middle class and came under increasing pressure as the development of the sport market produced skilled practitioners who could not support themselves by inherited or other means and whose services were much in demand. As Coakley *et al.* (2009: 317–18) argue with regard to that once great bastion of aristocratic amateurism, the modern Olympics,

> The wealthy aristocrats who organized the Olympic movement and sponsored the modern Olympic Games even used their power to establish a definition of *amateur* that privileged athletes from wealthy backgrounds around the world. This definition excluded athletes from working class backgrounds, who could afford to train only if they used their sports skills to help them earn a living. The definition of *amateur* was revised over the years and, by the 1990s, amateur sport was largely a thing of the past. The loosening of the definition of the 'amateur' and the professionalization of most sports has increased the chances of participation. However, money and economic power now operate in different ways as training opportunities for developing high-level skills has become increasingly privatized in many countries. Additionally, powerful corporations use the Olympics to expand profits by linking their logos and products to particular athletes and global sports images that serve their interests.

This pattern of development of sport from the initial domination of amateurism among local elites sharply differentiated from the folk pursuits of the subordinate classes, followed by an increasing professionalization and commercialization that partially 'popularizes' institutional sport while creating other, corporate–commercial inequalities, has been replicated (with considerable contextual variations) as sport diffused across the globe (Maguire 1999). Coakley *et al.*, though, in noting this important shift, rather play down the important development, evident in most countries, of a *mixed economy of sport*, through which the state underwrites strategic elements of the development of private athletic careers and subsidizes the expropriation of athletic labour power by private capital in exchange for powerful signifiers of national identity and prowess. However, they do demonstrate how class relations in sport have changed to some degree, with at least a semblance of sporting meritocracy appearing through which a tiny number of mostly male athletes from outside the upper strata – and, indeed, from beyond the most affluent countries in the world – can exercise their labour market power to sometimes extravagant effect.

Nonetheless, sport – especially its affluent individual forms such as tennis and golf – is skewed upwards in terms of socioeconomic class in ways that mirror the social structure of the amateur sport order and which demonstrate the articulation of inherited social and sporting power. As already noted, most participants (indeed, competitors in every sense) in the sports labour market don't 'make it', get by for only a short time or leave their sports career with only modest returns. Their chances of doing well in sport are, as before, greatly enhanced by inherited class privilege and, at least as important, their masculine sex/gender (see also McKay *et al.* 2001). Thus, the limited 'democratization' of the sports industry by no means affirms that it is open and equitable but merely that, as it has industrialized and become subject to commodity logic, the dominance of the aristocratic class has been partially ceded to that of corporate capital of an increasingly global and mediated kind. In this accelerated passage through the emergence of the global media sports industry, I have attempted to demonstrate how it exceeded, while never entirely transcending, the limitations of space and time; standardized some aspects while diversifying others and used numbers as its universal, convertible language; and produced an almost hyperactive global market revolving around events, celebrities, collective identities and multiple points of exchange. Although the preceding discussion was peppered with exemplars, it has been necessarily abstract in places, and it would be useful to illuminate pivotal, concrete features of contemporary global media sport in order to reinforce just how much has changed in the two centuries – no more than a sliver of human history – since sport became the social, cultural, political and economic phenomenon that seems, illusorily, always to have impinged on the collective consciousness. The following discussion takes in the point of origin of modern sport and the sport that most persuasively assumes the mantle of the world game – association football in England.

The global, organized, continuous and commodified

Having traced, in summary, the emergence of the institution of sport and its interconnected transformation into a global industry intimately related to the mass media that grew along with it, it is helpful to take stock of the contemporary economics of sport. It was noted earlier that the world's richest sports club is Manchester United, with sports magazines such as *Forbes* continuously tracking the economic fortunes of both sports entities and sports celebrities (such as the aforementioned Wayne Rooney), some of whom have become only their own brands, as signified by the frequent use of sonly their surnames (such as Ronaldo, Zidane and Beckham). Thus the media, which are indispensable elements of the global sport economy, report on clubs and athletes as particularly glamorous cases of companies and entrepreneurs, as, for example, below:

> [Manchester] United's lofty standing is in spite of the club's heavy load of debt, with Forbes factoring in endorsements, merchandise sales, sponsorship and television revenues when considering a company's value.

> Forbes rates Tiger Woods as the top earning athlete, with an estimated annual income of $30m. The world No 1 golfer is followed by the boxer Floyd Mayweather Jr in second and the basketball star Kobe Bryant in third. (Callow 2010)

Such discourse is now remarkably unremarkable, but it is important to register how comparatively quickly it became so. As discussed above, professional association football first developed, like most sports, in Britain in the late nineteenth century. It was historically associated with a male, working-class player and fan base that was deeply territorial, if not aggressively parochial. Now globally famous clubs, such as Manchester United and Liverpool, were established in the industrial heartland of north-west England, often growing out of teams formed first around factory workers. Over the twentieth century, as was addressed earlier, football became more professional and highly capitalized, developing a private ownership structure, a transfer system to manage (on almost a feudal basis) its labour market, acquiring sponsors as important income streams and participating in a major television market that offered both profile and broadcast rights revenue. Following the rationalization and quantified 'grading' of club teams using systems of promotion and relegation, Liverpool and Manchester were well established in the First Division of the English Football League, but like other large clubs they became increasingly dissatisfied, towards the end of the twentieth century, with having to share profits, especially from broadcast rights revenues, with 90 other clubs. Here, the weakening of collectivism and solidarity among leading clubs indicate the heightened intrusion of individualism and material competition. In 1992, these clubs joined with an elite group of clubs to form the English Premier League (EPL) and benefited enormously from the additional television rights provided by the newly established subscription service BSkyB, controlled by the media proprietor Rupert Murdoch. Again, the movement from a free-to-air to a restricted platform of sport on television and the sharp rise in ticket prices in refurbished stadia signify a 'farewell to the working class' among elite football clubs. Both Manchester United and Liverpool developed substantial international fan support and, like others in continental Europe such as Real Madrid, Barcelona (a club in which members also exercised substantial ownership rights) and AC Milan, sought to capitalize on them, especially through the sale of licensed merchandise and by drawing subscribers to their in-house television services.

At the same time, the EPL was actively pursuing broadcast rights well beyond its home base in the United Kingdom and parts of Europe, especially targeting the Asia-Pacific region, the most populous and fastest growing media sports market in the world. This is now a familiar story of 'sportsbiz' expansion, but it is also one in which sport's claim to be somehow set apart from more 'mundane' areas of commerce (the legacy of long-lost amateurism and now degraded myths of sporting ennoblement) was exposed. Clubs were publicly listed on the stock market and/or traded as publicly limited companies by multinational capital, with the EPL substantially departing from received notions of 'Englishness' in terms of players, managers (now often called coaches) and owners (Horne 2006; Taylor 2008). The United Kingdom's membership of the European Union (EU) ensured that barriers to regional transnational movement were greatly weakened (King 1998, 2003), and a more far-reaching Europeanization and globalization diversified and enriched a game whose *embourgeoisement* and cosmopolitan character contrasted starkly with the largely homogeneous working-class culture that preceded it. Football's integration into global capitalism meant that it was also more directly subject to its vicissitudes, including the forms of debt financing that either created or exacerbated the global financial crisis that began in 2007 (Stiglitz 2007).

By October 2010, both Liverpool and Manchester United had accumulated massive debts. Liverpool's American co-owners Tom Hicks and George Gillett Kop Holdings company owed £280 million and were set to be purchased by another US concern, New England Sports Ventures (NESV), owners of the Boston Red Sox baseball team, for £300 million (BBC 2010a). Manchester United was in a better position but had just posted an £80 million loss (BBC 2010b) and also was experiencing considerable fan discontent with its own US owners, the Glazer family, which had purchased the club (via substantial borrowings) for £800 million in 2005:

> Critics say the family has saddled the club with massive debts, and this has led to protests by supporters' groups ...

> Many fans are continuing to boycott the team's traditional red shirts and scarves, and instead wearing green and gold, the original colours of Newton Heath, the amateur side which was founded in 1878 and went on to become Manchester United.

> A group of wealthy Manchester United supporters known as the Red Knights also proposed making a takeover bid. (BBC 2010b)

The original purchase by the Glazers had also prompted the in-protest establishment in 2005 of a breakaway club (starting out again in the lowest divisions of English football), Football Club United of Manchester (2010), positioning itself as the authentic heart of the club in declaring 'This is how it feels to be FC. This is how it feels to be home'. Although such traditionalist, topophiliac sentiments are common in British football (Rowe and Gilmour

2009; Rowe, Ruddock and Hutchins 2010), they are deeply at odds with the powerful economic structures of the game that have moved far from 'home', while locally owned and managed capital like the Red Knights has found it difficult to match the resources of foreign owners and bidders. As noted above, the EPL was overtly set up as a financial elite that would benefit directly from greatly increased broadcast income gained through the monopoly subscription service of the other major beneficiary, BSkyB (Horsman 1997). Its broadcast income constantly rose, sometimes running into trouble with European regulators who believed the close connection with BSkyB to be anti-competitive, but 'riding out' periodic political and market turbulence, such as the collapse of Kirch Media (which acquired FIFA's World Cup rights), ITV Digital and the UK division of Setanta (with the United States' Disney-owned ESPN taking over its EPL broadcast rights in 2009 – a year before, ironically, Setanta closed its US operation) (Mason and Moore 2009; Rowe 2004a).

Thus, the first rights agreement with BSkyB of £304 million over five seasons more than doubled in value over the next four (£670 million, 1997–8), and then exceeded a billion pounds sterling (£1.024 billion) over the next three, with the next broadcast rights deal involving BSkyB and Setanta reaching £1.7 billion, with further income coming from broadcast organizations such as the BBC. Of particular interest in this context is international broadcast rights revenue, which was £320 million for the seasons 2004–7 but grew very considerably afterwards, doubling from £625 million in the following triennium to £1.4 billion for 2010–13. As was discussed earlier, this global economic appeal was not accidental but the product of astute marketing in both mature and key emerging media sport markets that, in the latter case, made its branded consumption an attractive signifier of global cosmopolitan identity, to the detriment of the local game (Rowe and Gilmour 2009 – and discussed in Chapters 3 and 5). As one journalist notes, not only has the EPL become a significant part of media development in other parts of the world, it also produces some of its own packaged content directly, so beginning to bridge the organizational–operational divide between sport and media:

> The overseas rights bonanza underlines the global appeal of England's top football division, and has been fuelled by intense bidding wars in key areas, mainly between pay-TV rivals in Asia.
>
> The Abu Dhabi royal family, from which Manchester City's owner Sheikh Mansour hails, has also played its part. The ruling elite's Abu Dhabi Media Company has won the rights for Premier League matches across the Middle East and North Africa from the incumbent holder, Showtime Arabia.
>
> The League has 98 broadcast partners, as well as its own new TV station, Premier League TV, which will provide 'viewer ready' action, commentary and analysis for nations wanting to buy rights 'off the shelf'.
>
> In the future, the League hopes PLTV can attract non-traditional buyers to the market, for example entrepreneurs who want to enter the football market but don't have broadcasting capabilities themselves.

The Premier League's live domestic rights for 2010–13 raised £1.782 bn when sold last summer. With such enormous growth in international sales, and room for expansion, foreign rights should overtake home sales in the future. (Harris 2010)

That (setting aside diagnoses that television is a dying 'old medium') a nationally based football league should earn more broadcast rights income in distant territories than at 'home' lays bare the economics of contemporary global media sport. It is not floating entirely free of history and place but has, through a combination of the old, the new and the futuristic, created an economic framework founded on the 'live broadcasting of history' (Dayan and Katz 1992) – that is, the unrepeatable, real-time sports contest – with myriad mediated uses and forms. It attracts not only advertising and subscription-based commercial media but also publicly funded media outlets as well as sponsors, sport and leisure goods providers, and diverse ancillary industries (such as tourism and hospitality – Hinch and Higham 2004; Weed and Bull 2004).

The globalization of English football takes many forms – the aforementioned foreign ownership of clubs (including Chelsea, owned by the Russian oil oligarch Roman Abramovich), of managers (such as, in the 2010–11 season, Italians Carlo Ancelotti, Roberto Di Matteo and Roberto Mancini, to which could be added the Italian coach of the England national football team, Fabio Capello) and of players (although more accurately there is a strong, legislated regional framework given the United Kingdom's membership of the European Union and, in particular, the renowned Bosman Ruling that reaffirmed freedom of player movement within it), meaning that by 2010 fewer than 40 per cent of EPL players could qualify to represent England in an international tournament (Jackson 2010). This growth imperative has meant that, for some parties, even the EPL and its equivalent leagues in Spain (La Liga), Italy (Serie A), Germany (Bundesliga) and others, plus the existing club-based European competitions (the two largest being the Union des Associations Européennes de Football (UEFA) Champions and Europa Leagues, both of which have been restructured and expanded in terms of numbers of teams and/or games), have been insufficiently lucrative. Hence, there has been frequent agitation for a European Super League that would enable even greater concentration of clubs, brands and capital (see, for example, Hawkey 2009). Of course, association football is by no means the only instance of the intensification of the economics of sport, with, for example, the NBA holding games in London in 2011 (BBC 2010e) and Major League Baseball underwriting the revival of the Australian Baseball League in 2010. Both initiatives demonstrate that sport, having escaped the confines of the local, haphazard, occasional and the amateur, now traverses the globe in finding new sites for action and in the certain knowledge that it will – indeed, must – be digitally encoded and displayed on screen everywhere that a viewing market exists or can be cultivated. This 'pulling power' of sport, furthermore, has had an increasingly 'sportifying' impact on other areas of culture, notably television, and especially in its 'reality' and quiz show genres, infiltrating and cannibalizing popular culture in sometimes bizarre, hybridic evocations, adaptations and parodies of sport in such programmes as *Beat the Star*, *Wipeout* and *Shaque Vs.*

Thus, it is important not to have too narrow a focus on the economics of global media sport, given that the general cultural prominence of sport also creates conditions that naturalize its ubiquity. The 'unconscious' market power deriving from the presence of 'sport-like' elements in diverse cultural contexts makes it especially difficult to pin a critique of sport on a constantly shifting target, while maximizing the opportunities for the cross-promotional exploitation of a range of cultural commodities. For example, the ready recognition of sport logos and celebrities in non-sporting contexts diffuses the operations of the sport market across news, entertainment, fashion and so on. It is, therefore, easier to turn this quotidian investment in sport into related forms of consumption and to advocate public expenditure on sports mega events that advantage the sport market as committed to the collective national interest.

The core business of contemporary sport, though, is arranging, playing and televising contests. It has been shown above that behind this seemingly simple remit there is much struggle and uncertainty – and potential financial reward and risk. By March 2011 NESV had completed the acquisition of Liverpool, but its former owners were pursuing a £1 billion damages claim against the Royal Bank of Scotland and three directors of the club at the time of the sale, and Manchester United have the same owners, a debt of over £1 billion (in the same month that, symbolically in terms of EPL-initiated inequality in English football, saw League 1 team Plymouth Argyle go into administration and subsequent relegation with a debt of £17 million, only to be purchased subsequently for £1), and have denied rumours of a takeover bid by the investment arm of the Qatari Royal Family. At the same time, the UK Culture Secretary had given permission for News Corporation to prepare an £8 billion full takeover bid for the remaining 61 per cent of BSkyB that it does not own (Sweney 2011a) and which, if successful, would have entrenched the dominance of British sport television by the Murdoch family. As is now history, the subsequent phone 'hacking' scandal (*Guardian* 2011) saw in July 2011 the takeover bid withdrawn, the *News of the World* closed, and various current and former employees of News International charged. Both Rupert and James Murdoch appeared before the British House of Commons Culture, Media and Sport Committee, at which the former stated, "This is the most humble day of my life". In sport's world of screens, as this chapter has amply shown (and is developed in Chapter 5), fortunes are made and lost, but it is also one in which there is continuing contestation over its priorities. Here, the injunction is not only that the money be shown but that it should also be justified. The case of the EPL highlights how, in some respects, it is a case of classic cultural imperialism, a Western export that colonizes and crowds out manifestations of local cultures (in this case, the football systems of, especially, the Asia-Pacific). But it also shows how it has been a global 'attractor' (Urry 2003) that at the same time has substantially eroded the Englishness of English football (Magee and Sugden 2002), as a combination of transnational capitalism and cosmopolitanism has re-fashioned the form that is being exported across the world. This paradox of global media sport is explored next in addressing the dream of every media sport corporation – to establish a powerful, profitable global television operation.

3

Television

Wider screens, narrower visions?

Moving images and home comforts

global media sports cultural complex comprises many different forms, es, technologies and practices that work together – and sometimes against a other – in remorselessly insinuating sport into almost every conceivable space of the contemporary life world. As I argued in Chapter 2, television has, since the middle of the twentieth century, occupied the prime position among sport media. As television passed from the status of luxury consumer durable to routine domestic technology, sport was made available in the home in a manner that brought vibrant stadium action into that mundane environment's most sociable space – the aptly named 'living room'. This was not an uncontroversial development, given fears that televising sport would drain the will to attend the unique stadium event and undermine not only the economics of sport but also, paradoxically, the appeal of a screen text that is highly dependent on the co-present crowd ambience. The first problem was partially settled when the sale of broadcast rights to sports events became more lucrative than the sale of turnstile tickets and the latter by the enduring social appeal of 'being there' and the improvement of the in-stadium experience including, ironically, the installation of large television screens.

But the media sport sphere, just like the wider world surrounding it, does not stay still for the convenience of its inhabitants. Sharing the handsome spoils of sport television is of necessity a contested process, and the contests between vested interests – including those of the state and the citizenry – have disturbed the relatively orderly arrangements surrounding airwaves and cathode ray tubes. Broadcast television itself has come under challenge from new technologies, especially the Internet, creating new points of reception and audience types. The globalization and marketization of television sport have posed problems for the nation state, which once exercised sovereign power over the delivery infrastructure and in many countries much of the content of television, and in variable ways across the globe is still a significant 'player' able to intervene in commercial relationships struck between sports, communications corporations and media organizations. It is impossible and, indeed, undesirable to underplay the economic forces at work in television and sport highlighted in Chapter 2, but also important not to be so dazzled by audience and broadcast fee numbers as to neglect the important interweaving of sport television and cultural citizenship that occurred and intensified once watching landmark sports events in the home mutated from elite privilege to common right (Rowe 2006).

The title of this chapter is a deliberate echo of Joseph Maguire's (1999) summation (itself drawn from Cas Wouters's (1990) conceptualization of trends in international class and state relations) of global sport as characterized by 'diminishing contrasts and increasing varieties', a dual process through which major differences between sporting forms and practices are reduced while smaller ones proliferate. Murray Phillips (2001: 27–8) sees this position as a useful 'mid-road' in globalization debates revolving around homogeneity and heterogeneity in explaining, for example, the development and diffusion of amateur sport:

> [W]hile amateurism provided a degree of homogeneity to a range of sporting practices, there was an underlying diversity that enabled sports to maintain their intrinsic qualities, service the conflicting needs of their vastly different clienteles, and in fact to interpret amateurism in a number of ways. For these reasons, the mid road between homogeneity and heterogeneity – diminishing contrasts and increasing varieties – as articulated by some within the globalization debate, resonates particularly well with amateurism at the turn of the century. At the level of diminishing contrasts, very similar definitions of amateur sports are highlighted in key documents from local and national competitions. At the level of increasing varieties, the accepted definition was interpreted differently and selectively or was modified by adding a number of clauses that effectively differentiated within sporting activities, between sports, and in different geographical locations. (Phillips 2001: 27–8)

This model may also be applied in a qualified and specific way to sport on television. No one who has walked into an electronics store or private home in recent years (at least in the West) can fail to have noticed the growing dimensions of televisions. It is not unusual to see whole rooms in households dedicated to the home theatre for sport and film watching, the screen apparatus often of such size as to outgrow the traditional living room, and what was once 'the box in the corner' occupying an entire wall. Of course, this is not to deny that there are many smaller screen experiences increasingly on offer, from computer monitors to touch screen mobile phones. The biggest screen in the house, though, irrespective of its mode of delivery as broadcast televisions become increasingly Internet enabled, still stands as a key focal point for the moments when televised sport is at its most socially engaged. Screen size, however, is no guarantee of breadth of content or interpretation. That is, the privileging of some sports at the expense of others continues despite the increased number of TV channels (including those dedicated to 24-hour sport) and – despite the multiplication of camera angles, simultaneous viewing of different events and the ability to call up information – an overall absence of interpretive imagination to the point of presentational cliché. Criticism of sport television, especially of commentary, may have evolved into its own parlour game, but nonetheless, there are serious questions to be addressed about both the quality and purpose of sport television as it undergoes profound change in the digital age (Boyle and Haynes 2004). Before this analytical assessment takes place, though, it is necessary to take stock of its global reach and influence.

A world in transmission

According to a 2008 PricewaterhouseCoopers Report, and even taking into account the global financial crisis in the middle of the projected period (which, in any case, does not appear to have had a long-lasting deleterious impact on media rights), television and other media continued to expand the size of the global sport market (here to a projected US$141 billion by 2012):

> Growing broadcast rights deals, and mobile and Internet spending will help drive the expected compound annual growth rate of 6.5 percent from 2008 through 2012, the report by consulting firm PricewaterhouseCoopers said. That is comparable to the 6.4 percent rate seen from 2003 through 2007.
>
> National sporting events also will boost revenue as companies look to align themselves with sports that draw consumer attention, PwC said. It cited international cricket rights boosting growth in Asia Pacific as an example.
>
> The strongest growth will be seen in the Europe, Middle East and Africa, Latin America and Asia Pacific regions, all of which are expected to see annual growth in the range of 6.5 percent to 7.1 percent, the report said ...
>
> Global revenue growth is projected to be strongest in Olympic years. PwC projected growth will hit 11.4 percent in 2008, 11.2 percent in 2010 and 9.9 percent in 2012, compared with growth of 0.4 percent and 0.3 percent in 2009 and 2011, respectively.
>
> The U.S. market accounts for the biggest piece of the pie, as sports revenue there is expected to hit almost $69.1 billion in 2012, compared with $46.9 billion in Europe, Middle East and Africa, PwC said. Revenue[s] in Asia Pacific, Latin America and Canada are expected to reach $19.4 billion, $3.9 billion and 1.3 billion, respectively. (Cited in Klayman 2008)

The PricewaterhouseCoopers Report highlights several important characteristics of, and trends in, the contemporary sport economy: that it is an integrated market in which the media are pivotal; it is a mixed media market, still led by broadcast television; and that it is a global media sport but one in which there is historically inherited unevenness in development and intensity. Here I will concentrate on the resilience of sport television and so will treat with some scepticism diagnoses of its decline, although recognizing that change is happening and that the few-to-many broadcast model that provided its first platform of dominance must inevitably 'share the podium' with other, more flexible ways of seeing live sport at a distance. Thus, apocalyptic pronouncements that old or legacy media such as television are being swept away underestimate the power of media 'incumbency' and the capacity of established media to adapt and, in many cases, cooperate with new developments as well as the tendency of many media users to combine and mix media rather than make zero-sum choices between them. There is also a curious ahistoricism about much of the analysis of imminent decline when considering, for example, the ways in which newspapers, radio, television and online media across the past century have, even if uneasily, interacted, while what passes for assessment of media trends is all too frequently special pleading by interest groups (either seeking protection in the case of older media or incentives by 'start-ups' marketing themselves in the case of newer media).

The media sports cultural complex is distinguished by an intricate network of different media forms feeding into, bouncing off and colliding with each other. Thus, a newspaper article about a sports team may encourage viewers to watch them perform on television, while encountering the team on television might draw the eye of the reader to a newspaper headline about it. Similarly, a radio news item may lead to a web search, which might stimulate an online purchase of a book on the subject. A visit to a website might prompt purchase of tickets to a game, watching an embedded video story, activating a hyperlink to a news story and so on and on. The key point here is that sport as a cultural item passes in and through the complex, attaching itself in some places, being modified in others and sometimes being diverted elsewhere. If sport is not, precisely, omnipresent, it is remarkably conspicuous – and much of the time, especially during global mega events like the World Cup and the Olympics, almost impossible to avoid.

Television plays a highly significant role in this cultural conspicuousness of sport, given its relative simplicity as a delivery mechanism and well-established place, as noted earlier, in domestic spaces and routines. There is a strongly habitual nature of media uses (Silverstone 1994), and levels of daily TV viewing indicate how the habit of watching television (or, perhaps more accurately, having the television on) is difficult to shake, even with many competing media and activities. As many authors have argued, sport is particularly well suited to television, especially in live form, as it concentrates attention on dramatic events happening in a delimited space in real time, drawing on, especially in international encounters, widespread passionate identification and a structure that enables anticipation and reflection, and which can be 'spun off' into many later uses, ranging from packaged highlights to the subject matter of quiz shows (see various contributions to Raney and Bryant 2006). There is no popular cultural form that regularly offers such a potent mix of 'liveness' and common language, the standardization discussed in Chapter 2 fostering sport participation and spectatorship as portable practice. When, for example, a tennis or football match is taking place on screen, those familiar with their fairly simple rules – the majority in most countries – can decode the fundamental elements of what is happening with ease. On the foundation of this common understanding is the necessary customization that might make it matter for more than the relatively small number of people around the world who will feel compelled to watch any tennis or football match because they are avid followers of the sport (fewer still of those people may be transfixed by *any* sport). This targeting of viewers requires them to be oriented by sport commentators – who is playing, why it matters, the 'back story' of the match, who should be supported or opposed and so on. Moving images of the most significant international sports, then, circulate the globe, with the 'live feed' provided by the principal broadcaster (such as NBC, which has had this role for the Summer Olympics since 1988) and local interpretation, in a language other than English where necessary, as well as an emphasis on the main concerns at the point of reception, usually by concentrating on 'our' players and teams, and others with shared cultural sympathies (de Moragas Spà *et al.* 1995).

This arrangement, though, begs the question of how a sport becomes global. By definition, sports can only aspire to global status if they are played in many countries and watched by many people. Sports that do not 'travel well', especially indigenous or local sports, may still be very popular in some countries and regions, and also demand the attention of expatriates, but they will not be global in any legitimate sense and so cannot exact substantial overseas broadcast rights fees. This does not mean that these sports cannot be seen in many countries, as the space of televised sports through multichannelling is now very large and can be accessed by diasporic viewerships on television and Internet platforms. Sports of little local appeal can appear on far distant television screens as sports (especially subscription) television 'fodder' for no more compelling reasons than ownership of rights and the need to fill programme schedules on sports channels with *something sporting*. For example, Australia, uniquely in the world, has four codes of professional football which in size (i.e. 'turnover') can be listed in the following order: Australian rules, rugby league, rugby union and association football. Thus, the last, the 'world game', is currently far behind the code that is played almost exclusively in one country (Hallinan and Hughson 2010), while the second most international football code (rugby union) is currently behind one played professionally in only a handful of parts of only a handful of countries – rugby league (Rowe 2007b).

The Australian Football League (AFL 2010), which governs Australian Rules Football, lists several international broadcast partners on its website, including the American broadcaster ESPN, which showed, among its territories, four games a week during the 2010 season and live coverage of the Grand Final as well as one 'game of the week', the Finals Series and the Grand Final in 2010 in Africa, Israel and the Caribbean. The Orbit Showtime Network, the website states,

> offers four dedicated sports channels featuring a wide variety of live international sporting action. We bring the best of the AFL to the Middle East and North Africa, including two live matches every round of the home and away season, plus the weekly highlights program showcasing all the action of the round every Wednesday evening on Show Sports 2. Our AFL coverage doesn't stop there – you can catch every moment of the Finals Series live, including the Toyota AFL Grand Final live from the MCG on the last Saturday in September.
>
> In addition to the AFL, we bring you live and exclusive coverage of the Barclays Premier League, Scottish Premier League and Portuguese Liga, plus cricket, rugby, golf and explosive shows from the WWE Universe and UFC. (AFL 2010)

This information reveals how the idea of global television sport and the claims of individual sports to wide international coverage need to be treated with some scepticism. That a sport like Australian rules football and its principal competition the AFL can be accessed in some way in the Middle East and North Africa via television indicates that it can claim to be global in technical terms, but this does not mean that it is a global sport with regard to status. Evidence that the AFL is avidly watched – or played – in Saudi Arabia or Libya is scant. So, although the total list of AFL international broadcast partners in television is impressive and also includes Australia Network (covering forty-four countries in Asia, the Pacific and the Indian subcontinent), Eurosport 2 (broadcasting a 'unique blend of team sports, alternative sports and new sports' to '40 million homes in fourteen languages across forty-six European countries'), Sky Television in New Zealand, TSN in Canada, MHZ Networks in Washington, DC in the United States and TG4 Television Ireland (AFL 2010), the reach of the televised game across the globe does little to disturb the status of Australian rules football as an overwhelmingly local game. Indeed, it is also available in live form online, either pay per view or without charge, through Big Pond TV and ESPN3.com in many countries and, no doubt, can be illegally streamed in many others. This could be seen as an example of niche TV sport in action using new digital technologies, but it can just as easily be characterized as a sport that is disseminated around the world because it *can be* – that is, the motive force is not demand but supply.

As the above quotation from Orbit Showtime Network reveals by mentioning – that is, advertising – other sports that it broadcasts (along with others on the AFL website, such as Sky Television New Zealand, which notes that it carries the Olympics and the Rugby World Cup in that country), Australian rules football is one sport among many that television makes available in many places but with highly variable levels of popular appeal. This is an unexceptional and even a desirable arrangement, provided that such global availability is not used to advance, either explicitly or implicitly, unwarranted claims about global audiences and also that the emphasis is on the practice and spectatorship of sport rather than its deployment as a vehicle for other commercial activities. Thus, for example, Tim Harcourt (admittedly, an enthusiastic follower of many sports), the Chief Economist of the Australian Trade Commission (Austrade), has noted that 'Aussie Rules Goes Global' and that, at the time of the AFL Grand Final,

> there'll be parties all over the globe with the MCG on the screen from Rio de Janeiro to Romania. In fact, in my travels as The Airport Economist around the world, I have noticed that wherever there are Australian exporters there are expatriates and wherever there are Australian expatriates there is sport and it's often Aussie Rules ...
>
> And thanks to the broadcast rights – through an agreement between the Shanghai Media Group (SMG) and the Australia Network, the game is being broadcast right across China. While Australian football contributes $3.4 billion annually to the Australian economy, with seven million people attending AFL matches each year a bit of broadcast action in the Chinese market would certain [sic] help the cause of footy exports. (Harcourt 2010)

In both servicing expatriates and enhancing 'footy exports' through broadcast rights (and through overseas development of the game), mainly nation-based sports like Australian rules football are inevitably drawn out of their home bases to varying effect. But to be able to boast of many broadcast partnerships and countries taking coverage of sports events and competitions attests to the seductive nature of global sport discourse. Few sports wish to be regarded as hyper-local or even nationally confined, in that to be so suggests that they are backward looking and lack flexibility, portability and professionalism. As has often been pointed out, even a large national competition like US baseball is anxious to declare that it is, in fact, a World Series. Television (and increasingly online and mobile media) is, then, a highly effective mechanism for at least enabling a rhetoric of globalization that, while mostly unconvincing, cannot be simply 'laughed out of court'. Thus, another Australia-dominated football code of limited international appeal, rugby league, can declare, like the AFL,

> The 2010 Rugby League Four Nations tournament [involving Australia, England, Papua New Guinea and New Zealand] is set to be broadcasted [sic] around the globe with thirteen broadcasters taking all the action to more than 60 countries.
> (Rugby League Four Nations 2010)

These countries and broadcasters include Brunei (Astro), Bosnia (SportsKlub) and Yemen (Orbit Showtime Network), which are not conventionally regarded as rugby league strongholds. The intention here is not to mock the size and status of countries or their standing in the sport but to re-emphasize that global sport television can mean very different things. In the case of major sports and sports events, simultaneous 'live' audiences that can be measured, as indicated earlier, in the billions, prompt declarations that the whole world (or at least a substantial component of it) has been brought together in a single screen spectator activity at the same time. The resultant image is of cultural globalization in its strongest sense of overcoming space, time and social division, if only temporarily, in the production of the universal human experience of the sports mega event (Horne and Manzenreiter 2006; Roche 2000). By contrast, minor sports servicing what are likely to be tiny audiences on specialist media platforms presents a much weaker picture of globalization as the provision of myriad cultural choices for increasingly fragmented audiences. Such provision is partly in response to the global circulation of 'home' audiences, the diasporic populations described above by Harcourt (although these can be very sizeable depending on the sport and the pattern of migration) and partly a matter of marketing and technological convenience. In this way, television sport emerges as little more than useful, inexpensive content for broadcasters in the digitized, multichannelled phase of television that began at the end of the twentieth century and for sports the exchange of broadcast rights for global bragging rights.

These arrangements ought to advantage sports that have had difficulties in getting on television in an earlier broadcast television environment of spectrum scarcity that revolved around established major sports and 'blockbuster' events. But although television is more extensive than before, it is nonetheless still hierarchical – as, of course, is sport itself. For this reason there is now less of a problem for many sports to be displayed somewhere on television, but in something of a replication of 'vertically structured' sport divisions and leagues, the key televisual allocations regarding national and international broadcast right payments, principal channels and time slots are concentrated on a relatively small number of sports such as association football and events like the Olympics, consigning most others to more marginal TV locations.

So, for example, the instance of Eurosport 2 (established in 2005) presented above, with its 'unique blend of team sports, alternative sports and new sports', is that of a supplementary channel to Eurosport (established in 1989). Such sports channel hierarchies on subscription platforms replicate those within the free-to-air sector, where digitization has advanced the stratification of content. When sports and sport events are carried live on general, major television channels rather than sport-specific ones, this is a sign that they are genuinely considered to have gone beyond the realm of sports appreciation and have assumed the status of national cultural 'property'. This is the value position, for example, behind the insistence that 'protected' sports events on Australian free-to-air television channels should in all but exceptional circumstances be shown on their main rather than subsidiary channels (Australian Government Department of Broadband, Communications and the Digital Economy 2009, 2010a). As will be discussed in detail later, the implications of this difference are profound because they draw sport television onto a highly political terrain of history, identity and citizenship that is nationally grounded but can also be global in scope as inalienable from the cultural commons of all peoples, irrespective of their material conditions.

The profile of sports within and across countries, though, is tied in various ways to deep, resilient structures of power across generations. For example, in a country such as India, which was once under the control of imperial Britain, popular indigenous sports played in the villages, such as kabbadi (which is popular also in other Asian countries and has its own substantial tournaments), were actively suppressed as 'uncivilized' under imperialism and struggle to match 'introduced' sports such as cricket in both their countries of origin and among diasporic (often socially and culturally marginalized) communities surrounded by Western sport (Johal 2001; Mills and Dimeo 2003). Such sports may survive and even to a degree thrive, but grass-roots popularity is no guarantor of elevation when confronted by sports that have the momentum of global television circulation and sponsorship. Thus, a sport like netball that is played predominantly by women in Commonwealth (i.e. former British Empire) countries does not generally receive the sustained, 'prime-time' television coverage that matches its player base, with consequent restrictions to professional sports careers for women (Coakley *et al.* 2009, Chapters 8 and 10). Such barriers of race and gender, therefore, operate in global media sport – although not uniformly or entirely predictably – to restrict opportunities while appearing to follow objective market principles of supply, demand and consumer sovereignty. Television, with its varying combinations of state control and regulation, public provision, and commercial oligopoly and competition, has from its base in individual nations fanned out across the globe, with major media organizations establishing the infrastructure and making the agreements that enable them, at least notionally, to be purveyors of universal media sport content. One company, News Corporation (as noted earlier, controlled by the Murdoch family and especially associated with its patriarch Rupert) has been particularly prominent as the first that could make a persuasive claim to be a truly global television sport entity. In the next section, I will consider what could be called the 'Murdochization' of media sport.

Towards a global sports network

Moving images of sport can now circulate freely around the globe, requiring little more than a small TV camera and a website. But broadcast television prides itself on being of an industry-standard broadcast quality – a standard that is constantly rising with the continual sharpening of images through high-definition and even 3D TV. Also, as argued earlier, the computer and the television are still largely distinct domestic technologies, and the cultural practice of television viewing so well installed in everyday lives that the design and layout of the main social and leisure space in the home (with the possible exception of the kitchen/dining room), the living room, are oriented around the world's most popular recreational activity – watching television. It can be objected that there are still many people across the globe who lack these 'creature comforts', but recent data on the diffusion of television indicate that it is still advancing rather than retreating. An article grandly announcing 'Revolution in a Box' by a development economist, Charles Kenny (2009), in noting the increasing television access and use across the world, is prefaced with the statement that '[i]t's not Twitter or Facebook that's reinventing the planet. Eighty years after the first commercial broadcast crackled to life, television still rules our world'. As both access and choice widen, Kenny notes that preferred viewing 'seems to be pretty much the same everywhere – sports, reality shows, and, yes, soap operas. Some 715 million people worldwide watched the finals of the 2006 soccer World Cup, for example' (Kenny 2009). It is probable that he is exaggerating the uniformity of viewing preferences and taking insufficient account of both local variations and the dynamic process through which different types of programming can emerge after an initial establishment period dominated by currently dominant, imported genres. Nonetheless, there is no reason to expect that major sports events will not be immensely popular as such television markets mature.

Many sports, as acknowledged earlier, are anxious to exploit new territories. Indeed, some major sports entities, such as the football clubs Manchester United and Real Madrid, have their own international subscription television channels. Cutting out the 'middle person' – that is, media companies – may be attractive in some regards (such as greater control and higher revenues) but also has many costs and risks. These include the cost of production, negotiating transmission and arranging marketing, and perhaps having to exchange 'blockbuster' broadcast rights revenue with major media corporations for a large number of smaller broadcast deals. It might also be argued that doing sport media 'in house' destroys any possibility of independent, fourth-estate vigilance in sport, if it were not for the fact that very little sport television has any journalistic interest in the ethics of sport (Boyle *et al.* 2010). Thus, while (inter)national sports governing bodies and clubs may have aspirations to become major media producers – indeed, in a recent Australian inquiry into reporting sports news and digital media this was precisely the accusation made by the Group Editorial Director for the Australian division of News Corporation (hereafter called News Corp), News Limited (Hutchins and Rowe 2009b) – the experience, expertise and capital wealth of media corporations operating across many areas of sport invest them with enormous advantages in piecing together a global sport television network.

News Corp has been the most aggressive force in acquiring, solely or through partnerships, media sport properties around the world. I and others have previously noted the company's commitment to sport as its 'battering ram' and main offering used to break into television markets and to get through to consumers by offering sport-led subscriptions that would establish a relationship with the company that would facilitate their take-up of other television and new media services (Boyle and Haynes 2009; Rowe 2004a). The extent to which this relationship has been consensual is a matter of considerable dispute. Certainly, for example, nobody is forced to subscribe to News Corp's (majority-owned and, as noted, attempted-but-aborted sole-owned) BSkyB (generally called just Sky) to watch live EPL or England test cricket, but its exclusive availability on Sky demands a stark choice: subscribe, go to a commercial premises (and sometimes to a public viewing site) to watch or do something else. Although still the most powerful global force in sport television, News Corp has been contained to a degree by competition regulators such as the European Commission and Ofcom, and has been required to share some of its broadcast sports and platforms, while, earlier, seeing its attempted takeover of Manchester United Football club blocked in the United Kingdom. Its aforementioned (discontinued) attempt to assume 100 per cent control of BSkyB caused further argument about concentration of ownership and control in such key areas as television news (McVeigh 2010) and, of paramount importance in the context of this book, of sport.

These matters of access and equity are discussed in greater detail below, but they are noted here to counter the more benign, naive or self-serving emphases on freedom of choice. The advantages of News Corp and other media corporations such as Disney gaining major broadcast sport properties in one country are obvious. They are then well positioned to acquire international broadcast rights (if sold separately, as is now increasingly the case) and to 'populate' its screens around the world with both sports of international appeal and, as noted earlier, with a good deal of 'filler' material that can fill vacant slots on secondary channels and flatter nation-based sports that they are, at least technically, 'global players'. Their investment in broadcast rights is very considerable – according to the company's 2010 Annual Report at the middle of that year its total, multi-year commitments to sports programming were well over a billion US dollars (US$13,320 million) and with further contingent guarantees of almost half a billion (US$429 million) (News Corp 2010a: 70). Once total costs of programming are taken into account (including technology, salaries, buildings, travel and so on), the scale of News Corp's investment in sport (and especially in sport television) is shown to be massive, with the concomitant cost recovery and profit imperatives of even grander proportions. The global News Corp sport empire encompasses the United States, Britain, Ireland, parts of continental Europe and Asia, and Australasia, composed of sole-owned operations, coveted ones (as in the aforementioned case of News Corp's (abandoned) £12 billion full takeover bid for the remaining 61 per cent of BSkyB, a company that made a profit of a little under £900 million in 2010 – Robinson 2010) and strategic partnerships. A key example of the latter is the ESPN STAR Sports joint venture with Walt Disney, which according to News Corp (2010b) was formed

> to deliver a diverse array of international and regional sports to viewers via its encrypted pay and free-to-air services.
>
> ESPN STAR Sports showcases a variety of premier live sports from around the globe, 24 hours a day, reaching more than 310 million viewers in Asia. ESPN STAR Sports has 17 networks covering 24 countries, each localized to deliver differentiated premier sports programming to Asian viewers. Networks include STAR Sports Asia, STAR Sports Hong Kong, STAR Sports India, STAR Sports Malaysia, STAR Sports SEA 2, STAR Sports SEA, STAR Sports Taiwan, STAR Cricket, ESPN SEA, ESPN China, ESPN Hong Kong, ESPN India, ESPN Malaysia, ESPN Philippines, ESPN SEA 2, ESPN Taiwan, MBC-ESPN (Korea).

Showing live sport from around the globe *to* the globe on a 24-hour basis constitutes a combination of Fordist continuous production and the 'immaterial' circulation of symbolic commodities that need not be constrained by the logistics of physical transportation that apply, for example, to bottles of wine or tennis rackets. Furthermore, as suggested in Chapter 2, there is comparatively little that needs to be done by means of customization, such as by 'patching in' some local commentary and context. While the product is at its most valuable in live form and so more 'perishable' even than fresh fruit or flowers, televised sport retains considerable value when it is replayed, discussed, summarized and 'highlighted'. Each new event can be deployed to stimulate interest in the next and forms part of a massive archive that is available for multiple uses, from documentaries to replays of 'classic' sports contests and moments (Brookes 2002).

That there is regular movement and display of TV sport texts around the globe, though, does not reveal very much about which ones are most prominently screened. This question goes to the 'narrower visions' raised in the chapter title and, essentially, that there might be a privileging of a small number of sports, predominantly Western in origin, leading to overexposure of some and the marginalization of others. In order to explore the content patterns of News Corp's global sports network, a detailed schedule analysis (executed by Callum Gilmour) was conducted of Australia, New Zealand, Taiwan, India and the United Kingdom during one week (6–13 May 2008). By examining which sports appear courtesy of News Corp in national contexts, and their origins, the flows of global media sport can be traced and analysed (see Tables 3.1–3.6). For example, in Australia, the subscription Fox Sports One Channel's (owned by the Premier Media Group, which is co-owned by News Corp and Consolidated Media Holdings, the main shareholders of which are Seven Network Limited, 40 per cent owned by media entrepreneur Kerry Stokes, and Consolidated Press Holdings, the private investment company of James Packer, son of the late Australian media proprietor and leading media sports figure Kerry Packer) sports by nation/region of origin is shown in Table 3.1:

Table 3.1 Fox Sports One (Australia), origin of content[a] and programme hours, from 6 May 2008 to 12 May 2008

Nation/region	Hours	Percentage
United States	63.5	38
Australia	47.5	28
Europe (except United Kingdom)	25.5	15
United Kingdom	22.0	13
Asia	4.5	3
Middle East	2.0	1
New Zealand	1.5	1
South Africa	1.5	1

a. Origin of content can be difficult to determine in the case of inter- and transnational sports events and competitions. In this case, the location of tournaments, principal broadcasters and rights holders may be taken into account in making a judgement about points of origin. However, most broadcast sport takes place routinely within nations and regions.

Here it can be seen that there is considerable concentration in the origins of sports programming in this major subscription sports channel in Australia. It should be immediately acknowledged that, as will be discussed in greater detail below, there are strong 'anti-siphoning' regulations in Australia that prevent pay TV from exclusive broadcast of key sports, which must first be acquired by free-to-air TV channels. So there are key local sports such as Australian rules and rugby league that cannot be 'monopolized' by pay TV in Australia, as has occurred with major sports in other countries. Nonetheless, US-originating sports constituted 63.5 hours (40 per cent) of programme content on Fox Sports One in the sampled week. The asymmetrical nature of content is evident, for example, by comparison with the 4.5 hours (1 per cent) of sport content originating in Asia. This concentration of countries/regions of origins is, furthermore, reflected in the range of sport that was broadcast.

While seasonality must be recognized (May is late autumn in Australia, when three of the four local football codes are playing), it is evident that a small range of sports dominate the schedule, with golf alone (not in season in Australia in the sample week) absorbing 65 hours of content (39 per cent) and roughly corresponds with the US-originating content (although the data do not indicate precisely which sports emanate from which countries). This may only be one sports channel in one country, but it reveals something of the unevenness of the flows and content of TV sport – indeed, to a degree supporting rather traditional notions of media and cultural imperialism. This point is reinforced by considering the other two Fox Sports channels in the sample week – Fox Sports Two and Three. The former has more 'local' (in this case, Australian) content in the form of rugby league in particular, while the

Table 3.2 Fox Sports One (Australia), type of content and programme hours, from 6 May 2008 to 12 May 2008

Sport [content]	Hours	Percentage
Golf	65.0	39
AFL	35.0	21
Soccer	21.0	13
Other	12.5	7
Rugby Union	8.5	5
Motorsport	8.0	5
Tennis	7.5	4
Ice hockey	3.0	2
Baseball	2.5	1
Snooker	2.0	1
Poker	2.0	1
Athletics	1.0	1

latter is dominated by European-originated programming, especially tennis. When the three Australian Fox Sports Channels are combined, an overall picture can be gained of their sports television schedule in terms of dominant origins and sports.

Table 3.3 Fox Sports One, Two and Three combined (Australia), origin of content and programme hours, from 6 May 2008 to 12 May 2008

Nation/region	Hours	Percentage
Europe	157.0	31
Australia	149.5	30
United States	113.5	22
United Kingdom	51.0	10
New Zealand	13.5	3
South Africa	9.0	2
Asia	6.5	1
Middle East	4.0	1

Table 3.4 Fox Sports One, Two and Three combined (Australia), type of content and programme hours, from 6 May 2008 to 12 May 2008

Sport [content]	Hours	Percentage
Tennis	100	20.0
Golf	82.0	16.0
Rugby League	58.5	11.5
Other	51.0	10.0
Soccer	45.0	9.0
Rugby Union	43.5	9.0
AFL	36.0	7.0
Motorsport	34.0	7.0
Netball	17.0	3.0
Baseball	14.0	3.0
Ten-pin bowling	8.0	1.5
Ice hockey	6.0	1.0
Magazine/news	3.0	0.5
Poker	2.0	0.5
Basketball	2.0	0.5
Extreme	2.0	0.5

It is not my intention to produce large amounts of undigested and largely indigestible programme schedule data, but counting and aggregating broadcast sport in this way provides a useful take on the kinds of 'choice' made available under the rubric of global sport television. The combined Fox Sports channel data in Australia reveal that 30 per cent of the programming in the sample week came from the country in which it was broadcast, but that over twice as much (63 per cent) came from Europe (including the United Kingdom) and the United States, leaving only 7 per cent 'sourced' from the rest of the world. Of the 500 hours of sports TV on these channels, two sports (tennis and golf) accounted for over a third of them (36 per cent), and only seven sports providing almost four/fifths (79.5 per cent) of content. The category of 'other', representing 10 per cent of programming, constituted multiple, minor 'snippets' of many other sports barely covered during the week. Thus, this case – and it must be emphasized that it is a single case, although informed by other data discussed at various points in this book – highlights how global television sport (here on a subscription platform) is highly concentrated in production and content terms (here exacerbated by a quasi-monopoly of sport subscription television), so challenging familiar claims of a cornucopia of varied sporting fare. As will be discussed below, state regulation does prevent pay TV from exclusive 'capture' of many key national sports and sports events in Australia, but this restriction applies overwhelmingly to the small number of sports, such as the four football codes, that are already well represented on subscription television. As a result, their removal would be likely to lead to more rather than less concentration of TV sport, with much 'imported' sports content of lesser local popularity only substituting for coveted premium content that is prevented from siphoning. Thus, as suggested in the introduction, there is no necessary correlation between expanding screen size and diversity of sport on screen.

So it is possible to travel around the world inspecting various sites and ascertaining the extent to which televised sport is inserted into other TV markets by the dominant ones, as well as the health or otherwise of local/regional sports broadcasting. The Asia-Pacific media sport market is especially alluring for those media and sport organizations that see in them an opportunity for lucrative expansion by, predominantly, re-circulating what has already been produced and sold at home base (Rowe and Gilmour 2008). Increasingly affluent and/or populous nations such as Taiwan and India constitute links in global chains that involve cultivating new sporting tastes, catering to established ones and providing surplus content to fill in the schedule gaps at negligible additional cost. In the same sample week, the combined statistics for ESPN and Star Sports in Taiwan are shown in Tables 3.5 and 3.6.

Table 3.5 Combined ESPN and Star Sports ESPN Star Sports, Taiwan, origin of content, from 6 May 2008 to 12 May 2008

Nation/region	Hours	Percentage
United States	159.5	48.0
Asia	118.0	35.0
Europe	27.5	8.0
United Kingdom	27.5	8.0
Middle East	1.5	0.5
Australia	1.0	0.25
New Zealand	1.0	0.25

Table 3.6 Combined ESPN and Star Sports ESPN Star Sports, Taiwan, type of content, from 6 May 2008 to 12 May 2008

Sport [content]	Hours	Percentage
Baseball	117.5	35
Other	46.0	14
Golf	32.5	10
Motorsport	30.5	9
Basketball	30.0	9
Billiards	21.5	6
Soccer	16.5	5
Extreme	16.0	5
Magazine/news	14.0	4
Table tennis	11.5	3

In the case of ESPN and Star Sports in Taiwan, almost two thirds of sports programming (64 per cent) came from the United States and Europe (including United Kingdom), with over a third (35 per cent) coming from Asia (excluding the Middle East, including Taiwan). This pattern appears to be common in global media sport that, in fact, is not so global – a high concentration of sports content from the region/nation and the main production centres in the West and negligible 'transported' sports material from Africa and South America. Sports are highly concentrated, with only four (baseball, golf, motorsport and basketball) responsible for 62 per cent of programming in the sampled week. In India, aggregating three channels (ESPN, Star Sports and Star Cricket), Tables 3.7 and 3.8 reveal some pattern variation, with Asia accounting for a little more sport (40 per cent) and Europe (including United Kingdom) and the United States rather less (48 per cent) – although even here local/regional sports content is outweighed by that originating in the West. The main variant here is the popularity of cricket, which introduces significant coverage from Australia, South African and the West Indies (as it is known in cricket but generally as the Caribbean) on its dedicated channel (18.5 per cent in total). Again, there is a tight clustering of sports, with four – cricket (unsurprisingly), soccer, tennis and golf – responsible for almost three quarters of sports content (72 per cent).

The sampled sports network schedule data (which took a considerable amount of time to assemble by, necessarily, a mainly manual counting method) make no claim to global comprehensiveness and clearly aren't broken down further into individual nations or the precise origin of each sport, nor do they

Table 3.7 Combined ESPN, Star Sports and Star Cricket, India, origin of content, from 6 May 2008 to 12 May 2008

Nation/region	Hours	Percentage
Asia	199.5	40.0
Europe	88.0	17.0
Australia	77.0	15.0
United Kingdom	72.5	14.0
United States	55.0	11.0
South Africa	7.0	1.5
West Indies	4.0	1.0
South America	0.5	0.25
Central America	0.5	0.25

Table 3.8 Combined ESPN, Star Sports and Star Cricket, India, type of content, from 6 May 2008 to 12 May 2008

Sport [content]	Hours	Percentage
Cricket	189.5	38.0
Soccer	74.5	15.0
Tennis	53.0	11.0
Golf	40.0	8.0
Other	26.0	5.0
Magazine/news	26.0	5.0
Motorsport	25.5	5.0
Hockey	22.0	4.5
Basketball	21.5	4.0
Extreme	12.0	2.0
Baseball	12.0	2.0
Rugby Union	2.0	0.5

explore the intriguing areas of sports programming (only loosely defined as appearing on a dedicated sports channel) such as magazine/news, extreme sports and poker. Nor has there been any attempt here to probe questions of sociocultural power, such as those revolving around gender, sexuality, 'race', ethnicity and class, as they relate first to which sports are shown in which context and how. I and other scholars address these vital questions in other places (see, for example, Birrell and McDonald 2000; Carrington 2010; Carrington and McDonald 2001; Caudwell 2006; Rowe 2004a; Wenner 1998), but my intention in this instance is to concentrate on the major flows of sports and its principal vehicles via broadcasting. Societies, nations and regions are not the only concerns for critical media sports scholars and are by no means the guardians of social progressivism. But they remain, despite strong criticisms of their analytical, explanatory and empirical integrity (see, for example, Urry 2000), significant reference points in seeking understanding of the global power dynamics in this field of culture.

What these statistics do reveal, then, is the complex dynamism of global media sport, which sees sports such as association football, motor racing, tennis, golf and basketball range freely around the world from their Western power bases but simultaneously having a differential impact in various regions and nations, and also having to come to terms with contextual preferences. For example, the historically US-dominated sport of baseball is popular in Taiwan but barely registers in India, while the historically UK-originated sport of cricket is of enormous interest in India but means almost nothing in Taiwan. Australian rules football and rugby league, however, do not 'travel well' outside that country to India or Taiwan. Media sports corporations such as News Corp and Disney, therefore, have considerable transnational power, but it is not unfettered. As noted, they can exert power over what is seen and this, undoubtedly, can encourage the popularity of intensively displayed and marketed sports, but there are historically inherited preferences, some of which have their origins in imperialism, colonialism and post-war occupation, that present considerable obstacles to the establishment of globally popular sports. There is also the apparatus of the state – much stronger in some countries than others in the field of national popular culture – that can still exert its authority on questions of cultural citizenship and the rights pertaining to broadcast sport viewing.

A screen with a view: sport television and cultural citizenship

In the previous section there was an examination of the flows of sport television across world zones through the agency of media sport corporations such as News Corp and Disney. This content is crucial in the more competitive television environment of the twenty-first century, when a familiar industry catchcry is that 'content is king'. It could be objected that this was always the case, but in a digital world where free-to-air and subscription broadcast television has splintered audiences through ever-increasing multichannelling choice menus, and television can be delivered by others means, especially through online and mobile platforms, and there are many other electronic media leisure options such as gaming and social networking, it has never been more important to draw in viewers with screen material that is compelling and unavailable elsewhere. It is for this reason that there is such intense disputation over intellectual property (Hutchins and Rowe 2009a,b) and access to mediated sport texts. Sport, as we have seen, is just such content, but it is not only that – it cannot be approached exclusively in industrial and commercial terms. As an important popular cultural form, sport draws its content appeal precisely from the claims to ownership by those who engage in and identify with it. In the past century, as television became integral to national culture and sport a pivotal symbol of nation, sport television became part of the 'national estate' (Whannel 1992). There has been, though, considerable international variation as to the type of broadcaster that pioneered sport television. For example, in the United Kingdom, continental Europe, Canada, South America and Asia, national public, free-to-air broadcasters carried 'emblematic' sports events as moments when the nation could assemble in real time, while in the United States, in particular, commercial sports networks broadcast sport in the absence of a strong public broadcasting sector (Chandler 1988).

In countries where commercial free-to-air networks were given access to sport content and then came to dominate it, supporters of public broadcasters were unhappy about the marketization of sports television (with paying for sports rights initially resisted and then acquired for very modest sums) that saw them 'dethroned', but this discontent (spurred by unwelcome exposure to high levels of advertising) was greatly exacerbated when subscription television restricted access to those willing and able to pay for them. In many countries, therefore, and especially those with a strong history of public broadcasting mixed with commercial free-to-air television, there have been intense debates about protecting sports events of national cultural significance from exclusive capture by commercial pay television. These issues go to matters of cultural citizenship (Miller 2006; Stevenson 2003) – that is, the right of any citizen, irrespective of their class position or personal financial circumstances, to be included in mediated sporting festivals of nation. These questions are not exactly vital when television has failed to reach most households but become so when, as has occurred across much of the globe, it becomes an everyday domestic facility requiring only TV reception, a rudimentary device for screening it and the necessary electrical power to activate it. In such cases, the state or the market are put under pressure to ensure delivery of major sports events live and free-to-air to the citizenry at large.

Across the world, therefore, the right to watch global mega media events like the Olympics or sports of particular national significance without charge remains a highly 'charged' area. For example, the member states of the European Union are permitted under the European Audiovisual Media Services Directive to designate events of cultural, national or public importance (almost all of which are sports events, apart from state weddings and funerals, the Eurovision Song Contest and a smattering of other televised occasions of moment) that must be made available 'live and free'. The EU framework enables parliaments to make such decisions, and as a result there is intense political lobbying by sport organizations that tend to strive for maximum broadcast rights, media corporations who want to purchase them to their advantage, and fan groups and viewer associations who demand the right to watch without unnecessary impediment.

Two recent legal cases reveal the nature of conflicts over televised sports access and rights. FIFA and UEFA attempted to prevent the United Kingdom and Belgium from reserving all of the World Cup and European Championship for free-to-air television because they

> wanted the freedom to sell certain matches within the tournaments to the highest bidder and have long argued that not all games can be considered to be 'events of major importance for the public' ...

> But the general court of the European Union ruled that both tournaments could legitimately be classified by national governments as 'single events' that could be protected with free-to-air legislation.

> The court said that it could not be predicted which games would be important for which country. 'It cannot be specified in advance – at the time when the national lists are drawn up or broadcasting rights acquired – which matches will actually be decisive for the subsequent stages of those competitions or which ones may affect the fate of a given national team', it ruled. (Gibson 2011)

Intriguing in this case is not only that the court ruled in favour of wider public access to major mediated sport events against FIFA and UEFA's argument that 'the current set-up interfered with their ability to sell television rights at the best price' (Wilson, B., 2011), but also that the competitive uncertainty of sport means that the importance of a sports contest to a particular member state viewership cannot always be determined in advance (e.g. they may wish to watch a match not involving their national team that is nonetheless relevant to their progress in the overall tournament). In a second ruling in the European Union in the same month, it was the subscription broadcaster BSkyB and the EPL that felt aggrieved when the Advocate General of the European Court of Justice, in the so-called Landlady Case, found in favour of a public house in the English coastal city of Portsmouth in overturning an earlier judgement that it had breached exclusive territorial copyright by showing EPL games using an imported satellite card from the Greek satellite broadcaster Nova (Fenton and Blitz 2011). Again, the contending issue was the capacity to maximize revenue from the sale of broadcast rights as opposed to its freer circulation among citizen-viewers.

This structural framework of interests and conflicts can be found in some form in all spaces of televised sport, irrespective of specific sports broadcast histories. For example, in the Middle East and North Africa, the Al-Jazeera Sports and ART Sports subscription platforms are challenging the traditional state-controlled sports TV sector, whereas in Argentina the reverse seems to be the case, with the ending of the Torneos y Competencias company's long-standing monopoly to broadcast football effectively 'nationalized' by the government in 2009. Meanwhile, the public Canadian Broadcasting Corporation (CBC) has managed to sustain its free-to-air telecasting of key National Hockey League (NHL) games. In countries such as Israel,

Singapore and Malaysia, subscription platforms have increasingly come to dominate sports television and yet, in the United States, with its prominent development of cable and satellite television sport, a 2008 House Energy and Commerce Subcommittee examined ways in which access to National Football League (NFL) and Major League Baseball games could be enhanced on free-to-air commercial networks (see various contributions to Scherer and Rowe 2012).

Countries as close (regarding regional location and broadcast history) as New Zealand and Australia have dealt with sports broadcasting differently in the past decade. The former has, since 1996, allowed the nation's dominant subscription broadcaster, the Murdoch-controlled Sky TV, to monopolize live broadcasts of the country's major sport, rugby union, and increasingly those of other sports, such as rugby league, cricket, netball and the 2008 post-Beijing Olympic Games. A 2009 change of government (from Labour to National) saw the abandonment of a broadcast policy review that might have legislated a place for free-to-air television. However, in Australia, the election and subsequent re-election of a Labour government (in 2007 and 2010) saw a review of sport on television reaffirm, while also to some degree reforming, the nation's anti-siphoning regime. Here a range of matters was addressed, including the rise of new media, digital multichannelling and programme hoarding as set out in its discussion paper (Australian Government 2009). It is worthwhile noting here what is described as the 'way forward' in the final report in reflecting both a continuing commitment to widely available sports television and a recognition of the changing environment brought about by digitization:

> The Government remains strongly committed to the free availability of sport on free-to-air television. Sport is central in Australian society and the objective of ensuring free public access to events of national importance and cultural significance remains a relevant public policy objective. However, the media landscape is changing rapidly as a result of the shift to digital technologies and amendments to the operation of the anti-siphoning scheme are needed to keep pace with these changes ...

> The Government's position is that nationally iconic events, such as the Melbourne Cup and domestic football grand finals, should continue to be shown on main channels first, and therefore be available in both analogue and digital until digital television switchover is completed in 2013. Even after digital switchover, the level of consumer awareness and broadcaster promotion of 'main' channels may still justify some retention of this restriction. However, there is a case for other events on the anti-siphoning list to be permitted to be shown first on digital multi-channels. This will provide free-to-air broadcasters with greater flexibility to utilise the capacity of the digital platform and enhance free-to-air coverage of significant sports events, and also drive digital take-up, which is a key priority for the Government.

> Finally, the Government is alert to the potential for new media to challenge the effective operation of the anti-siphoning scheme. Platforms such as Internet Protocol Television provide the *potential* for sporting content to migrate exclusively from free-to-air television, and no longer be available freely to the general public.

> While sports coverage on new media platforms appear to be predominantly supplementary to that of traditional television at this time, it is possible that in the future subscription-based new media services may indeed pose a threat to free access to sport for Australian audiences. (Australian Government 2010b)

While there is much here that is specific to the Australian context – its anti-siphoning regime being the most stringent in the world for a range of reasons, including the political influence of the free TV sector and the centrality of sport to Australian culture – it is also apparent that such issues of access, technology, culture, economics and citizenship register across all global sites where television shows sport – that is, almost everywhere. The rapidly changing media landscape discussed above has not seen the end of television, but there is no doubt that it is in transition. For example, the familiar idea of a 'main channel' on which to watch the main sports events may fade (like the concept of an 'original' paper document and its copies after word processing), although there is some industry concern that the resultant fragmentation of audiences across sport and non-sport platforms on the same day will lead to some viewer 'churn' and a reduction in the impressive audience figures on single channels that allow a premium to be extracted from advertisers and sponsors.

This discussion of sport television and cultural citizenship reveals that globalization is not about homogeneity but a highly contextualized and variable working through of responses to developments that are both endogenous and exogenous. As will be shown in Chapter 4, digital technologies both change the structures and relations surrounding sports media such as television and create permutations that seem in some ways to revive practices often deemed to have passed into history. Thus, the screens on which sport is watched become both larger and smaller, and what can be watched on them expanded and narrowed according to who controls the content supply chain and the outcomes of struggles over the relations of production and consumption. Sport television under a regime of digitization, therefore, is becoming more synthetic and its contexts and practices more variable. As Jinna Tay and Graeme Turner (2010: 46) suggest,

> [A]s the consumers of digital television increasingly embrace the opportunities for customization and individualization and so on, it would seem reasonable to assume that some of the preceding versions of co-presence – the national, the local, the broader and less personal social framings – are likely to become less important to the experience of television than they have been in the past. This will vary, though, according to the social, political and regulatory context – and not just merely in relation to the actions of consumers or the enabling capacities of the technology. There are plenty of locations where broadcasting has declined in importance but where the embedding of the national has remained a major discursive component of the television programming produced.

Such uncertainty and analytical tentativeness about the consequences of globalization and digitization may be intellectually frustrating but is preferable to the wilder 'apocalyptic' or 'utopic' projections of television's future – or, more accurately, futures – that have proved so consistently unreliable. As is pointed out below, some of those agents and organizations closest 'to the action' have had great difficulty in anticipating the next shift in television in general and sport television in particular.

Global sports television and its futures

This chapter has concentrated on highlighting important aspects of how sports television is constructed as global but has developed in ways that are highly contingent and even idiosyncratic, the product of powerful forces that can shift both in-demand and incidental sports onto the screens of the world in a curious mixture of strategic placement and content 'spraying'. It can lead to the massive over-concentration of some sports (such as association football) and a serious neglect of others (like most sports played predominantly by women or those deemed to be too localized and 'downmarket'). In focusing on the broader processes out of which a global television sport apparatus is being constructed, the prospect of it being dismantled – or even dismantling itself – has come into view. Ironically, at the very historical moment when sport television is more watched and more valuable than ever before, the medium of television is often represented and represents itself as in crisis (see various commentaries: Spigel and Olsson 2004; Turner and Tay 2009) and, especially, under siege from what has come to be called new media, but which is in some respects becoming so familiar as to be losing its veneer of novelty. The more intense 'competition for eyeballs' created by many screen types and uses (computing, gaming, social networking, niche programming) is feared by sport TV programmers to be depleting the peak audience levels that deliver them cultural reach, economic prosperity and political influence. However, some recent evidence suggests that the social ritual appeal of television viewing can be supported rather than undermined by the very social networking that is predicted to dissipate it. Thus, for example, the 2010 Super Bowl between the New Orleans Saints and the Indianapolis Colts (with its post–Hurricane Katrina emotional charge regarding the former team) had a record audience of over 100 million people, and television executives partially attributed this success to the 'grass-roots' promotional impact of social networking:

> CBS [the Super Bowl Broadcast Network in 2010] Chief Executive Leslie Moonves said social networking tools such as Twitter have encouraged TV viewing as Americans exchange opinions on what they're watching:

> 'They've bucked the trend,' said Andy Donchin, director of media investments at Carat, a media-buying unit of Aegis Group PLC. 'As much as we're pulling away and watching different things, there are some things that we want to watch together.' (Schechner and Ovide 2010)

Thus, although aggregate viewing may be falling to a degree in mature television markets like the United States, the sociality of televisions and its rituals (Silverstone 1994), and the relationships of reinforcement between media (as opposed to assumptions that they are always involved in zero-sum competition), means that the already socially engaged nature of major event sports television reproduces and extends itself. In the following year, the Super Bowl audience for the Green Bay Packers versus Pittsburgh Steelers game was even larger, and there were frequent references to it 'making history', such as:

> History was made last night on FOX when Super Bowl XLV became the most-watched U.S. television program ever, and FOX became the first network ever to exceed 100 million viewers (100.9 million) for a night in prime time, according to fast-national ratings released today by Nielsen Media Research.

> FOX Sports' broadcast of Super Bowl XLV averaged 111 million viewers and is the most-watched television program in U.S. history, obliterating the prior record of 106.5 set last year during Super Bowl XLIV by 4.5 million viewers.

> This is the fourth consecutive Super Bowl to set a viewership record, and attracted 13.5 million more viewers than FOX's last Super Bowl broadcast in 2008 (97.5 million) for the New York Giants upset of the undefeated New England Patriots. No other major sporting event has ever hit a record high in four consecutive years. This also marks the sixth straight year that Super Bowl viewership has increased, and over that span average Super Bowl viewership has increased from 86.1 million in 2005 to 111.0 million, a gain of nearly 25 million viewers.

> The game posted a 46.0/69 household rating/share tying Super Bowl XXX in 1996 (Dallas-Pittsburgh) as the highest-rated since Super Bowl XX in 1986 (48.3/70, Chicago vs. New England). Only eight of the 45 Super Bowls played had a higher rating, and all were played in a nine-year span between 1978 and 1986.

> Super Bowl XLV also set a new mark for total viewership of any program in U.S. history (persons age 2+ watching all or part of the game) with 162.9 million people watching, 9.5 more than the record set a year ago (153.4 million).

> The airing of Super Bowl XLV goes down as FOX's most-watched night of prime time ever, as well as FOX's highest-rated night ever among Adults 18–49. It's also the most-watched night on any network in at least 20 years, and the highest-rated night on any network among Adults 18–49 in 15 years (dating to the night of Super Bowl XXX on NBC). (Seidman 2011a)

That Super Bowl continues to make history – of an approved kind, especially for the News Corp–owned FOX television network) – in US television, and the manner of its interpretation, reveals the close relationship between quantification in sports competition and television viewer ratings, both of which are presented in the form of scores and records (see also Buteau and Fixmer 2011; Schechner 2011). These statistics reveal the capacity of sports television to breach some demographic divides during events of national significance – for example, despite widespread perceptions that the United States's Hispanic population is interested in and watches association rather than American football, Super Bowl 2011 'reached an average of 10.0 million Hispanic viewers making it the most-watched show in U.S. television history among Hispanic viewers' (Seidman 2011b). It is for this reason that a 30-second commercial can be sold for between US$2.5 and US$3 million (Buteau and Fixmer 2011; Sweney

2011b), both displaying (in the form of film trailers) and connecting with other media (including online, mobile):

> The 30-second TV spots for Super Bowl XLV cost about $3 million each and sold out months ago. According to Kantar Media, the cost of Super Bowl ads has risen by 36% in the last ten years, with a 30-second spot costing around $2.2 million a decade ago.

> The biggest advertisers in 2011 include Anheuser-Busch (Budweiser beer), with the largest buy for the game. Dot-com firms also take a sizable portion of commercials from CareerBuilder.com to E*Trade. Film spots will include a preview of the sci-fi Western Cowboys and Aliens starring Daniel Craig and Harrison Ford.

> The peak advertising event of the year is joining the digital age by going beyond the 30-second TV spot to include online features, social networks and mobile media. Ad agencies are incorporating Facebook and Twitter as well as contest sites such as http://beonthefield.com. (*The Independent* 2011)

On top of the very large US audience, Super Bowl is also shown live in over 200 countries and, while its international viewership is dominated by neighbours Mexico and Canada, the use of international pop stars in the half-time entertainment (in 2011, the Black Eyed Peas) helps to draw some international attention, although the actual international viewership is difficult to ascertain and historically prone to exaggeration (Martin and Reeves 2010).

The oscillation between excessive optimism and pessimism that pervades the occupational culture of 'legacy media' tends to forget certain sociological verities, such as that humans are social and capable of combinatory rather than sole-focused activity, and is also unduly focused on the West. The constitutive global sociocultural complexity means that the latest 'American way' of television and Twitter plays out quite differently in other social environments across the globe or within sub-environments within the same country (hence, while overall viewership for the Super Bowl has increased, the percentage of households watching has fallen below half (Schechner 2011). As Raymond Williams (1974) influentially argued about the rise of television as a cultural form, and has since been borne out by the emergence of Short Message Service (SMS) and the Internet, very little can be reliably predicted or known about the uses and abuses of media until they engage, unpredictably, with those for whom they have been designed – or have appropriated them (see also Hill, 1988). In typically witty fashion, he states,

> If we cancel history, in the sense of real times and real places, we can conceive of an abstract human nature which has specific psychic needs and which variable forms of technology and intercourse come to satisfy.

> Any cancellation of history, in the sense of real times and real places, is essentially a cancellation of the contemporary world, in which, within limits and under pressures, men[sic] act and react, struggle and concede, cooperate, conflict and compete. A technology, when it has been achieved, can be seen as a general human property, an extension of general human capacity. But all technologies have been developed and improved to help with known human practices or with foreseen and desired practices. (Williams 1974: 129)

For Williams, the horizon of the 'original intention' of a technology's use is initially limited by the social group that first controls it, but this hegemony cannot be maintained perpetually, and other groups – often subordinate – find new uses for and adaptations of it. Indeed, its uses and effects may be quite different from the original conception and intention, unforeseen and unintended by any particular social group, but emergent in the relationships between them and in processes of trial and error (see also Hill 1988; MacKenzie and Wajcman 1998). Thus, in counselling against both technological determinism and 'determined technology', Williams shows how structural forces set limits to what can occur (it is not generally possible, for example, for individual sport fans to acquire the rights to sport) but that cannot police them entirely (that same fan might 'hack into' and distribute digital signals of sports contests). He sees television as a particularly striking case of a technology invented for 'military [as with the Internet], administrative and commercial intentions' (Williams 1974: 130) which became dominated by the commercial in some contexts (as in the United States) but for purposes of 'social training and social control' (which occurred in Britain). These 'conditions of complex or of privatised mobility' were also understood by 'the many people who were experiencing this process as subjects':

> To controllers and programmers they might seem merely objects: a viewing public or a market. But from their own side of the screen there was a different perspective: if they were exposed by need in new ways, they were also exposed to certain uncontrollable opportunities. This complicated interaction is still very much in the process of working itself out. (Williams 1974: 131)

Williams's words, published in 1974 in the analogue era when colour television was still in its infancy, resonate even more effectively at a time when television is no longer the acme of communications technology. In late 2010 the television guide of the leading Australian newspaper, *The Sydney Morning Herald*, tried to replicate an exercise from the turn of this century of asking a group of television industry experts to predict what television would be like a decade later. Intriguingly, only one of its previous TV forecasters from 2000 agreed to go public again with their new predictions, such is the reputational risk of speculative forecasting in this volatile field. In an overview, its editor declared,

> Live sport will become increasingly valuable. Water-cooler moments will become rarer, although viewers will continue to seek out the communal viewing experience, enhanced by social media. (Hassall 2010)

Here, the aforementioned experience of the Super Bowl, Olympics and the World Cup is predicted to continue, in that a fragmented television audience comes together for important collective rituals (notably, here, a great sporting occasion attracting global interest), and its 'buzz' is stimulated by the social media which were initially believed to be the enemy of an old medium such as television. In the same edition of the TV guide, Stephen Conroy, described as the Communications Minister but whose full title, revealingly, is Minister for Broadband, Communications and the Digital Economy, 'avoids saying how changes in anti-siphoning laws might affect viewing in 2020 but does say: "The old regulations ensuring broadcasters produce and screen Australian stories won't work in the broadband age"' (quoted in Walters 2010: 4). As discussed earlier in this chapter, at the time that the minister made this comment he was involved in a highly controversial revision of the regulations governing the relationship between free-to-air and subscription television sport. In a nation such as Australia, where the state mandates the minimum proportions of prime-time and other hours of local content (which includes sport but privileges original drama) for commercial television providers, there is constant jockeying for position among established and emergent competing interests to change the rules in their favour and considerable pressure from less organized interest groups, such as sport television viewers, to maintain and enhance what they now regard as their established rights of cultural citizenship as they pertain to taking part by viewing, without an admission fee, in events of national cultural significance that, for most practical purposes, involve only sport.

But, in an age that has been characterised as both 'digital' and 'global', and so is less amenable to national government control, there is a (seemingly) perpetually confusing and contentious interplay of new possibilities, former entitlements and emergent opportunities for enclosure and exploitation. For example, the tension between showing the sports event 'warts and all' and dressing it up as 'must-see' television is constant. The live performance aspects of sport rely to a degree on faithful reportage – but what can be done when the action itself is underwhelming? Above, the advantages of sport's competitive uncertainty were seen in a European Court's rejection of FIFA and EUFA's attempt to anticipate national audience interest in an unfolding sports tournament. But the same live, spontaneous uncertainty that may make sport compelling viewing can also turn it, during unequal encounters, into a non-event for all but the most sport committed. Here the contagious impact of the live, co-present crowd is crucial – a game is worth watching because lots of other people noisily, colourfully attest that it is so. So if the crowd is neither noisy nor colourful, within the available repertoire of television tricks are not only audio maximization, dramatic close-ups and rapid intercutting of images, but also 'rent a crowd' techniques by sponsors and broadcasters that engage people to simulate spontaneous, idiosyncratic fan passion. Better still, 'some great technological innovations' can be used that can, as one broadcast television executive in Australia has argued (although by no means the first – see Rowe 2004a), effectively separate the representation of a sports event to the distant audience from any requirement for it to be faithful to the context in which it was performed for those present:

CHANNEL Nine has revealed a bold plan to repackage its Monday night programming with live AFL matches complete with virtual crowds.

Nine's executive director Jeff Browne said Monday night football was likely to underpin its push for a slice of the next AFL broadcast rights deal from 2012, but he regarded it as primarily a television game in which he would compensate for half-full stadiums with virtual crowds.

For example, if Etihad Stadium had a crowd of less than 20,000, thousands of spectators could be inserted into empty seats using digital technology.

'I think Monday night is the new franchise for the AFL, and we want it', Browne told *The Age*. 'It's a traditional timeslot in sports all around the world.'

'Obviously, being a Monday night, you'd attract less people to the match. But there are some great technological innovations we can put around it to make it a fantastic game for television, and we'd show it live.'

'People are being diabolically conservative about this. The fact is people are home on Monday nights and they are out on Friday nights.' (C. Wilson 2010)

This idea of 'made for television' sport, in which the authenticity of the live, in-stadium event is sacrificed to make the viewing experience more attractive in response to the rhythms of weekly leisure, exposes the dilemmas of a global medium for which digital innovation can turn to the faking of fandom. As we have seen, across the twentieth century, broadcast television sport became not only more accessible but also more commodified, more plentiful yet also more systematically rationed. Just as newspaper sport was confronted by the need for major adjustments to its *modus operandi* by the arrival of television, and the whole medium is now seeking to work out the terms of peaceful coexistence with the Internet, sports television faces a future in which its hold over major live mediated sports action is loosened. This adjustment is being made from a position of strength rather than weakness, but the combination of new, proliferating post-broadcast technologies and the difficulties of exercising proprietorial and territorial control are creating a very different, uncharted global media sport landscape. In Chapter 4, the ramifications of this struggle for possession in online sport, with its immediate promise of narrower screens but wider visions, are given further consideration.

4

Digital Media, Networking and Executive Fandom

Sports broadcasting under different gods

Chapter 3 was concerned with sports television as the dominant medium of the past half century, establishing itself around the world in the form of public and commercial free-to-air broadcasting and commercial subscription platforms by various means, such as microwave, satellite and cable. It was shown that the global television system is a mixture of nationally contained content combined with selected sports programming circulating into other countries and regions, sometimes regarded as crucially tied to the viewing rights of citizens (both of nations and of the world) and sometimes predominantly 'filler' for multi-sports channels that satisfy expansion and status aspirations of sports and sports events of limited international appeal while providing modest broadcast rights revenue. The screening of major sports events can be highly sociable encounters, offering 'water-cooler moments' when large numbers of people engage with the screen action, identify with and distinguish themselves from the contestants, organize social events based on them and so, by various means, feel connected to social groups ranging from suburbs to nations. It is for this reason that such collective sporting moments are often – though there are signal exceptions as indicated in Chapter 3 – protected by international sports organizations, regional political unions, national governments, public broadcasters and free-to-air network television corporations from moving beyond the reach of the general citizenry. Indeed, television can enable the simulation of 'being there' not just by watching from home but by attending what are called live sites or public viewing sites organized around watching prime sports events on large screens in public spaces (McQuire 2010; Rowe and Stevenson 2006). For example, during the 2010 World Cup in South Africa, FIFA established official Fan Fest sites in Rio de Janeiro, Mexico City, Berlin, Paris and Rome (although, surprisingly, none in Asia) and in nine South African cities, while many others were set up under the aegis of cities and local governments (Rowe and Baker 2011). However, watching sport on screen, even collectively, is qualitatively different from being part of the sport spectacle being screened, a component so important that, as noted in Chapter 3, some television programmers have considered digital crowd simulations to provide atmosphere.

Indeed, there is a broader critique that watching television, even in company, is a rather passive activity. It is my intention here only to acknowledge, rather than to engage deeply in, the debates about 'active audiences' and 'active viewers' that proliferated in media and cultural studies as a response to mechanical accounts of helpless readers victimized by media propaganda and disempowered by trivial entertainment (see, for example, Brooker and Jermyn 2003, Part 3; Rowe 2011b). This position, especially where associated with the *oeuvre* of John Fiske (1987), and notably in his key work *Television Culture*, is that audiences actively make meanings out of the culture provided to them by industrial media capitalism, and so they cannot be wholly controlled by – and may be resistive in some respects to – the texts and messages that they receive. This recognition of the complexity of reception is, then, a counter to those who simplify it as simple absorption and acceptance. As Fiske (1989) puts it,

> We live in an industrial society, so of course our popular culture is an industrialized culture, as are all our resources; by 'resources' I mean both semiotic or cultural ones and material ones – the commodities of both the financial and cultural economies ...

> However, the fact that people cannot produce and circulate their own commodities does not mean that popular culture does not exist ... The creativity of popular culture lies not in the production of commodities so much as in the productive use of industrial commodities. The art of the people is the art of 'making do'. The culture of everyday life lies in the creative, discriminating use of the resources that capitalism provides. (Fiske 1989: 27–8)

In the area of sports television, this combination of audience creativity (e.g. turning the sports commentary that is supposed to determine how viewers interpret events on screen into a source of comedy) and social intercourse (such as using televised sports events for purposes well beyond simple viewing, including the reinforcement of sociocultural identities) produces a very different picture from that of the mythical inert (usually male) sporting 'couch potato' (Bryant and Cummins 2010). This is especially so when the users of sports television are also involved in different types of fan community, both place based and 'de-territorialized' (Sandvoss 2003), that display a considerable degree of active involvement and organization in the conduct and experience of fan life. Garry Crawford (2004: 159), focusing specifically on sports fans, stresses the everyday social rather than the politically resistive aspects of sports fandom, while recognizing the wider societal constraints imposed on it:

> Cultural texts (such as sport) have always played a role in many individuals' lives, as a source of conversation, recall, individual and collective memories and as a constituent of individuals' identities. However, we live in a society increasingly based upon social performance and spectacle, where individuals will draw on cultural texts in the construction of their identities and their social performances.

Thus, although there are many ways in which TV sport can be put to use by its viewers, limitations to the structure of orthodox sport television viewing in any context are always present given the one-way flow of images and sounds, and the inability of viewers to 'speak back' directly to the spectacle that they are watching. There are, of course, many other modes of communicating about sport other than responding to screen action or to other professional media, such as radio, newspapers and magazines. Sports fans have for some time engaged in their own mediated sport production, such as through fanzines, the 'cottage industry' alternative to the sports pages of major newspapers (Haynes 1995; Rowe 1995). However, since the highlight of the paper fanzine, the digitization of media technologies has created many more opportunities for interactivity rather than straightforward reception and new ways of exceeding the usual spatial 'footprint' of media use. Here the 'active audience' is more commonly described as the 'active fan' because implicit in the concept of fandom is not just a matter of taste (liking sport) but also of communal identity and even of organized collective action. Without descending into the realm of caricatures of yesterday's and today's sports media, it is undeniable that many new possibilities of mediated sport fandom now exist. At its worst, the old system of (analogue) sport television constituted a rationed menu of fixed alternatives, with a small number of broadcasters and sports organizations determining what could be seen and when (King 1998). Viewers would have to 'make appointments' with televised games shown live, 'as live' (a trick to simulate real-time transmission), by delayed telecast, replays and highlight packages. Surrounding the action would be other programmes involving preview, review and discussion also scheduled by broadcasters. The innovation of, first, video tape recorders and, later, personal or digital video recorders allowed the kind of time shifting that matched the increasing fluidity of everyday lives. Digitization also allowed split-screen simultaneous viewing, information requests and so on, thereby enriching the experience of sport TV viewing as the menu of available sports widened, especially for those who subscribed to dedicated sports channels.

However, these innovations were still spatially restricted to the fixed sites of television reception. The development of mobile and computing devices enabled sport to find its fans in myriad spaces, rather than requiring them to find the limited spaces in which sport was displayed. News Corp's promotional information signals the potential of this shift:

> On the ground, the ESPN STAR Sports Event Management Group manages and promotes premier sporting events across Asia. ESPN STAR Sports reaches consumers at any time, any place and through all media platforms. The multilingual, online platforms, espnstar.com, espnstar.com.cn and espnstar.com.tw and footballcrazy.tv interact with millions of users, providing them with in-depth sports news, results and competitions.
>
> Developed for the sports fan who is constantly on the move, *mobile*ESPN and STAR Sports Mobile deliver differentiated mobile content. *mobile*ESPN enables the serious sports fan to follow his or her favorite sports more closely than ever before with a combination of specially produced video news clips, in-depth news coverage and analysis. STAR Sports Mobile provides interactive and entertaining opportunities to engage with sports, delivering exclusive video excerpts from leading football clubs Arsenal and Liverpool, as well as highlights from STAR Sports original programs covering opinions, instructional tips and the latest online game reviews. (News Corp 2010b)

It can be noted here that there is still a careful restriction of access to live sport, without which subscriptions could not be extracted from consumers (as revealed in the so-called Landlady Case briefly discussed in Chapter 3), but the online platforms operate as global media spaces that direct viewers towards their regional television schedules, while the mobile platforms constantly prime the interest and attract the attention of the 'serious sports fan' in ways that serve and foster a consumer-oriented sports culture. The amount of available sports coverage and 'data' is extraordinary and could not possibly be embraced comprehensively by even the most dedicated sports fan. For example, clicking on to espnstar.com (8 December 2010) illuminates sundry aspects of cricket, football, motorsport, tennis and golf (all of which featured strongly in the sports television programme schedules presented in Chapter 3) as well as US sports (basketball, baseball and so on) and other sports (such as athletics, boxing, Asian Games, MMA Martial Combat and Kia XGames Asia). There are games such as Maxis Football Manager, Super Selector and Maxis Voice of a Fan (Maxis being a leading Malaysian information and communication technology company), the latter involving a fan video competition: 'Football transcends all boundaries and the love of soccer is universal. Show your support to a fellow football fan by voting for your favourite BPL [Barclays Premier League] fan video! The video with the most votes will win fantastic prizes so vote now to aid a fellow fan's victory!' Here there is a clear interpellation of association football fans in a manner that also recruits them as co-presenters of media sport, although under conditions of standardized formatting, duration and questioning (e.g. 'You are the manager for the day. What would you change in your favourite team?') and a requirement that they declare support for a specific team (such as Liverpool, Chelsea, Manchester United, Everton), although not always in the English language. There is an Opinion section with regular columnists and bloggers (the latter described as 'presenter or journalist, this group are [sic] – like you – fans first'), and others for sports videos and sports widgets, a TV schedule, news feeds, Facebook site, links to sponsored content and substantial advertising (of cars, cameras, sports clothing, beer and so on).

During the Cricket World Cup in 2011, at the same time as the association football season in the Northern hemisphere is in full flow, visitors to the website were offered the choice of two 'styles' – one with more football and the other with more cricket. By all these means of guidance, a web of technologies and uses connects sport viewers/fans to sports, media organizations, advertisers and other viewers/fans – although live broadcast television remains the most prized content around which other material pivots. The convergence with computing and telecommunications, though, indicates that what was once regarded as a distinct media sector is now a more complex system of networked media sport (Hutchins, Rowe and Ruddock 2009). Having considered at some length in previous chapters the histories and structures that have mediated sport and increasingly taken its cultural experience beyond the boundaries of nation – Maxis Voice of a Fan from espnstar.com cited earlier being a case in point, with fans from Asia commenting on an English association football competition in a forum sponsored by an Asian information and communication technology company – it is useful now to consider both the politico-cultural consequences of the intermeshing of broadcast and other technologies and the emergence of the figure of the global sports fan.

Determining sport news and the national interest

It is not so very long since selected live sports events were simply shown on television, heard on radio, reported in newspapers the day after and lavishly covered in magazines some time later. All of these activities still occur but in the context of other media and media combinations. For example, since the early twenty-first century newspapers progressively established an online presence. At first, these were shorter versions of the paper version, then they carried equivalent content and after that used the possibilities of the online medium to add multiple hyperlinks to other texts, advanced photographic and audio-visual material. Furthermore, sports organizations themselves set up substantial websites, while other sport and fan sites, and also telecommunications companies that had secured online and mobile rights to sports content, began to show more sports action and information. These developments provided greater opportunities for seeing mediated sports action (in still and moving forms) but also disturbed the established cultural 'genres' and legal frameworks according to which they were classified and the protocols by which they were handled (Hutchins and Rowe 2012). The 'de-specialized' nature of online technologies also meant that these media sports texts were normally available across the globe and without direct charge to users. As a result, the relatively established order of the media sports cultural complex that had held for several decades (involving a degree of 'strategic chaos' but with a greater degree of predictability when compared with a more converged media environment) has been shaken, especially for broadcast television companies holding expensively acquired sports rights and believing them to be increasingly infringed in the name of frequently updated sports news. The resultant disputation among interest groups has threatened to turn the wide world of media sport (that is almost compulsively described as 'exciting' by its producers and transmitters) into a litigious battleground.

In Chapter 3 it was noted that the Australian federal government, which oversees the most rigorous anti-siphoning sports television regime in the world, had reviewed its scheme in 2009–10 (as it had done periodically over two decades) and had sought to come to terms with the competing demands of media sport interests and the new horizons presented by technological innovations and accompanying audience/user expectations (Australian Government 2010a). Around the same time the Parliament of Australia Senate Standing Committee on Environment, Communications and the Arts held an inquiry into, and produced a report on, 'The Reporting of Sports News and the Emergence of Digital Media' (Parliament of Australia 2009) – the first formal inquiry of its kind in the world (Hutchins and Rowe 2010). It, no doubt, seems striking to many that a relatively small country with a population of 22 million should be so active in this area. The explanation lies partially in the often-noted cultural centrality of sport in Australia, which has been described, a little ironically, as a *Paradise of Sport* (Cashman 2010), afflicted by a *Saturday Afternoon Fever* (Stoddart 1986), wherein, according to Donald Horne's (1964: 37) famous pronouncement, 'sport to many Australians is life and the rest a shadow'. More importantly, in global terms, Australia is something of a 'testing ground' for media sport – a former White colony that inherited much of its institutional structure and societal ethos from Britain, before becoming increasingly influenced by, and politically aligned with, the United States in the twentieth century, belatedly recognizing (but still not entirely reconciled with) its indigenous population, became a major destination for migrants first from Europe and then the Asia-Pacific. It is now one of the most ethnically diverse countries in the world, and is situated as an English-speaking country on the edge of Asia, the fastest growing continent in population and economic terms and so is regarded as something of a Western 'staging post' for the Orient, caught between East and West (Wiseman 1998). It is for such reasons – predominantly, that it is a country with a developed Western media sport system increasingly economically embedded in the burgeoning Asia-Pacific region – that Australia is a larger force in media sport than might be expected and why, in both aforementioned media sport inquiries, multi- and transnational interests participated and sought to advance specific agenda that could defend current 'entitlements' and promote new, advantageous precedents.

The Australian instance is instructive with regard to how national governments find it difficult not just to adjudicate between competing media sport interest groups but to regulate media sport production and use within its jurisdiction. For example, the 'Sport on Television – Review of the Anti-Siphoning Scheme Discussion Paper' notes,

> The sale of sports rights for new media platforms are not currently covered by the anti-siphoning scheme. At present, Internet Protocol television and internet video content of sporting events are not considered a 'broadcasting service' under the *Broadcasting Services Act 1992* and as such are not regulated by the Act. Sporting content carried on mobile phones is also not specifically regulated by the Act. Further, the provision of sporting content via internet video hosted on international websites is not regulated by Australian law. (Australian Government 2009: 22)

Here is a classic example of a nation state seeking to encompass new media sport technologies within a modified regulatory framework designed for an earlier technology, while also having to grapple with the problem of regulating content from other countries over which it has no direct control or authority. The patrolling of borders is difficult enough with physical cultural objects in the forms of books, compact disks, digital video disks, software disks and video games under so-called parallel importing laws (Rowe 2001), but it becomes even more so when they take on immaterial form via the Internet where they do not, in any case, fit easily into current legislative and regulatory frameworks. Interestingly, the report that followed the review was rather less than apocalyptic about the challenge of new media to the authority of the state, for no other reason that the proliferation of flat-screen televisions in the home and the resilience of the practice of television viewing as currently understood meant that new media were complementing, supplementing and even stimulating the use of 'protected' broadcast technology rather than supplanting it:

> The view of new media as a complementary viewing experience has [also] been noted overseas. In the United Kingdom, the Independent Advisory Panel's November 2009 report into the Listed Events Scheme found that television is likely to remain the first choice for sports coverage.
>
> > *... the Panel has been convinced that, at least in the foreseeable future, and as far as the biggest sporting events are concerned, most people's first choice of how to view them will be by means of what is still identifiably a television set.*
>
> Research conducted by US television network NBC Universal of its 2008 Beijing Olympics coverage revealed that while there were over 75 million streams of its online content, less than 1 per cent of the audience relied solely on the internet to view the Games, seeing internet use as complementary to traditional television viewing. This led NBC executives to declare that new media does not cannibalise television viewing.
>
> > *The internet hardly cannibalises – it actually fuels interest.*
>
> ... At present, sports coverage via new media platforms appears to be supplementary to that of traditional television. New media services such as IPTV remain in their infancy in Australia and there are no examples to date of sporting events being siphoned exclusively to these platforms. Submissions to the review commenting on this issue generally opposed extending the anti-siphoning scheme to new platforms. However, there are views that the pace of technology convergence and the ever increasing quality of broadband means that differences between traditional and new media platforms are being eroded and the delivery of robust, high quality audio-visual services via IP-based platforms is increasingly feasible. These submissions conclude it is possible that in the future subscription-based new media services may indeed pose a threat to free access to sport for Australian audiences. (Australian Government 2010a: 30–1)

So, for the 'foreseeable future', it is apparent from the above statement that after extensive consideration little needs to be done because 'traditional television' remains dominant, and in any case, almost all sport and media organizations now use the Internet to promote their 'product' across the globe. But the openness of free-to-air broadcast television may be challenged, ironically, by 'closed' Internet-enabled sport services.

Perhaps, though, there is also a recognition here that it is too onerous – and in some ways contradictory – a task for the state to intervene in the name of citizens at a time when more mediated sports content is being made available to them free of charge. Unless and until this freely circulating material is restricted, there is felt to be little point in intervening on such grounds, but there are other principles on which to stand, especially those concerning national sovereignty (controlling media space), intellectual property (defending copyright) and institutional order (settling debilitating conflicts). The last was the primary motivation for the second recent state intervention in the media sport sector in Australia, this time on the subject of sport news and digital media. The Senate Committee, in quoting a submission from the Thomson Reuters news agency, demonstrated a keen awareness of the intimate nature of the sport–media nexus and the capacity of media forms to travel freely beyond national contexts:

> 1.5 It became apparent to the committee during the course of its inquiry that there is much common ground between sporting organizations and the media on this issue. Both sporting and media organizations believe there is a need for news coverage of sport and wish for sports news reporting to continue. News organizations detailed the benefits of news reporting to sports:
>
>> There can be no better promotion for any sport than the availability of timely, unbiased information to as many newspapers, websites, broadcasters and magazines as possible ... news agencies have the ability to constantly and consistently deliver this information globally to both developed and emerging economies; to very large and very poor media outlets. (Parliament of Australia 2009: 2)

But it also recognized the increasingly fractious nature of the organizational relationships involved in this 'delivery' of sport in a 'new media environment' caused by the progressive, digitally inspired breakdown of the established division of labour, responsibility and ownership between sport and media domains:

> 3.1 The convergence of media technologies and the emergence of new media platforms have created new opportunities for news media organizations, sports broadcasters and sporting organizations alike. These opportunities also bring with them challenges as existing businesses and organizations attempt to adapt to the new media environment.
>
> 3.2 Changes to the media landscape have led to some conflict as all stakeholders seek to take advantage of new opportunities as they emerge. This conflict is primarily between some news media organizations and some major professional sporting organizations ...
>
> 3.3 There are two related concerns being raised.
>
> 3.4 First, news media organizations and large sporting bodies engaged in the debate each believe that the other is encroaching on what has traditionally been their domain. This has been most evident in conflict over Internet use of sports news and images, and also to a lesser degree in respect of mobile digital platforms.
>
> 3.5 News media organizations have claimed that sporting organizations are entering into the media domain. Ninemsn described this as sporting organizations 'trying to provide many of the same services that media companies are, such as up-to-date scores, news reports on matches, images and video'.
>
> 3.6 Similarly, sporting organizations have argued that news media organizations have expanded their traditional role to that of providing sports entertainment ...

3.7 Second, some stakeholders are unhappy with the way in which traditional regulatory and contractual mechanisms are coping with the challenges presented by the new media environment.

3.8 During the inquiry, the committee heard evidence of conflict between news media organizations and sporting organizations over accreditation agreements. Some news media organizations claimed that sporting organizations were attempting to use accreditation agreements as a means 'to alter or even displace the fair dealing provisions contained in the Copyright Act, the public policy underlying it and the right of news organizations to exercise their rights as copyright owners in the material they create'. Sporting organizations argued that their accreditation agreements were used 'as a means to ensure that without clear regulation or other guidelines the intellectual property of sport is protected and content is appropriately used in line with fair dealing principles'. (Parliament of Australia 2009: 15–16)

These disputes, which had resulted both in litigation and lockouts of news organizations from sports events and retaliatory media boycotts (Hutchins and Rowe 2010), have arisen out of not just the media convergence (of broadcasting, telephony and computing) but the convergence of media and sport whereby both sides have accused the other of doing the other's traditional job. Thus, some sports (such as cricket and Australian rules football) have accused the media of using their sports news gathering and reporting functions as cover for the commercialization of sports rights that rightfully belong to sports, while media organizations have argued that sports are trying to corral sports information, including legitimate news, so that they can monetize it through their own media outlets. Disagreements between sport and media (especially broadcast) sectors are by no means unprecedented – and to some degree endemic. Before television became pivotal to the economics of sport it was treated with considerable suspicion as a likely tempter of paying spectators to stay at home. When handsome compensation was made available through broadcast rights, their inflation (usually achieved by playing rival broadcasters off against each other) led media companies to complain about a power imbalance and to tactics including purchasing sports clubs (thereby placing themselves on both sides of the bargaining table) and even setting up their own sporting competitions, just as some clubs established their own television stations and, later, virtually all set up websites (Boyle and Haynes 2009; Rowe 2004a). However, as was noted in Chapter 3, the legal cases involving FIFA, Union of European Football Associations (EUFA) and BSkyB demonstrated something of a community of interest between rights sellers and current holders in defence of their intellectual property, although by extension non-rights sellers can be expected to seek to maximize their access to this content (often in the name of news but sometimes through simple piracy). The combination of rapid digital dissemination and the involvement of other communication players, especially telecommunications companies, have created more intense zones of conflict, including over the permissible number and timing of still photographs on websites. With similar conflicts occurring in other countries, such as the United States and the United Kingdom, Australia became towards the end of the first decade of the twenty-first century the ground for a 'proxy war' between major sport and media organizations, with global implications:

A NEW Senate inquiry might set a global precedent for online sports reporting and result in a digital 'anti-siphoning list' as administrators and media groups feud over where news footage taken at sports events can run ...

'The potential precedents for this are enormous,' the head of a major news agency said.

'This will set a global benchmark – it has been coming to a head for a long time.'

There has been growing tension between news organizations and a number of sports in recent years as the line between traditional newspaper, TV and radio reporting has blurred with the growth of digital media. (Canning 2009)

It is not, then, surprising that submissions to what was officially an inquiry of a national parliament were received from international interests, including Agence France-Presse, Getty Images, News Limited (a wholly owned subsidiary of News Corp), the International Olympic Committee, the International Cricket Council, Hutchison Telecommunications and the World Association of Newspapers. Yet, for similar reasons to those concerning the later, rather inconclusive outcomes of the engagement with the new media environment in the anti-siphoning review, the proposals of the Senate Committee were cautious. It recommended no changes to copyright law but that 'stakeholders negotiate media access to sporting events based on the principle that all bona fide journalists, including photojournalists and news agencies, should be able to access sporting events regardless of their technological platform' (Parliament of Australia 2009: 52) and that without such an agreement 'that the Minister consider initiating the process for consideration of a code under Section 51AE of the Trade Practices Act' (Parliament of Australia 2009: 52). In due course, a voluntary 'Code of Practice for Sports News Reporting – Text, Photography and Data' (Department of Broadband, Communications and the Digital Economy 2010) was framed, an administration committee formed and a dispute resolution process through an appointed mediator agreed, but with no ultimate impediment to legal recourse. The code explicitly does not venture into the most contentious area of all – the online retransmission of audio-visual footage from sports events:

1.1 The object of the Sports News Reporting Code of Practice (the Code) is to ensure that Media Organisations are able to access sporting events for the purposes of gathering News Content for News Reporting.

1.2 This Code applies only to the gathering of News Content for News Reporting as they are each defined in this Code. It does not in any way apply or establish a precedent in relation to the gathering of audio, vision or audio visual content for News Reporting. (Australian Government 2010b)

These closely watched and rather tortuous deliberations in one country reveal considerable anxiety about the trajectory of media sport under globalization and digitization. There is unquestionable change occurring but no clear direction except, paradoxically, in terms of multidirectional processes accompanied by the substantial 'drag' of a broadcast television sector that continues to wield substantial power and which has shown a capacity to adapt as well as to fret. As Raymond Boyle and Garry Whannel (2010a: 260) have noted, continuity and change are coexistent, not mutually exclusive, and 'the role played by television in the mediation of sport has diminished in the ways often [thought] likely in the 1990s'. In seeing the media sport experience become broader, complex and multi-layered, they argue that it is more useful to think about 'the relationships between screens and sports content' rather than concentrate only on the television screen:

> Large flat-screen televisions have spread rapidly since the 1990s into the living rooms of the viewing public. Even bigger screens are now a common and taken-for-granted feature in pubs, bars, stations and shopping malls. Small screens, too, on laptop computers, mobile phones and E-Readers are offering new modes of disseminating sport-related content. One issue of growing significance is how that sports content gets pulled down onto the screen and how it is paid for either as part of public media or commercial media content. The role of big media brands such as the BBC or Sky in organizing this process will remain crucial as we embark on the age that will see the ability to pull down content from the internet onto your living room television becoming a mass market activity over the next decade. (Boyle and Whannel 2010: 260)

Thus, for example, there is no doubt that IPTV will bridge the current space between computer screens and television screens, but the conventions and habits associated with television viewing are likely to display the resilience of cultural habit and domestic design just as they are changing and being supplemented. Similarly, while large media corporations struggle with this dynamic context, so do sports clubs, small to medium enterprises and fans. As Michael Real (2006) notes in drawing on both the medium-focused theory of Marshall McLuhan and the political economic perspectives of Herbert Schiller and Robert McChesney, the content of a new dominant medium (the world wide web) is likely to be that of the previously dominant medium (television), while the six current major transnational media conglomerates have increasingly drawn the web, the 'once unruly youngster' (Real 2006: 177), into their orbit. Therefore, at the very point when 'nightmare arguments about the future of television' were being made by some analysts,

> Web sites were successfully exploring webcasting and seeking out partnerships with television networks. Seeing the successful synergy of ESPN and its Web site and CBS and its Web site, SportsLine, the venerable sports publication *The Sporting News* spent years working up a partnership for its Web site, an effort which resulted in it joining forces with Fox television. The benefits shared between Sporting News Online, *Sporting News Magazine*, and Fox Sports included major cross-promotions of each other's offerings and a sharing of columnists/commentators and celebrity features.

> At the same time, streaming video technology had forged another bridge uniting television and the Web by making transmission of television over the Web

practical ... without the need to download large files before playback. Also, access-on-demand could be coupled with new miniaturized wireless devices for access everywhere. The move from online to television and back became more seamless, and television and computer screens began to be more interchangeable. (Real 2006: 176–7)

Such notions of seamlessness and interchangeability, across both space and time, have not figured notably in the world of proprietorial media dominated by competitively exclusive mindsets and business plans, whereby one medium's gain must be another's loss. However, cross-media promotion, such as that pertaining to print sports journalism and broadcast television, has been a feature of media sport throughout the analogue era, while conglomerate strategies involving acquisition of different sports media – and even of sports entities themselves – are well established. What is different about the digital context is that sport content in this form can be more rapidly dispersed and adapted, and so is more difficult to control. For example, a new area of concern has emerged over athlete (micro) blogging, especially via Twitter, and social networking, notably through Facebook (Hutchins 2011; Hutchins and Mikosza 2010). It has produced new protocols in tournaments, including the Olympics and the football and cricket World Cups, and a series of controversies, including in 2009 when Minnesota Vikings player Bernard Berrian tweeted a joke about a teammate's injury that 'went viral' and was widely believed, England cricketer Kevin Pietersen announcing in 2010 that he had been dropped from the one-day and Twenty20 teams with words including 'Done for rest of summer!! Man of the World Cup T20 and dropped from the T20 side too ... It's a f—— up!!' and leading Australia swimmer Stephanie Rice, who had seen photographs involving party poses from her unrestricted Facebook page published in newspapers in 2008, tweeting 'suck on that faggots' after Australia narrowly beat South Africa at rugby union in 2010. Apart from matters of protocol and taste, there is particular concern among sport organizations that Twitter can be used by sportspeople to make sensitive political comments (such as during the 2008 Beijing Olympics) or to circumvent sponsorship agreements. Such direct public communication, without recourse to established media outlets or sport body mediation, points to new, unregulated practices that undermine the careful media management that typifies contemporary institutional sport.

Much of the concentration in my discussion to date has been on the ownership, control and organization of media sport production in a global context. This is a crucial analytical area because questions surrounding them remain pivotal – in some ways even more so – when old routines of sender-message-receiver no longer (if they ever truly did) command the field of communication. Thus, the work of contemporary cultural theorists like Henry Jenkins (2006a,b) on 'convergence culture' and 'participatory culture' represents an important advance on our understanding of shifts between and around old/'legacy' and new/'newest' media, and in audience relations that prompt such neologisms as 'produsage' (Bruns 2008) and (following the visionary work of Alvin Toffler) 'prosumption' (Humphreys and Grayson 2008; Ritzer and Jurgenson 2010). It calls for a combination of critical scepticism and a close attention to what it now means to engage with media sport culture. Earlier I have discussed how transnational corporations, international and national sports organizations, sports clubs and athletes have negotiated media sport convergence and networking – or tentatively begun to do so. But there is a need for a closer focus on the implications for the sport fans now confronted, depending on their social and spatial location, with an increasing range of media sports experiences and possibilities. This is where heightened interactivity is especially important – the opportunity to talk back and to initiate talk, to get involved not just in watching or commenting on sport but also to help organize it – and from any global site with an online connection.

Executive fandom in a digital world

It was noted earlier that watching sport on television has often been regarded as a rather passive activity and that, even where it is viewed more positively in terms of social engagement and cultural creativity, it can hardly be described in unequivocally 'liberatory' terms. Other readings of sports fandom stress the fanaticism dimension and the connections with deviance, violence and other forms of 'unreason' (as summarized in various contributions to Brown 1998a; Crawford 2006; Raney 2006, 19 *ff.*). Against such perspectives are celebrations of 'pro-social' fandom and attempts to advance 'fan democracy' among sports fans, sporting institutions and across the social spectrum (see, for example, Brown 1998b). It is important to recognize the complexity of mediated sports fandom and consumption (Gray, Sandvoss and Harrington 2007; Hermes 2005; Sandvoss 2005). Despite attempts to reduce experiences and relationships to simple taxonomic binaries, they are highly variable not only across social and spatial locations but also with regard to the same human subjects. As Art Raney (2006: 313) notes in his survey of the research on motivation in 'the use and viewing of mediated sports', watching sport on television involves affect, cognition and sociality; can be intentional or serendipitous, involve deep engagement or passive distraction; and while it is for some an 'all-consuming passion', in most cases it is accommodated among the sundry responsibilities and activities of the diurnal round, so that '[w]hile some sport viewers are no doubt addicted to the action, most others have struck a balance between sport and the rest of life' (Raney 2006: 327).

But striking a balance between different spheres of life is not the same thing as seizing opportunities to change those circumstances. The term 'fan' does not connote empowerment – nor, indeed, does Crawford's (2006: 20–1) once preferred (but since discarded) descriptor 'supporter'. As sport has become increasingly professionalized, corporatized, mediated and commodified, it has become more difficult for its 'appreciators' (another descriptor, alongside 'supporter') to have a proactive impact on how it is organized. Sports clubs with member bases have, in general, progressively ceded power to their professionally structured associations, which in turn have traded much of it to media corporations. As a result, fans have become distanced, literally, from the game. This, though, is not a wholly disadvantageous development in that the process of mediation has made distantiated sports fandom possible. Nonetheless, it is difficult to see how a sports fan can wield much influence in sport except in a negative sense by, for example, demonstrating in or outside the stadium or refusing to be a disciplined consumer by declining to purchase tickets, merchandising, television subscriptions and so on, or even to figure in the TV ratings by switching channels. As mentioned previously, digitization can enrich the experience of watching screen sport by enabling multi-screening, online discussion groups, web sites and mobile connectivity. But it is also, perhaps, capable of fostering the development of active sport fan communities who may be able to use converged, networked media in a manner that advances their collective agency. Indeed, the capacity of these technologies to overcome at least some of the privileging of spatial proximity that creates hierarchies of 'authentic' sport fandom (Bale 1998) can potentially democratize mediated sport fandom by transforming it into a new mode of sports organization from below. Sports fans disillusioned by what they see as the takeover of their popular culture by capital have formed associations operating as pressure groups to improve the condition of sport in line with their own interests. For example, the UK-based Football Supporters' Federation (FSF) (2010) has declared 'The Fans' Blueprint for the Future of the Beautiful Game', the introduction of which (below) expresses its unhappiness at what is seen as the neglect by elites of supporters and the deleterious impact of 'power and money' on the game of association football:

1.1. Football in Britain is at a crossroads. Financially, the game's never been better off. It's never had more committed followers both at home and overseas. Yet never have so many clubs been on the brink of financial extinction, nor has the game been so ridden by short-sightedness and self-interest.

1.2. During last season the chief executives of both the Football League and the Football Association were forced to resign. The root cause of both departures? Power and money. The game's elite in England, Wales and Scotland seems intent on keeping an ever-increasing proportion of the wealth generated by the game for themselves.

1.3. The Football Supporters' Federation (FSF), formed on 1 August 2002, unites the former National Federation of Football Supporters' Clubs (NFFSC) and the Football Supporters' Federation (FSF). It represents over 100,000 of the game's most committed supporters in England and Wales grouped in 124 democratic fans' organizations. They follow teams from the Premiership to the non-League pyramid. They follow the English and Welsh national teams at home and abroad.

1.3. [sic] It's these supporters who travel thousands of miles throughout Britain and overseas every season. Without FSF members there'd be no game. We pack the grounds, sing the songs, provide the passion.

1.4. Yet supporters are the one group in the game which is most frequently ignored. No more. Football supporters are uniting around a set of principles which they believe are essential to the future of football. We invite all those who love the game and have its best interests at heart to join with us.

1.5. It's time to act before it's too late.

The tone of the Blueprint is familiar, especially for those well acquainted with association football in Britain, with its long-established connection to (especially masculine) working-class sociocultural formations that have undergone profound change in late modernity (Brown 1998a; Sandvoss 2003). It is concerned primarily with football in Britain, but it is not – and cannot be – limited to that national context given that its extensive website is available across national boundaries and its free membership (currently exceeding 180,000) is available to all those who accept the 'fundamental principles' of its constitution, which include promoting diversity, opposing discrimination, rejecting violence and promoting 'a positive culture of fair play and goodwill between all football supporters' (FSF 2010). The FSF works, within a primarily national framework, to fashion a constituency beyond an individual nation, attracting 'commercial and government sponsorship and support', without, it is claimed, 'ever losing its unique "by fans, for fans" character'. This popular conception of the fan is crucial to the discursive task of asserting the 'authentic' identity, interest and agency of sport fans against those that construe them as the disempowered constructs of the aforementioned 'game's elite'. Through such initiatives as holding an annual Fans' Parliament (in UK locations such as Wembley Stadium), providing a FSF Fans' Embassy service to assist travelling England fans abroad and publishing a paid magazine *The Football Supporter* and a free England print and electronic fanzine, *Free Lions*, 'complemented by a telephone helpline, website information, and a team of willing volunteers', the FSF is mainly oriented to English fan concerns, while acknowledging those of Scotland and Wales. This English/British orientation is tempered to a degree by developing links with clubs in Europe and, especially, through Football Supporters International (FSI), a supporters' network that covers Europe and international campaigns:

> Throughout Europe, and increasingly beyond, football fans are campaigning against the same threats to our game – commercialization, poor policing, the power of television, racism and more. The FSF is endeavouring to develop international campaigns around these international issues. (FSF 2010)

This apparent slippage between the national, regional, international and global within football fandom parallels the same movements within the wider sphere of sport, which simultaneously traverses and draws energy from place-based 'parish pump' concerns and identifications and much more diffuse and de-specialized phenomena. It is not possible to retreat to the local and pretend that the global can be kept at bay, and indeed, it is increasingly implausible to separate them in any absolute sense, with the globalization of football and fandom reflecting a complex intermeshing and synthesis of spaces and identifications (Giulianotti 1999; Giulianotti and Robertson 2009; Sandvoss 2003). However, the language and affective discourse of the authentically local, and of resistance to 'power and money', remains salient within 'by fans, for fans' value constructions. As noted earlier, this is not surprising given that, in Raymond Williams's (1977: 121) terms, sport (especially through its long-established manifestations such as association football) is deeply imbued with the cultural complexity that evidences 'dynamic interrelations, at every point in the process, of historically varied and variable elements' and which he describes as 'dominant, residual and emergent' forms. Thus, it could be conceded that corporate capitalist relations are currently dominant within media sport but that they co-exist with residual (which Williams distinguishes from 'archaic') 'experiences, meanings and values' formed in the past and still alive in the present, despite being at variance with the residual form (such as those elements of fandom that privilege uncommodified exchange within spatially proximate neighbourhoods) and also with emergent values and practices that, in this case, might involve a global cosmopolitanism that negotiates distantiated commodification and topophiliac communal identification. This necessarily abstract framework can be given some preliminary shape and texture in considering synthetic or hybridic forms of sport fandom that exploit digital media technologies and protocols while celebrating inherited values and practices.

A case in point is that of MYFC, which, although small scale in relation to major football clubs, has garnered worldwide attention as the most adventurous initiative to date of using online media and communication not only to watch and comment on sport and sport-related issues, but also to intervene directly in its ownership and management. As noted in Chapter 2, clubs in the major leagues of European association football, especially the EPL, are owned by billionaire entrepreneurs and consortia from around the world (Blackburn Rovers, for example, was acquired in November 2010 by the Indian Venkateshwara Hatcheries Group), with some (such as Borussia Dortmund in the German Bundesliga) publicly listed. Some association football clubs (including very prominent ones, such as FC Barcelona, and also in other codes of football, like the Green Bay Packers) are run by members (as opposed to shareholders) but are otherwise quite conventional operationally in terms of divisions of labour between elected board members, paid staff and fans. The innovation of MYFC was to experiment with a democratic structure that sought to use digital technology to, paradoxically, make decisions on the running of the club permeated with a pre- or early modern ethic of community. It is this arrangement of rights, responsibilities, duties and functions that coalesces around the concept I propose of the 'executive fan' which, in the context of networked digital media sport, lends itself well to active participation in sports clubs irrespective of the physical location and origin of the fans in question.

MYFC began in the United Kingdom in 2007 when, initiated by a former football journalist Will Brooks, over 20,000 members (reaching a claimed peak of 31,000 in late 2008 but falling to only 1,419 financial members by March 2011) formed a society with the aim of purchasing a controlling stake in a football club. The members voted in early 2008 to purchase a 75 per cent stake in a semi-professional football club, Ebbsfleet United, which was then in the fifth tier of English football. Especially audacious was MYFC's propositional motto 'own the club, pick the team' and, later, claim to be the 'world's first football club' and 'the world's first internet community to buy and takeover a real-world football club' (MYFC 2011). Of particular interest to some of the world's most prominent news media (including the BBC, CNN, *The Wall Street Journal* and *The Times* of both London and India) was the novel idea that an actual team and its tactics, in something of a reversal of the real-world simulations of games such as FIFA Manager (a game produced by EA Sports, a company that has sponsored the club), would be selected democratically by members by means of a ballot held on the club's website (Hutchins and Rowe 2009a). Instead of the manager/coach making decisions on behalf of the members, the latter would perform this task and instruct the manager/coach. Furthermore, while the purchased team Ebbsfleet United is physically located in Gravesend, Kent on the south-eastern fringe of London and based at its (modest) Stonebridge Road ground, decisions could be made by members in any location across the world. The ambitious sweep of MYFC is enthusiastically stated in the 'About MyFootballClub' section of its website and is worth quoting at some length in constituting almost a manifesto for global executive fandom:

> MyFootballClub is a unique internet venture that uses the principle of crowdsourcing and crowdfunding to run a real football club.
>
> Rather than being owned by millionaires with varying interest in the fortunes of a club, Ebbsfleet United is owned by thousands of members, who each contribute small amounts annually, and vote on key management decisions like the budget, transfer deals, kit supplier contracts, kit design, election of Club officials, and even approve the Manager's contract!
>
> This model brings a unique dialogue between the club and the community, with local fans sharing knowledge about the club, and global members contributing their expertise and skills that would otherwise cost the club. Members are able to bring fresh ideas, which are discussed and voted on as a community, for action by the Club.
>
> It also brings a level of transparency into the Club management which is rarely seen, with members even able to discuss line items from the Monthly budget with the Club accountant openly as a community. Can you imagine that at your main club?
>
> MyFootballClub isn't like playing FIFA Soccer, Championship Manager or Hattrick. There's no quick button to buy and sell players, no fast upgrade for the stadium, and certainly no cheat codes!
>
> Every decision we make could affect the fortunes of the club, the players and the staff. As responsible owners, we also have to scrutinise the information that comes

to us, challenge the Board and the Club management and make the decision that we feel is best for the club.

Debates are long and often heated, and it's sometimes hard to remember that we're trying to make a collective decision, but there's nothing like matchday experience as a MYFC owner, whether you're at the game or following at home. That's when we really come together as a *community*.

- *At the ground*, you'll meet other MYFC members, many of whom have travelled to Stonebridge Road from around the UK, Europe, even the World! It's thrilling to know that the contribution you made put those players on the pitch and every goal feels like you scored it!
- *At home*, whilst listening to the radio commentary, you can discuss the progress of the game with your fellow members in the chatroom or the forum.
- Out and about there's a free *text message service*, where your fellow members send updates and goal alerts from the ground.
- And we've partnered with TVMobili to bring you delayed *streaming of the matches* on matchday, as well as an archive of previous games and highlights. (subject to coverage and TVMobili subscription).

All of this makes for an experience that can't be matched anywhere else. So join the MyFootballClub community for only £50 and *make Ebbsfleet United your football club*. (MYFC 2011)

Each paragraph above proposes an organizational politics and ethics of MYFC that combines enduring, collective social concerns of fans with media technologies and uses that fashion new, dispersed community formations. It uses recent business, marketing and organizational concepts like 'crowdsourcing' and 'the wisdom of crowds' (Howe 2009; Surowiecki 2005) that challenge the centralization and elite concentration of knowledge and power, and emphasizes transparency and accountability. It draws on the current of collective sport fan resentment that it has become the plaything of the rich, many of whom have little 'authentic' interest in sport. It references sport gaming but insists on the responsibilities of owner-members to 'flesh and blood' players, support staff and fans. Both the local and the global, and community (undefined, but implicitly in north-east Kent, where Ebbsfleet United is based) and club, are brought together. The diverse, multi-layer means of connectivity are highlighted – physically through ground attendance, listening on the radio, watching on television, exchanging text messages and contributing to online chat rooms and forums. The 'solemn' duty of voting and so making management decisions on budgets, sponsor contracts, player contract, ticket prices, home and away playing kit design, Society Board Membership and so on is also shown to be crucial to shaping the future of the club, although it did not ever extend to the much trumpeted area of player selection, team tactics and structure. This lack of follow through on the club's most audacious claim led to some discontent among members and, as is discussed here, to the formation of a dissident, breakaway fan group, FreeMYFC (2009).

Broadly conceived, then, the MYFC and FreeMYFC phenomena could be said to evidence what David Harvey (1989: 238) sees as a significant aspect of the condition of postmodernity, in which

> [m]ovements of opposition to the disruptions of home, community, territory, and nation by the restless flow of capital are legion ... Movements of all sorts – religious, mystical, social, communitarian, humanitarian, etc. – define themselves directly in terms of an antagonism to the power of money and of rationalized conceptions of space and time over daily life. The history of such utopian, religious, and communitarian movements testifies to the vigour of exactly this antagonism. Indeed, much of the colour and ferment of social movements, of street life and culture, as well as artistic and other cultural practices, derives precisely from the infinitely varied texture of oppositions to the materializations of money, space, and time under conditions of capitalist hegemony.

MYFC – which it must be re-emphasized is a small, tenuous but intriguing experiment in an alternative politics and organization-mediated global sport – is, in its own field of popular culture, an expression of resistance to the capital-centric power formation of twenty-first century association football and a manifestation of 'executive fan power'. However, as Harvey observes of all such movements, they are 'all too often subject to the power of capital over the coordination of universal fragmented space and the march of capitalism's global historical time that lies outside of the purview of any particular one of them' (Harvey 1989: 239). The level of capital investment and professional organizational commitment required at only a modest-level stratum of contemporary sport is considerable, and for this reason the desired concentration on the sporting aspects of the operation is largely subordinated to that of financial management and fund raising (the earlier discussed case of FC United providing a salient example of the stark mismatch between the grass-roots 'start-up' and the world's richest sports club (Manchester United) from which its members had seceded). MYFC, therefore, cannot transform the condition of sports clubs and fans, and is beset with contradictions regarding, for example, its relation to the rationalized structures of sport that it finds unresponsive and its reliance on the corporate media and telecommunications organizations that are integral to the industrial-capitalist complex of which it is in various ways critical. It is not surprising that this is the case, not least because, as noted above with regard to the theoretical framework of Raymond Williams, the coexistence of the dominant, residual and the emergent, and the many ideological inconsistencies and compromises inherent in working within and against a dynamic institutional context, militate against straightforward outcomes of success and failure.

For example, an arrangement in which spatial constraints can be ameliorated, so that MYFC's members have equal voting rights and access to official information irrespective of their global location, does not mean that space is of no consequence. According to MYFC's (2010) information for members, as of 16 December 2010 its membership breakdown (3,065 in total, and which was halved a few months later, but at the time of writing was the last available figure) by country in descending order was as follows:

United Kingdom: 1,368 (44.8 per cent)

United States: 236 (7.7 per cent)

Australia: 64 (2.09 per cent)

Ireland: 43 (1.4 per cent)

Norway: 41 (1.34 per cent)

Canada: 41 (1.34 per cent)

Sweden: 32 (1.04 per cent)

Germany: 27 (0.8 per cent)

Italy: 23 (0.75 per cent)

Netherlands: 20 (0.65 per cent)

Finland: 12 (0.39 per cent)

Unknown: 1,013 (33 per cent)

Others: 133 (4.35 per cent)

It can be seen that the United Kingdom has the largest number of members, although the second largest cohort is 'stateless', while it might safely be assumed that the majority is UK based and has simply declined to provide a 'street address'. Membership clusters in the United States, Canada, Scandinavia, Australasia, Ireland and other parts of Europe represent about 18 per cent of the known membership locations, and 26.4 per cent of the unknown category is excluded, with the others (including Asia, the Middle East, Eastern Europe and South America) accounting for less than 5 per cent (4.35) of members (and 6.5 per cent excluding the unknown category). This distribution of members calls into question the global nature of the club, if to be 'global' is taken to mean an even spread across the world. However, as has been noted in Chapters 2 and 3, global media sport is patterned and uneven, following, variously, the lines and flows of imperialism, colonialism, technological development, capitalist market development, population movements, cultural traditions (including 'invented' ones), language concentrations and so on. These are not immutably fixed, uni-directional 'passages', and shift with the tides of history, but they cannot be 'wished away' by appeals to the annihilation of hierarchies and borders that are notionally enabled by changes in communications technology, trade liberalization and so on.

Therefore, it is not surprising that all the members of the elected Society Board have (as of late 2010) been based in the United Kingdom, nor that tensions have arisen between the long-term Ebbsfleet United fans who live close to its spatial hub, and the more recent and scattered members who joined MYFC, took part in the purchase of their club, eradicated its debt and so gained the right to vote on its management without, in many cases, ever seeing the team play under co-present conditions or visiting its home ground (Rowe et al. 2010). As will be discussed in Chapter 5, such divisions between fans based on posited hierarchies of history, knowledge, proximity and commitment are also a common feature of major professional clubs that have sought to expand their operations and fan base in new spaces – even, in some cases, in the same country. MYFC's audacious self-proclamation as 'the world's first internet community to buy and takeover a real-world football club' is perhaps sustainable in that its Internet-based governance structure is more 'radical' than most supporters' trust arrangements, but there are comparable initiatives in other places, including the United Kingdom, South America (Brazil), Northern Europe (Denmark, Germany, Poland) and the United States. Indeed, one minor Israeli club, Hapoel Kiryat Shalom, did institute in 2007 a 'pick the team' arrangement (Lewis and Khadder 2007) – subsequently modified after alleged 'sabotage' by rival teams' fans – that was promised but never introduced by MYFC. As noted above, disgruntled MYFC members who did not believe that the club had done what was promised in this respect, and who believed that it was in other ways undemocratic and were critical of its (now departed) founder, established a rival web-based organization, FreeMYFC, which sought (unsuccessfully at time of writing) to establish its own football club (Ruddock *et al.* 2010). The slight absurdity of a fragile experiment such as MYFC being challenged by another one (with only just over 300 members, none of whom are required to provide a subscription fee, and which was largely inactive by 2010) reveals something of the debilitating politics of 'movements of opposition' in materially and politically unpropitious circumstances as outlined earlier by Harvey.

The difficulty of sustaining interest and involvement in a socially networked environment and in online communities is well known (Ang and Pothen 2009), with the frequent incidence of drifts in levels of participation and high levels of 'following' and 'lurking' rather than posting and an over-representation of a small number of posters (Neilsen 2006). For example, a content analysis of the FreeMYFC website discovered that 60 per cent of members said nothing and only intermittently used the site, with most contributions coming from less than 10 per cent of members who were also, predictably, very heavy users of the site (Ruddock *et al.* 2010: 305–60). Indeed, one FreeMYFC member (Alter) who did a seven-day content analysis of MYFC's 'Society' and 'Soapbox' forums noted,

> [It] highlights a serious lack of engagement by the members – there appears to be no appetite by the majority of members to contribute anything to the running of the Society. Across two forums, there have been a total of 180 posts over 21 threads by 59 unique posters. This equates to an average of just over 3 posts per posting member and only 1.61% of the membership engaging – although the majority of the unique posters only made a single post. (FreeMYFC 2009)

Furthermore, a recent content analysis of MYFC voting (as noted earlier, with overall membership now below 2,000 from a peak of over 30,000) found, as demonstrated in Table 4.1, that the levels of participation were highly variable in terms of votes, hits and comments. These variations were in part attributable to different levels of importance – for example, negotiations over the coach's contract (540, 1,693 and 47, respectively) engendered much more member activity than whether the club should advertise on Facebook (86, 299 and 1, respectively). The table also reveals the routine nature of the functions of the executive fan, in voting on proposals (from both ordinary members and the

Table 4.1 My football club votes, December 2010–February 2011

Topics	Total votes	Hits	Comments
Donate MYFC T-shirts to the ultimate football pub quiz?	72	194	0
Outstanding loan from Phil Sonsara: a proposal to clear this debt immediately	159	473	10
Should we advertise in *The Guardian*?	60	337	7
MYFC Cup pre-season	219	624	14
Should we begin negotiations over the coach's contract?	540	1,693	47
Should the society allow Ebbsfleet United Football Club (EUFC) footage to be used in an amateur movie?	221	623	5
Vote: extending our website maintenance contract	249	722	8
Should we stop using Paypal?	301	926	23
Welcoming members to Stonebridge Road	141	529	4
Permission to approach premiership players to join MYFC	171	672	14
MYFC to buy shirt sponsorships from EUFC?	152	540	14
How should we respond to the VAT rise?	323	927	9
Thurrock 25th January promotional game	92	409	6
Facebook advertising vote	86	299	1
Offer to purchase majority stake in Ebbsfleet United	310	1,377	53
MYFC accounts	281	735	12
Free tickets for fleet in the community youths	288	692	5
Fleet Learning Zone building hire vote	288	727	16
Potential FA Trophy Droylsden Replay prices vote	137	389	2
New membership fee	590	1,656	23
EUFC £5 match promotion v Lewes, New Year's Day	176	552	15
Preparation of MYFC accounts	81	302	2

Society Board) that are normally the province of paid, professional executive staff and directors who are not required to run every decision, major or minor, past a shifting electorate of members, a significant proportion of whom (like this author) are in other countries, continents and hemispheres. Thus the 'real-world' nature of the project, as a variant of volunteering, begins to shift the nature of the activity from leisure to work-like. Under such circumstances, it is unsurprising that MYFC has been subject to considerable churn and non-participation and that the commitment to its mission has waned after the first flush of enthusiasm.

Despite – or perhaps because of – these difficulties, the idea of supporter-owned clubs and various conflicts over models, fan organizations and fans, and the use of new media technologies, continues to intrigue major media outlets such as *The Guardian* (in whose *Weekend Magazine*, in something of a reversal of interest, MYFC members voted in February, 2011 to purchase a discounted advertisement). For example, the following story refers to a range of aforementioned tensions surrounding MYFC and presents its web-based community status as a liability:

> The story-telling machine which is the FA Cup draw has produced an intriguing contest in the first round proper tomorrow afternoon, between the flourishing, supporter-owned AFC Wimbledon, and Ebbsfleet United, the club still forced to bill itself as 'owned by a web-based community'.
>
> Wimbledon, formed by fans in 2002 who refused to see their club purloined into becoming Milton Keynes Dons, are the favourites, having progressed through promotions from their genesis in the Combined Counties League to current second place in the Blue Square Premier.
>
> Ebbsfleet, renamed in 2007 but with a solid non-league history latterly as Gravesend and Northfleet, were purchased in February 2008 by myfootballclub, a website venture which invited people to subscribe for £35 and buy a football club. At its height, 30,000 people were attracted to join by the idea of having a say in owning a club, which was a frustration to Supporters Direct, Wimbledon and others where genuine, lifelong fans work hard to promote democratic supporter ownership of clubs. (Conn 2010a)

Here the familiar distinction between 'genuine, lifelong fans' and those lured to 'buy a football club' is made as well as reference to another UK-based sports fan advocacy group, Supporters Direct, which declares in its Mission Statement that '[o]ur goal is to promote sustainable spectator sports clubs based on supporters' involvement & community ownership' and among its listed activities includes the following: 'campaigns for the wider recognition of the social, cultural and economic value of sports clubs', 'aims to create the conditions in which supporters can secure influence and ownership of sports clubs', 'provides guidance and support to groups in more than 16 countries throughout Europe' and 'promotes the value of supporter ownership to sports fans, empowering them to set up supporters' trusts or become members of existing trusts' (Supporters Direct 2010). With the now mandatory communicative tools of website, blog, Facebook group, Twitter, Delicious, Yahoo Groups, Wiki, RSS and Keep in Touch, along with member services, academic publications and Social Value Research reports, advocacy organizations like Supporters Direct paint a very different picture of sports clubs, television viewers and fans than that typically represented, as outlined above, of the 'couch potato' and the 'disempowered consumer'.

This does not mean, though, that the global media sports cultural complex is entering a new phase of wholesale retreat from aforementioned driving forces of commodification, mediatization and corporatization that have significantly shaped its expansion – though never in a one-dimensional, uncontested manner. It should also be acknowledged, of course, that not all sport fandom is politically engaged in orientation and experience, often resembling a straightforward leisure consumption framework with little in the way of activism and deep commitment, while sport fans may also drift in and out of political engagement and activism in a manner that defies consistent classification (Crawford 2004; Horne 2006; Richardson 2004; Rowe and Gilmour 2008). Indeed, in cases where the purchase and exchange of sport memorabilia seem to dominate fan priorities, sport fandom appears to be no more explicitly political than train and plane spotting or attending Elvis Presley impersonator and Star Trek conventions.

Although the emphasis in this discussion has been on the 'world game' of association football, and especially in Britain, these questions are by no means confined to one sport or dominated by one country. Control over sport and communication of and about it is always subject to some level of disputation. There is never a neat fit between the blind, inexorable impulse to capitalize on sporting affect and the manifestations of that affect among the human subjects who give life to sport as intensely experienced popular culture. It is evident in unlikely places, for example in the heart of the United States' 'sports biz' in the case of the Green Bay Packers football team, which is located in a comparatively small city and has a strong element of community ownership. Or in the local resistance to franchise relocation in a range of American sports (Josza 2004; Nunn and Rosentraub 1997; Rosentraub 1999). The main point, then, is that discussing the mediation of sport cannot be reduced to technical enhancements of the viewing screen experience or the financial advantages that flow from expanding the reach and range of available media services. The convergence of broadcasting, computing and telephony makes sports consumers more accessible to media sport producers but also to each other as social actors. The networking of media enables many more textual forms and experiences to be made available and targeted more precisely to individual tastes, but it also creates a host of new ways by which media sport followers might be galvanized to defend and extend their collective interests. Finally, the major sports organizations and print and broadcast sports media that once did most of the 'authoritative talking' within the sphere of sport are now in more direct dialogue with alternative voices, many from neglected sporting social spaces and even from points of the globe once believed to be beyond their orbit (as is addressed in Chapter 5).

New prospects for global media sport

Just as television has dominated the mediation of sport for several decades, so media sport scholarship has privileged television. There is, of course, much more to media sport than television, and the media sports cultural complex is, in fact, an intricate global web of media that is constantly being woven and broken in new ways, catching and releasing its 'prey' in ways that are both systematically planned and the outcomes of overt resistance and unpredictable contingency. Sports media range from newspaper articles to the semiotically encoded bodies of athletes and fans, from the dedicated programming of live events to the incidental texts, such as competitively structured 'reality television', that consciously and unconsciously, explicitly and implicitly, evoke meanings that are customarily attached to the world of sport (Rowe 2011b). If the process of 'mediatization' is taken in its widest sense – that there are more media, a greater range of media genres and forms and that the influence of the media can be felt almost everywhere – then sport is unequivocally an integral aspect of it.

But media sport, like sport itself, is never what it used to be. In this chapter we have seen how there has not just been a proliferation of its forms – an extension of a trend that has been evident since radio sports commentators pre-empted the descriptive accounts of the following evening's or day's sports press – but that they are increasingly combined and recombinant, feeding into and off each other using the multi-modal potentialities of the digital. Therefore, media sport no longer consists primarily of a series of distinct forms and genres that can be accepted or rejected but as a nexus of intersecting, interpenetrating sports discourses and practices. It is synthetic rather than unitary and hybridic instead of stylistically coherent. It is also less tethered to place and nation (though these remain important anchor points) and more dynamically global, but not in the straightforward, mechanical and functionalist sense as a 'single, clear and unambiguous "causal" entity' (Urry 2003: 96), whereby, in John Urry's conceptualization via complexity theory,

> global complexity is not simply anarchic disorder. There are many pockets of ordering within this overall patterning of disorder, processes involving a particular performing of the global and operating over multiple time-space with various feedback processes. Such pockets of ordering include various networks, fluids and governance mechanisms. These different pockets of order develop *parallel* concepts and processes of what we call the global. At different levels there are what we call 'global fractals', the irregular but strangely similar shapes that are found at very different scales across the world, from the household say to the UN.
>
> And, as such pockets of ordering emerge, so various often very substantial non-linear effects of 'global–local' objects, identities, institutions and social practices develop. These come to form and to elaborate the strange attractor of glocalization. (Urry 2003: 102–3)

The simultaneous ordering and strange occurrences that Urry describes applies conspicuously to global media sport and its flows, forms and futures, with the synthetic concept of 'glocalization' – first developed by the marketers of products and services in territories very different from their point of origin – that seeks to capture the merging of the local and global in ways that deny the possibility of the restoration of their separation. It reveals how

> globalization-deepens-localization-deepens-globalization and so on. Both the global and the local are bound together through a dynamic, irreversible relationship, as huge flows of resources are drawn into and move backwards and forwards between the two. Neither the global nor the local can exist without the other. (Urry 2003: 19)

From the marketing strategies of the sports media to the intervention policies of national governments to the attempts by some fans across the world to reclaim 'their game', we have seen the constant interplay and infusion of the global and the local in the field of media sport. Networked digital media have been crucial to this process and have required media sport scholars and researchers to engage with them in ways that do not deny the enduring power of sports television but situate and analyse it appropriately within contemporary and future-leaning media ecologies. At the same time, no nation states – or, indeed, national or international sports and/or media organizations – are able now in a digital environment to exercise the degree of control that they once could over sports broadcasting and other capital-intensive forms of media sport communication, including newspaper reporting and radio commentary.

Two special journal issues in 2009 and 2010 have grasped this necessity, exploring such topics as multiple media sport platforms, blogging by athletes and others, video gaming and fan networking and activism (Boyle and Whannel 2010b; Leonard 2009a). But much more work of this nature needs to be done in the face of the rather static prevailing models of old versus new media and the virtual versus the real. As David Leonard (2009b: 12) puts it in programmatic terms,

> Scholarship must push beyond the boundaries that see old and new media in opposition and that devalue the knowledge, representations, and identities disseminated through new media technologies as insignificant, kid's stuff, and the extreme to see, theorize, and analyze the continuities and links ... We must continue to react to the ever-changing nature of sporting landscapes resulting from innovation and technological changes, not simply categorizing metamorphosis as indicative of the new media era of sport but reflecting on the impact and significance of these transformations. In other words, what is new beyond the technology and tools; what remains unchallenged and constant within sporting cultures?

In answering Leonard's challenge, we turn in Chapter 5 to global media sport flows that both reproduce and problematize familiar theoretical conceptions of imperialism and postcolonialism (Bale and Cronin 2003). As argued above, globalization is not a smooth, even process of homogenization but one in which the flows of people, capital, ideas, technologies and media (Appadurai 2001) ebb and flow, responding and adapting to new environments and creating new sporting formations in the interplay of history, place, mediation and orders of power. Just as the centres of media sport export their signs and symbols to new territories, the former Empire can also strike back in diverse ways. As Arjan Appadurai (1996: 105) argues with regard to cricket:

> At the reception end, decolonization involves the acquisition of cultural literacy in cricket by a mass audience, and this side of decolonization involves the sort of appropriation of competence that we are all inclined to applaud. But there is also a production dimension to decolonization, and here we enter into the complex world of entrepreneurship and spectacle, of state sponsorship and vast private profits.

Analysing these contradictory phenomena can advance a critical understanding of the balance of power within the global media sports cultural complex, where the game is not always in the hands of the West and the Global North; the digital information technology that enhances sport, media and ancillary industries may be developed far from Silicon Valley, and the first language of large cohorts of fans (executive or otherwise) is unlikely to be English.

5

From West to East – and Back Again

Sport beyond nations?

When considering global media sport, it is crucial to consider the nature and balance of its flows around the world. As indicated in various places in this book, it is banal and misleading to talk about 'the global' as if it were evenly spread and without histories, origins and destinations. Nations are not irrelevant to sport and media – only a brief glance at locational variations in the popularity and prominence of various sports, and the involvement of national governments in it, quickly disabuses the analyst of that misconception – but not all nations command equal power over the production and circulation of sport. The institution of sport, its practices and protocols emerged, as argued in Chapter 2, in the West, as did the first major media institutions capable of transmitting the images and sounds of sport across the globe. Therefore, there is a close historical relationship between the development of global sport and Western imperialism and colonialism still evident in the twenty-first century, but as is also apparent, control over the flows of media and sport is not all one way, and just as there is something of a shift in geopolitical economic power towards Asia, this trend is also registering in sport and its mediation. It is no simple task, though, to disentangle what might be regarded as media sport imperialism from the necessary development of sport in a new context before it is 'indigenized', adapted and even 're-exported' to its places of origin (as has occurred with other Western-dominated cultural forms, such as popular music – Robinson, Buck and Cuthbert 1991). It is also conceivable that sports and forms of sport originating outside the West may become globally popular. Indeed, it has been argued that some so-called Western sports originated in other regions and were appropriated, changed and then reintroduced in their places of origin (e.g. physical practices resembling association football and golf have been recorded in ancient China – Xu 2008: 14). I am not going to delve deeply into these debates, as they tend to rely on disputes between historians about the origins of sport and its cultural predecessors – one example concerns whether Australian rules football originated among colonists as an adaptation of British football forms, especially rugby union football (Blainey, 2010), or among Australian Aborigines in a cultural practice known as Marn-Grook (Judd 2005). The specific focus of this chapter is on the extent to which the flows of media sport are uneven and whether the consequences of such an imbalance entail the subordination and, at worst, extinction of local sport structures.

It is important, though, not to fetishize or romanticize nations, which are in long-view historical terms recently constructed entities prone to 'invent' traditions (Hobsbawm and Ranger 1983) stretching back to antiquity, often operate through national mythologies as ways of shoring up inequalities by invoking the 'enemy without', and can be used as vehicles for chauvinism, often of a highly racialized kind, militating against cross-border initiatives in pursuit of social justice and citizenship rights that are deemed by local elites as interference in a nation's 'internal affairs' (Calhoun 1997). At the same time, the idea of nation is often crucial in mobilizing diverse, divided populations to throw off the yoke of colonial and neocolonial oppression or to resist military aggression and territorial ambition (see, for example, various contributions to Delanty and Kumar 2006). Sport is particularly effective in symbolizing the nation, for good or ill, according to context, aim and outcome. As Garry Whannel (2008: 108) notes in an influential early (now reprinted) work on the subject from a socialist perspective,

> National sport has proved a highly successful element of bourgeois ideology. A popular cultural activity is linked to national identity, an unproblematic unity over and above political difference. It creates a largely artificial sense of national-belongingness, an imaginary coherence. It masks social divisions and antagonisms, offering a unity which we all too easily fall in with ...
>
> Judgements about the relations between national sport and nationalism cannot be made without considering the particular social context. National sport plays a different role in developing and post-colonial countries from that which it has in imperialist powers. Similarly its role in industrialised communist countries is rather different from its role in capitalist countries.

Thus, the mobilization of sporting nationalism to express a sense of superiority over 'inferior peoples', demand political fealty (Miller *et al.* 2001) or, in classic 'bread and circuses' style, to distract the populace from the pressing political questions and outrages of the day (Eco, 1986), are quite different uses of sport to that of, say, giving a once subordinated and, perhaps, arbitrarily combined people a sense of purpose, pride and unity (see various contributions to Bairner 2001; Bale and Cronin 2003). Globalization has not on the evidence in sport diminished national sentiment, and it is unthinkable to consider an international sports tournament without the *frisson* of national competition. However, global media flows have powerful effects on significant elements of the sporting infrastructures and cultures of nations, and it is important to understand the extent to which these have positive or negative sociocultural consequences. For example, connecting nations to other nations through respectful sporting contact is generally regarded as a benign phenomenon, but obliterating local sporting cultural cultures through sports commerce is not. If mediated sport figures as a key agent of global neo-cultural and economic imperialism, a critical media sport studies is required to intervene in debates concerning the cultural politics of sport. A conspicuous point of return for such an analysis is a sporting competition from the place of origin of modern sport and now its 'world game' – the EPL. In previous chapters I have highlighted at various points the significance of the EPL as a nationally based competition that has transmuted into a hybrid of local and global, its images and signs flowing outwards as its labour and capital moved in the other direction. It is useful to track and examine these flows in greater detail in seeking to grasp the dynamics of power in the global media sports cultural complex.

Founding a global media sport behemoth

The EPL might be described as a national sports league with an initially national media focus but with a formative logic that turned it into a global media sport phenomenon. Its history is well known but in short can be traced to the frustration of a small number of leading English association football clubs in the 1980s that they were, essentially, 'carrying' the majority of the ninety-two professional clubs that comprised the four divisions of the Football League stretching from Carlisle near the Scottish border to Plymouth in the far south-west. The so-called big five (King 1998) of the time – Arsenal, Everton, Liverpool, Manchester United and Tottenham Hotspur (later reduced to the 'big four' with the addition of Chelsea since its purchase in 2003 by the Russian oil billionaire Roman Abramovich and the relative decline of Everton and Tottenham) – were especially keen to gain a greater share of collectively negotiated broadcasting, sponsorship and marketing revenue rather than be required to share part of it with other, smaller clubs. One key justification for the breakaway by the twenty-two clubs (reduced to twenty in 1995) in the English First Division to establish the Premier League (thereby creating the taxonomic absurdity of a descending hierarchy with names such as Championship and League One) was, though, international in nature – that English football was falling behind richer southern European clubs, in particular, and so English clubs were underperforming in European competitions. As Anthony King (1998: 110) has noted, television income, especially the prospect of a greater inflow of capital from subscription television, was crucial to the formation of the EPL:

> The Premier League was created to prevent the loss of income to the lower leagues which the top clubs had found increasingly intolerable throughout the 1980s, but the League was also established to maximize the bargaining position of the top clubs in their re-negotiation of a new television contract which was due in 1992.

The EPL's decision to exchange the broadcast reach afforded by free-to-air television for the unprecedented funding offered by the (Rupert Murdoch–controlled) BSkyB did not only create disputes over cultural citizenship rights in the United Kingdom (as discussed in Chapters 3 and 4) but also accelerated the globalization of football in England. The capacity to charge viewers for access to the best live club contests of the nation's most popular sport created an increasing influx of television capital in football that saw the EPL's broadcast rights contracts rise in value from £304 million for the first five seasons (1992–6) to almost £1.8 billion for domestic rights alone (2010–13) among its broadcasters (European competition authorities having insisted on splitting 'packages', although without destroying BSkyB's overall dominance). The large amount of money flowing into the English game reversed the (quite modest) leakage of English footballers to continental Europe, attracting a large number of top players from Europe (assisted by the 1995 Bosman Ruling, which guaranteed footballers freedom of contract and mobility throughout the EU) and many from other regions, especially Africa and South America (Giulianotti 1999). These flows across the global 'ethnoscape' (Appadurai 1996), or shifts in the 'new international division of cultural labour' (Miller et al. 2001), transformed the complexion of the English football labour market, especially the Premier League. According to one calculation from 2007 concerning the Premier League,

> Research by BBC Sport has revealed the extent of the challenges currently facing the national team as the pool of talent available to the manager decreases.

- 76% of the starting XIs that played on the first weekend of the first Premier League season in 1992 were English, only 37% were English on the first weekend of this season
- Only 10% (23 players) of the starting XIs in 1992 were from outside the UK, this season that number had increased to 56% (123)
- Non-English players have scored 69% of Premier League goals so far this season – they have even scored two of the three own goals
- Of the 118 goals scored so far, only nine have been scored by seven English strikers
- According to the latest Deloitte figures for disclosed transfer fees, spending by Premier League clubs rose from £333m in 2006 to £531m in 2007
- Half of that went to non-English clubs. (Slater 2007)

This increased European cosmopolitanism of English football, it is argued here, jeopardizes its 'Englishness', as foreign players are purchased from overseas and come to dominate the Premier League, the wealthiest division and also the expected source of most players in the England national team (as discussed at the end of Chapter 2). It should be noted, though, that there has also been a spillover effect for the lower divisions of English football (and in other UK leagues such as in Scotland, which formed its own Premier League and lower divisions structure in 1997), where there has also been a considerable influx of overseas players. In contrast to the success of English club teams packed with non-English players in international competitions such as the European Champions League, the failure of the England football team to win a major international tournament for over forty years has led to criticisms that players eligible to play for England are, as noted earlier, being disadvantaged by the influx of overseas players to its best league. Thus, after every tournament, newspaper stories such as the following appear:

> England's dismal failure at the World Cup can be blamed on the Premier League's inability to promote home-grown talent, according to the president of Spain's La Liga.

> José Luis Astiazarán has questioned the number of young foreign players at Premier League clubs and said the principal reason Spain have reached Sunday's final against Holland is that '77.1%' of footballers in their domestic league

are Spanish-qualified, a direct result of home-grown players being given the opportunity in their clubs' first teams. In the Premier League fewer than 40% of players are English.

'In La Liga there are 77.1% Spanish players, 16.7% European and 6.7% non-European', Astiazarán said. 'Our strategy is to work very hard with young home-grown players and to try to have a mix between them and experienced players.

'Why is it not a high number of foreign players in La Liga? Because we invest more and more in young Spanish players than in young foreign players. England has many times taken young players from outside who are 14, 16 years old. These kind of players are not English. This is one of the most important differences between Spain and England. We invest in young Spanish players. In Arsenal, Liverpool, Manchester United there are a lot of young Spanish, French and Italian players – maybe this is why at the moment you are not creating young English players.

'These [young foreign] players cannot play for the English national team. It's good to have goalkeepers from outside. But how many English goalkeepers are in the Premier League?' (Jackson 2010)

Such comments by the president of one prominent national league of association football in Europe about another, of course, may be read as political and do not recognize other national variations, such as the capacity in Spain for individual clubs to negotiate their own broadcast rights contracts and the related domination of two clubs, Barcelona and Real Madrid, with these two clubs alone supplying over half of Spain's 2010 World Cup–winning squad (twelve out of twenty-three). However, the above statistics and commentary reveal not only national variation in the organization of sport but also the ways in which the nation can be problematized by regional and global sports flows. In what sense, for example, is the EPL 'English' in any more than a territorial sense when over half of its players (and most/many of its owners, managers and coaches) are from other countries and when this arrangement appears to undermine the performance of the principal signifier of nation – the team that competes in the UEFA European Football Championship and the FIFA World Cup. In that sense, the 'English' in EPL may refer only to where it is hosted or to the majority of in-stadium spectators – where cities override nations as the principal units of organization and identification – rather than in a deeper, more expansive sense of national identity. In this regard, the primacy of 'multinational', city-based football clubs over nation states invokes the analyses of theorists of globalization and transnationalism – such as, notably, Manuel Castells (1996, 1998) – that new networks of major cities are able to some degree to bypass nation states and might even constitute the revival of the city-states that preceded nations as the most powerful units of sociopolitical organization. Anthony King (2003: 27–9) has related this development of region-states or city-states to football, which he regards as the 'primary public ritual in the new Europe' (King 2003: 32). It can be seen, for example, in the constant pressure by Europe's largest football clubs to form a 'European Superleague', which would effectively subordinate national domestic competitions in the same way as, for example, the EPL has done with the other English football leagues. The arguments in favour of a European Superleague are similar to those for the EPL – that smaller clubs were gaining too much of the industry's turnover from broadcasting, sponsorship and marketing; that the standard of play would be enhanced by pitting 'the best against the best'; and that there is much more popular interest in watching the glamorous clubs, which in turn would create higher revenues through television ratings and subscriptions, thereby elevating association football in the entertainment market.

That a European Superleague is still yet to be formed despite over thirty years of agitation may be ascribed both to the mutation of the European Champion Clubs' Cup into the UEFA Champions League as a hybrid 'knockout cup' and league competition that has created more contests between Europe's dominant clubs, and to the resilience of passionate local rivalries in intra-national competitions (not all of which are between the leading clubs, which, in any case, do not retain that status in perpetuity). It can also be attributed to the power of the supranational sport bodies like UEFA and FIFA, who are able to wield power in governance through 'diplomatic' interventions in European and world football. This does not mean that nation states do not retain power in some key respects – for example, no international sports event can take place without, effectively, the consent and often direct support of the host nation. Also, although the United Kingdom cannot under EU law prevent the citizens of member states gaining employment in its football clubs, as a sovereign state the United Kingdom is free to impose restrictions on those from non-EU countries. Nonetheless, it has largely fallen to supranational bodies like UEFA and FIFA to, perversely, buttress domestic sport competitions. For example, a 2009 newspaper report referring to coverage in various European media outlets stated,

> A European 'Super League' is a non-starter for Uefa chief Michel Platini, senior officials within European soccer's governing body said today, playing down media reports it was mulling plans for such a competition.
>
> Platini was quoted by France Football as saying Uefa was prepared to discuss plans from European teams to create a continental league to replace the Champions League and Uefa Cup ...
>
> The European Club Association (ECA), which represents 137 leading teams such as Manchester United and Real Madrid, talked about a 'Super League' during a meeting last week in Nyon, Switzerland, France Football reported.
>
> The Super League would be made up of three divisions with 20 to 22 clubs in each tier, the two newspapers said. Promotion and relegation would occur between the divisions each season.
>
> European domestic leagues would remain if a Super League ever got the go-ahead, Gazzetta said, but the number of matches in individual championships would have to be reduced so that top clubs could play in both competitions. (Ennis, Reuters 2009)

Here the political dynamics of sport seem to have little bearing on the interventional role of nations, as clubs and the governing body negotiate over competitive structures and resource distributions. Governing bodies such as

UEFA (despite occasional threats of secession by dissident clubs), while important economic entities in their own right, are also involved in regulating the 'rampant' football capitalism that individual clubs may engage in while pursuing their individual interest. It falls to peak sporting bodies to manage individualist motivations among sports clubs, which if given full rein, would destroy the variety, novelty and competitive uncertainty that is integral to the appeal of sport. For example, EUFA has sought to 'even up' the relationships between clubs and reduce the instability resulting from their collapse through excessive debt and trading imbalances by intervening in the increasingly 'wild' and speculative football market:

> Michel Platini has warned clubs who are running at huge losses, notably Manchester City, that Uefa would not shirk from issuing Champions League bans if new rules governing 'financial fair-play' are broken.
>
> The principle of the new Uefa regulations is that clubs must not spend more than they generate and thus either accumulate debts or be reliant on billionaire benefactors such as Roman Abramovich at Chelsea or City's Sheikh Mansour bin Zayed al Nahyan.
>
> According to recent annual accounts, only four Premier League clubs met this principle, though Uefa's assessments will be over two or three-year periods, beginning in 2013. Even then, clubs will be allowed to accumulate as much as €45 million (£37.3 million) in losses in that first period as long as it has been written off as equity by a benefactor ...
>
> Uefa also unveiled its latest report into the finances of European clubs and believes that the findings – a record combined loss of €1.2 billion (£996 million) – highlights [sic] the need for reform.
>
> The report shows that it is not just English clubs who are struggling to balance their books. More than half of the 664 clubs across 53 leagues are currently running at a loss. It is only in Germany, Belgium, Austria and Sweden that the overall income of the clubs exceeds their outgoings. (J. Wilson 2011)

The reliance on speculative borrowing and (increasingly multinational) benefactors, as well as questionable accounting practices tolerated, notably, in Italy and Spain, has created enormous capital imbalances within European football that require new market development in other regions. UEFA's European Club Footballing Landscape Report (2010) of the 732 clubs that it licensed in 2008 found that

> [English] Premier League clubs owe more money than all the other clubs in Europe's top divisions put together ...
>
> It calculates the combined debts of just 18 Premier League clubs at just under €4bn (£3.5bn), around four times the figure for the next most indebted top division, Spain's La Liga ...
>
> The Premier League made much more money from television and other commercial income than its rivals, €122m on average at the 18 clubs; the next wealthiest was the German Bundesliga, whose clubs made an average €79m. Yet despite that commercial advantage, the 18 English clubs were hugely more reliant on borrowed money from banks and club owners than the 714 other clubs

combined. 'English clubs contain on their balance sheets an estimated 56% of Europe-wide commercial debt', the report says. (Conn 2010c)

While the EPL's assets (£3.8 billion or 48 per cent of total club wealth across Europe) were also the most valuable in Europe, the UEFA figures did not even include its most indebted clubs, Portsmouth and West Ham United, to which, ironically, it had denied licences in the accounting year because of their extraordinary financial problems (although it also found that 47 per cent of Europe's top clubs made a loss in the year assessed, despite the highest ever revenue levels). Reliance on benefactors is particularly common among English football clubs, which is a clear indication of the unreliability of a business model that not uncommonly leads to insolvency, according to the 'very generalised picture' provided by Beech, Horsman and Magraw (2008: 12–13):

- A trend of poor performance on the pitch leads to relegation and reduced revenues.

- Costs are not cut back, in particular players' wages, and are wrongly prioritized.

- If the club owns its stadium, as the most valuable asset this becomes an issue. If the club does not own its stadium, it raises different issues – borrowing becomes extremely difficult, but creditors may hold off as there is no major asset to strip.

- Management faces a dilemma of whether to spend in the hope of improved performance on the pitch and hence promotion with its attendant financial gains or whether to release its better players in order to reduce costs.

- Bad management is widespread, with a worrying number of instances of unethical and even criminal management.

Increasingly, the 'benefactor' is an overseas entrepreneur using football as a point of entry into UK business networks and often, given the importance of sport stadia to the urban fabric (Frank and Steets 2010; Gratton and Henry 2001), with perhaps a greater interest in the redevelopment of land in and around football clubs, than in the sport itself. This pattern, which is by no means restricted to English football, is presented here only by way of illustration of some of the key factors in the indebtedness of many football (and, indeed, other sports) clubs despite enhanced levels of turnover. UEFA's 'financial fair play concept', which includes banishment from a key international competition if prudent financial management has not occurred in clubs, has been developed to stabilize and equalize a sport market in which the EPL, especially, has been characterized by continuing club difficulties in an era where rising revenues, both from broadcasting and the 'gentrification' of the game (King 1998), might be expected to achieve those outcomes. However, as has been demonstrated, the concentration of market power in a small number of clubs has created a perverse situation whereby the majority of clubs receive a slight proportion of total revenue and a minority uses its increased revenue to leverage more debt for higher expenditure.

Thus, just as football fans are often said to be eternally optimistic about 'next season', many football clubs are similarly naively hopeful with regard to the 'next market'. For example, to return to the EPL's recruitment of overseas players, a key justification is not only enhanced strength of the playing squad but also increased interest in the club from their countries of origin, which in turn creates the conditions for major marketing pushes into new territories. This does not mean, though, that English football did not have a substantial overseas following prior to the establishment of the Premier League. The flows of sport and television in the twentieth century took football fandom both to 'likely' places (diasporic settlements across the world) and rather unlikely ones where the signs of football affiliation took root. With regard to the latter, for example, Grant Farred (2008: 4) has described in passionate terms how

> [he] became a Liverpool fan ... by accident. It was an arbitrary decision, a choice made by a young boy in apartheid South Africa from a very long way, geographically and conceptually, away from the city of Liverpool and the club's Anfield Road Stadium. The full ethical complexity of that choice, a disenfranchised coloured kid supporting an almost uninterruptedly white team for almost two decades in a supposedly democratic metropolitan society ...

However, such 'arbitrary decisions' and 'accidents' became more systematically induced as the development of a global television infrastructure (as discussed in Chapters 2 and 3) and of sports markets in new zones created important new revenue streams when mature sports markets began to show signs of saturation (Miller *et al.*, 2010). The £1.4 billion (2010–3) garnered for the overseas broadcast rights to the EPL signified its value in competitive subscription television markets, especially in Asia, which in turn raises questions about the impact on football production and consumption in those places. The flow of such intensively marketed sport broadcasts involving 'glamorous', high-production quality content, it can be argued, is likely to have a deleterious effect on equivalent, local sport formations. As noted above, this process may manifest itself as media-cultural imperialism, whereby the sport experiences offered on the 'periphery' appear inferior and, indeed, as a sign of 'backwardness'. The EPL (and other major Western sports discussed as follows) has judiciously played on this comparative advantage, seeing in the Asia-Pacific region in particular a rapidly growing sport consumer market that is ripe for cultivation, if not exploitation. Just as the EPL has 'sucked in' overseas labour and, as noted in Chapter 2, overseas (particularly US but also Eastern European, Middle Eastern and Indian subcontinental) capital, it has spread out in an attempt to counteract the high degree of indebtedness and balance sheet failure described earlier.

Global sport: export markets and local sustainability

The Asia-Pacific region has been consistently identified as the primary growth opportunity for global sport, given its population of over 4 billion and economic growth rate that far exceeds that of other world regions (Rowe and Gilmour 2008). There is consistent concern with 'opening up' Asia to sport by a variety of means. These include, as noted at various points in this book, awarding mega media sports events to it (in recent times, these include the 2002 Korea–Japan World Cup and the 2008 Beijing Olympics) as well as the growing role of Asia on tennis, golf and motor sport circuits. It also involves the prominent televisual presentation of Western sports competitions like the EPL and the NBA, backed by team tours and heavy promotion of licensed merchandise, as well as the strategic recruitment of Asian athletes to competitions such as the EPL, NBA and Major League Baseball in a manner that draws 'hometown' viewers in large numbers (notably, for example, the Chinese NBA basketballer Yao Ming – Farred 2006). These are not simply 'innocent' extensions of leisure options to new audiences across the globe – the sophisticated barrage of sports brands articulates with the development of consumption-oriented cosmopolitanism in Asia that tends to reflect unfavourably on local sports products. Indeed, securing a visit of a major European football team, often involving public subsidies alongside local commercial sponsorship, is commonly regarded in Asian cities as a highly desirable goal. Thus there are frequent media stories concerning such attempts, like the following from Taiwan:

> Taipei – Taiwan is trying to woo Real Madrid to play on the island while the Spanish club is on its Asian tour in August, a sports marketing company said Monday. Real Madrid has been invited to play an exhibition match in Beijing in August as part of activities to mark the second anniversary of the 2008 Beijing Olympics, said Chin Hsi-yueh, the manager of Bros Sport Marketing Inc.
>
> Taiwan, Japan and Vietnam are all vying to lure Real Madrid, the world's richest football club, to their venues after Real's Chinese sponsor Great Gate Sports & Entertainment Co Ltd, agreed to add one more stop to the tour, Chin said.
>
> 'We hope Real Madrid can play one game in Taipei on August 4 before it goes to Beijing,' he said …
>
> Chin said the Chinese sponsor favours Real Madrid playing in Taiwan but said Taiwan must come up with the funds.
>
> Taiwan's biggest rival is Tokyo, which is offering 7 million euros (10 million US dollars) for a friendly, while Bros Sport can only offer 3 million euros.
>
> 'We hope our government and the Sports Affairs Council can allocate funds and join us in inviting Real Madrid,' he said. (*Earth Times* 2010)

Despite, in this instance, the tour not occurring because of the extended commitments surrounding the 2010 World Cup in South Africa, the contest between nations to host star sports visitors is a continuing feature of each off season. A frequent justification for these invitations is that they stimulate the sport in the host country, encouraging young people to take it up on behalf of their country and providing a 'benchmark' for local teams' performance. However, evidence of this outcome is slight, with commonly expressed complaints that the impact is, in fact, negative in that local sport may be overshadowed and even denigrated. For example, Malaysia's hosting of the 2007 Asian Cup (the major tournament of the Asian Football Confederation (AFC)) was a major disappointment in terms of spectator numbers and national attention, and its domestic club competition remains in severe decline (Gilmour and Rowe 2010). By contrast, Manchester United Football Club's 2009 promotional tour garnered intense interest, with 30,000 fans attending the team's training session and many Malaysians in the 85,000 crowd in the match between Manchester and the Malaysian national team (itself a questionable pitting of club against nation) wearing the visiting team's colours and merchandise and cheering for them (Gilmour and Rowe 2010).

It is not intended here to represent association football in Asia as entirely in a state of disrepair. Japan's J-League, for example, has seen attendances rise annually since 2006 to reach almost 10 million in total by 2009, although Japan, as part of the dominant global economic triad with Europe and North America (now challenged by China), can hardly be regarded as on the economic periphery (Hirst and Thompson, 2009). But this success contrasts with that of even those countries with strong performing teams and economies, such as Korea's K-League (whose 2009 season-average attendance was barely half of the J-League's 20,000 – AFC 2010), or with large populations and considerable potential but with poorly organized football leagues, as is the case in corruption-ridden China (Montague and FlorCruz 2010). It is also notable that, in the 2011 Asian Cup held in Qatar (which had at that time recently been awarded the 2022 World Cup), '[o]nly 3,481 turned out to watch Uzbekistan beat Kuwait on Wednesday at the 22,000-seat Al-Gharafa stadium while 3,639 were at the 12,500-seat Qatar Sports Club on Tuesday to watch United Arab Emirates play North Korea' (Casey 2011). This attendance, though, was substantial when compared with the 2009 Malaysian Super League match at which there were only eleven paying spectators (Samuel 2009, cited in Gilmour and Rowe 2010). The overall argument is that in Asia, as in other world regions, the development of football is much more uneven than is generally acknowledged in such claims as 'Asia's footballing potential is boundless' (FIFA 2004).

In East and Central Africa, there is a similar pattern to that found in parts of the Asia-Pacific region, with massive support for the EPL among local fans while local football often struggles. The turmoil caused by war and internal discord, the debilitating impact of underdevelopment and poverty, and institutionalized corruption have all helped to contribute negatively to the conditions that have fostered the export of the EPL to countries such as Kenya, Ethiopia, Uganda and Tanzania that reveal a deep global imbalance. As Peter Musembi (2010) records in a BBC World Service (2010) radio feature,

> No country from the east of the continent qualified for [the 2010] South Africa [World Cup] – not that there is anything unusual in that ... And it is certainly no surprise that Kenya will not to be at the World Cup ... A feud has been raging there for over six years between two bodies claiming to be the legitimate administrators of the game in the country. As a result, football standards have plummeted, and there has been a growing passion for the English Premier League.

> In Kibera slum [the largest in Africa], just outside the capital, Nairobi, people pay 20 Kenya shillings (25 cents) to watch Premiership matches in TV halls. One hall is

called San Siro Stadium, named after the home ground of Italy's Inter Milan, where Kenya's most successful international footballer, McDonald Mariga, plays. Kenyan teams play to just a handful of spectators. Other halls are called [after English football grounds] Old Trafford, Stamford Bridge and Highbury. Bernard Otieno, an Arsenal supporter outside San Siro hall, says it is a disgrace that Kenya is not in the World Cup. 'We have very good players like McDonald Mariga who can represent us in international matches, but our league is surrounded with a lot of politics that is why we can't prosper,' he says. 'We are left with the consolation of watching the English Premier League, since we are not entertained by our own football.'

Such postcolonial accounts involving the 'consolation' of the EPL give a much less positive interpretation to that of Farred's (2008) symbolic embrace of English football under the South African apartheid regime. By 2010, post-apartheid South Africa hosted the World Cup for the first time on the continent, and yet association football in Africa is widely regarded as afflicted with substantial difficulties. According to Steve Bloomfield (2010) (whose book's prologue contains an anecdote in which he is released from brief detention by the Sudanese security agency after claiming to be a friend of English celebrity footballer David Beckham), different histories of imperialism and colonialism have created different patterns, with footballers from ex-French colonies like Senegal finding it much easier to move to European clubs than from ex-British colonies, given the more restrictive immigration arrangements in the United Kingdom. But it is not clear how enhanced labour mobility in East and Central African football would automatically be of benefit to the local game, although the banning of such movement by the Zaire (now the Democratic Republic of Congo, a former Belgian colony whose official language is French) government after that country reached the World Cup Finals in 1974 had a clearly deleterious effect on the development of the game in that country. In Kenya, though, the media are perhaps coming to the rescue, with its sixteen-team Premier League for three years carried and sponsored by the South Africa–based, pan-African satellite broadcaster SuperSport (which also, ironically, has the rights to the EPL), creating the necessary infrastructure for a professional football system that, for example, can now pay its players reasonable wages and is required to display greater transparency in governance. The global interdependency of media and sport is well illustrated here as in other regions of the globe, with a familiar contrast between flourishing fandom for glamorous overseas sport competitions and the struggling attempts of local competitions to overcome a vast gap in prestige and 'packaged' spectator appeal.

The problems of football in Africa, signified for some by the general failure of African teams in the World Cup, are frequently ascribed to internal factors (such as inefficient and corrupt governance) and, above all, to the reproduction of historical inequities deriving from imperialism and colonialism as they are played out in the flows of labour, capital and images of contemporary global sport. Following is one assessment from within the African online media (Inou and Akinyosoye, 2010), listing among 'Six Problems with African Football':

The alienation of African football and neo-colonialism: Five out of six trainers of African teams, excluding Algeria, are of European origin. Thus one can assume that African countries, fifty years after having achieved their so-called independence, are still not able to believe in themselves …

European coaches continue to convey a colonial image in football schools, where football talents are 'produced' for European clubs. Young African football talents serve as fresh supply for European Clubs. What happens to national leagues is irrelevant. This leads to a depreciation of African football leagues and to an extremely fragile national consciousness …

Depreciation of African football leagues: African players, who play in national leagues have almost no chance of playing for the national team. Such a depreciation of the national league pushes players to emigrate. During the last FIFA World Cup, the South African Soccer team was the only one in which the majority (14 out of 23 players) of the team also played in the NFL. In the Ivory Coast and Cameroon teams only one player came from national clubs …

In Algeria no single soccer player of the national team played for the national league.

Migration as the only way to success: Since soccer players are not appreciated in national leagues, African soccer players tend to emigrate from their countries. More than 400 African soccer players play in 36 European top-leagues … Dishonest agents attract young players between the age of fifteen and sixteen to Europe on the grounds of false promises and the intention to exploit them. If the players do not perform as expected, they are simply disregarded and abandoned. Traffickers of soccer players no longer use traditional ways and means, transporting players from an African country to a once occupying country (Nigeria–Great Britain, Cameroon–France). Players are trafficked via Eastern European countries where entry requirements are not so tight. For many European Clubs African players are cheap goods. They are imported to Europe on the sidelines of human trafficking and thanks to the cognisance of high-ranking officials and criminal networks.

This very negative picture of neocolonialism in African football sees the top positions occupied by Europeans and the local players as a source of cheap labour, 'trafficked' into the main European leagues (sometimes via exploitative football academies) in the certain knowledge that most young aspirants will not prosper, while importing the seductive imagery of Western sporting glamour and success (Darby, Akindes and Irwin 2007; Sparre 2007). However, this is not a random or open process of the movement of sporting labour. As Raffaele Poli's (2010: 499) research has revealed, the increased flow of footballers between countries has 'not been reflected in a significant spatial diversification of transfer networks. On the contrary, it has led to a quantitative reinforcement of older channels'. These channels include 'geographical proximity' within Europe and, outside it, 'historical links (Spain–Latin America, Italy–Latin America, France–old African colonies, England–United States and Australia)'. The same channels, as noted above, carry their structured symbolic dominance back to the places where athletic labour is sourced and so stimulate consumptive spectatorship directed less towards the local sports competitions that have been 'vacated' than to the global, cosmopolitan sport seen as the 'gold standard' by which all excellence is measured.

Association football has been extraordinarily successful in its 'global diffusion', which can be partially attributed to the 'relative simplicity of football's laws, equipment and body techniques' (Giulianotti 1999: xi), qualities that facilitate ready adoption by players and spectators alike. But such a purely formal analysis cannot explain its global spread – there are many other simple, easily adopted and appealing sports, and at least one other, basketball (discussed below), could just as easily fit this mould. Instead, a range of other factors has contributed to association football's spread, from imperial and colonial imposition (especially from its British 'home' – see, for example, Mills and Dimeo 2003) to more everyday encounters through international trade, educational provision and cultural exchange. Giulianotti (1999) also emphasises the game's adaptability in meaning and use in very different contexts, its formal characteristics meshing in a range of ways across continents with different antagonistic formations (articulating with its pronounced, though by no means unique, binary competitive structure), cultural and religious belief systems and so on. But the master narrative has not been one of universal uptake with various local adaptations and variations. In Australia, for example, association football has lagged behind other codes despite its strong connection with Britain (to the extent that it was stigmatized in Anglo popular culture as the 'wogball' of migrants from non-English-speaking countries (Hay 1994) while, most strikingly, the United States has been resistant and ambivalent towards it (Markovits and Hellerman 2001). There is a revealing debate (paralleling in some ways critiques of the inconsistency of US agricultural protectionism and advocacy of free markets for its own exports) about how much the country most associated with global sport resists those that it does not dominate – especially association football. Toby Miller (2010) has argued that, despite the evident popularity of the sport in the United States, there is a tendency in some quarters to see it as 'un-American':

A potent brand of amateur intellectualism and reactionary academic scholarship celebrates a putative American exceptionalism, which supposedly seals off American sport from outside influence. The concept of exceptionalism began as an attempt to explain why socialism had not taken greater hold [t]here. It has since turned into an excessive rhapsody to Yankee world leadership, difference, and sanctimony. So we encounter claims made – in all seriousness – that 'foreignness' can make a sport unpopular in America.

Perhaps the most notorious instance of American exceptionalism was applied to soccer by the Reaganite Republican Jack Kemp, who derided it as a 'European socialist' sport, in contrast to its 'democratic' rival (the 'football' that he had played in college and professionally). Similarly ethnocentric denunciations of soccer – predicated, of course, on letting Latinos and migrants know they're not 'American' – still flow from angry white men. Frustrated at the prominence and popularity of the sport, they are desperate to attack what a *Wall Street Journal* opinion essay calls its taint of 'European … death and despair'. The American Enterprise Institute's journal says Americans insist that 'excellence should prevail' while Europeans and Latin Americans are happy with second-best – so they enjoy soccer.

It is a little curious to see association football regarded as in some way 'alien' or 'un-American'. Its national men's team is currently the top-ranking Confederation of North, Central American and Caribbean Association Football (CONCACAF) member and eighteenth out of 203 in the world, took part in the first World Cup in 1930 and has qualified for every tournament since 1990 and hosted it in 1994. Its women's team is ranked first in the world and has won the World Cup twice and the Olympics five times (indeed, it is this success that may have led to a sexually stigmatized 'feminization' of football in the United States, where the patronized figure of the 'Soccer Mom' is associated with a certain kind of stifling suburbanism – see, for example, Swanson 2009). While there is clearly a substantial foundation of practice and support for association football in the United States (especially at the school and community level), the intemperate comments of some critics and, less dramatically, its continued lagging behind the professional, 'home-grown' team sports of gridiron, basketball, baseball and ice hockey are a salient reminder that the flows of global media sport are complex, variable and multidirectional. The kind of critique that Miller advances – essentially that in the United States there is an ethnocentric suspicion of association football – has often elicited defensive complaints that the game is, indeed, an important part of the American sporting fabric. For example, Bill Saporito (2010) demands,

> Please stop lecturing us. We know that it's called football everywhere else and that it's the global game, the beautiful game. Americans call it soccer because there's a perfectly great sport here already called football, one that is not inclined to surrender its moniker anytime soon. So don't get your football knickers in a twist about it.

> Soccer it is. And stop asking that question, 'When is soccer ever going to be big in America?' Soccer won't ever be NFL big or Major League Baseball big, but in so many ways, soccer has become a big and growing sport. An American sport. Americans love to play it, certainly. Soccer trails only basketball in the number of participants. It's the most popular sport for women among NCAA schools. That's been true for a long time. Indeed, the game has deep roots in the U.S., arriving with immigrants from Scotland, Germany, Italy and elsewhere, who brought their work skills and their game with them.

The United States, as a 'nation of immigrants', would be expected to be the site of many sports, but just as racial and ethnic hierarchies persist within it, the sphere of sport is also unequal and, as noted earlier, may be so through association (pun not intended) with those already marginalized and disadvantaged. It is not possible here to engage in a thorough, detailed analysis of the social complexion and power structure of each sport. But it should be remembered that although, following Pierre Bourdieu (1978, 1984), capital in all its forms (social, economic, symbolic, cultural and educational) is crucial to how sport is structured, deployed and experienced, it is accumulated and exchanged in diverse ways including, perhaps perversely, foregrounding human subjects who are exploited and degraded in substantial proportions as image-exemplars and promotional vehicles (notably African American men – Carrington 2010). This point is made because the United States is not only a developer of domestic sport and recipient of externally produced sport but is also a major exporter of it, especially in mediated form. Indeed, it was the United States that first developed the commercial mediation of sport that was subsequently mimicked and adapted all around the world (Chandler 1988;

Goldlust 1987; Rader 1984; Rowe 2004a; Wenner 1989). US-identified sports have, therefore, pioneered the global promotion of sport and sports brands, while tending to display a certain defensiveness towards those that have moved onto their 'patch'.

Probably the most successful US-originated sport in this regard is basketball, which (as discussed in Chapter 2) was developed in the United States (by the Canadian James Naismith) in the late nineteenth century explicitly as a sport for young men that was easy to play in inclement weather indoors. Basketball, though, was adaptable to a range of spaces (such as external urban squares, streets and waste ground), its popularity at the informal, community-based level accompanying its progressive establishment as a professional sport in the United States, first at city and college level before the NBA was founded in 1946 (WNBA wasn't formed until 1997). Basketball leagues have been set up on all inhabited continents, with an international governing body, now known as Fédération Internationale de Basketball Amateur (FIBA) and currently with 213 national member federations, and its own World Championships since the middle of the twentieth century (first held in 1950 for men and 1953 for women) and a long-established participation in the summer Olympics (since 1936 for men and 1976 for women). FIBA presents the following 'Key Numbers' among its 'Quick Facts':

- A study conducted by TGI Europe in 2006 in the four European markets UK, FRA, ESP and GER and based on 56.00 [sic] interviews, shows that the 33 million basketball fans in these four markets are mainly young (15–24), male and deriving from high social grade categories.

- A global study, conducted by Roper Starch Worldwide in April '97 based on 35,000 interviews, showed that 11% of the world plays basketball. Basketball has even replaced football as the most popular sport in areas like Asia and Australia and is on the way to surpassing football worldwide.

- Over 450 million people play basketball on competition and grassroots level in 2007, but the number of licensed players has also risen drastically since 1992. (FIBA 2011)

While such statistics are promotional in nature and so in various ways questionable (including the claim about regional popularity and the apparently approving four-country European player profile as 'mainly young (15–24), male and deriving from high social grade categories'), they do reveal that basketball is a major global sport that has acquired a player and spectator appeal that extends well beyond its technically sporting characteristics. Basketball, more than any other sport, has wedded the 'style power' associated with popular music with the performative, competitive cultural characteristics of organized sport (McComb 2004; Rowe 1995). In particular, as has often been discussed, basketball's association with a certain 'cool' form of African American masculinity (drawing on, in particular, the studied insouciance of hip hop's presentation of self) created a 'cultural package' that was highly visual and globally portable (Andrews 1996; Baker and Boyd 1997; Carrington 2010; McKay 1995). The NBA's global expansion has been on several fronts, including, as already noted, the circulation of content on television, with its influential Commissioner David Stern assiduously placing it on screens in a multitude of countries by direct negotiation with broadcasters from the early 1980s onwards (Williams 2009) and encouraging overseas players in a manner that would later 'globalize' basketball more fully by reversing the flow of sporting labour in its originary American contexts. As one journalist commented after viewing Stern at the 2008 Beijing Olympics,

> Last summer, when the gold, silver, and bronze medals were handed out after the Olympic basketball tournament in Beijing, China, to the members of the teams representing the United States, Spain, and Argentina, 24 of the 36 medals went to NBA players, past and present.

> Standing with hand over heart as the U.S. national anthem played and the flags of the three medal-winning nations were raised in the Olympic basketball arena, NBA commissioner David Stern felt his heart swell with pride – equal parts patriotism and self-realization.

> The globalization of the NBA, long a goal Stern had envisioned, seemed an unquestioned fact.

> FOR DECADES, Stern has understood the global appeal of basketball in general and of the NBA in particular …

> Today, NBA television programming reaches 215 countries and territories, and games are broadcast in 45 languages.

> And Stern has watched the rosters of his league's teams swell with players born outside the United States. In the 1983–1984 season, there were eight international players on the NBA's 23 rosters; by the 2006–2007 season, there were 83, from 37 different countries and territories. (Monroe 2009)

This history of basketball's development reveals the familiar correspondence of elements of globalization and Americanization, with contrasting readings that basketball's spread beyond the United States through promotional and marketing campaigns and the flow of foreign sports labour into the NBA can represent the diffusion or re-concentration of US control over, and identification with, the sport. Similarly, 'socially responsible' outreach work such as 'Live, Learn or Play' as part of the 'NBA's commitment to youth and family development', involving 525 'new and refurbished basketball courts, libraries, playgrounds, homes, fitness facilities and technology rooms [are] created in conjunction with NBA league and team community and business partners' in over twenty-two countries since 2005 (NBA 2010), can be seen as either philanthropy or marketing by stealth – or, indeed, as both and more besides. I prefer here to argue that the NBA and US basketball in general, as with other cultural-material forms and sub-forms (including film, blue jeans, soft drinks, fast processed food and pop music) in which the United States played a seminal (and often resiliently powerful) role in international circulation, communication and exchange, have overtly and systematically taken its 'product' to the world. This, though, as was observed in the case of English association football, could never be a one-way process of sports exportation, with the flows of people, capital, identities and practices moving in other directions and also setting up alternative centres of power (notably in Europe). That 300 million people in China might watch an NBA game (sometimes exceeding its US audience) is testament to its televisual sporting pulling power, but it is also a sign of Chinese sporting nationalism in the particular attraction of that audience to contests involving their compatriot Yao Ming (Farred 2006; Oates and Polumbaum 2004). Here, as with the EPL and its aforementioned influx of foreign players and increased emphasis on cultivating external markets that are potentially larger than the foundational one, the status of, strictly, a 'national' competition becomes problematic.

Nonetheless, the extended forays of the NBA into Asia, especially its two largest markets China and India (now often conflated as 'Chindia'), represent a US-initiated expansionism with mixed evidence of a positive effect on the sport in the 'recipient' country. In India, NBA financial support for competitions, coaching programmes, strategic organizational advice and 'Live, Learn or Play' sport community-infrastructure building have been generally less successful than its television coverage of games in the United States and website NBA.com/India. The NBA-India fan page on Facebook is able to create a local 'buzz', but (as discussed in Chapter 4) this medium of exchange can be directed towards, and provoke interest in, major sports events such as the NBA finals, rather than stimulate local, grass-roots participation and spectatorship (Dawson 2010; Klayman 2010; Singh 2010). Whether an imported sport 'takes' in its introduced site is not determined by a formulaic application of standard principles of exposure, marketing and persuasion. The NBA is one among many sports viewing India as an alluring commercial opportunity, but it must confront a range of socioeconomic obstacles, such as the widespread urban and rural poverty that make even establishing a basketball court, club and small competitive league inordinately difficult. In addition, there is the national sporting disposition – supported by massive economic investment and media coverage – which, as is discussed below, leans so heavily towards cricket in India as to overshadow all others.

The NBA expansion strategy extends beyond Asia to Africa (Means and Nauright 2007) and, as with other sports with global ambitions, is enthusiastic about 'tapping' mature and emergent media sport markets and anticipating the next to embrace branded sports consumption. Although this process has much in common with imperialism, it is never a simple process of invasion and obliteration. For example, as Mark Falcous and Joseph Maguire (2006: 74) argue in their analysis of NBA coverage in the United Kingdom,

Status, prestige, power, and control underpin established–outsider relations: without hegemonic control, the claim to higher status and the specific charisma of a particular sport and nation (the NBA and the United States) would have no basis. Power differentials of this kind generate contrasts between group charisma and group stigma – established groups enjoy the former, while outsiders suffer the latter. Established groups are better able both to organize, within specific zones of prestige, their high status public image while at the same time constructing a negative image of outsider groups. This uneven balance of power – at local, national, and global levels – is the decisive condition for any effective stigmatization of an outsider group. Accordingly, dominant reflections of both US and UK culture(s), both national contexts characterized by complex heterogeneity, are reinforced in NBA coverage. The NBA seeks established status in global terms. Yet, the political economy of UK media production, and the dynamics of global ideological exchange, moderate their strategies. This study shows that the selling of the global involves 'concessions' to the local. These findings confirm the assertion that, no matter how apparently powerful the global, it is obliged to negotiate with the local, especially when the 'local' is a former 'super power' with a well-established media industry.

Basketball is a popular sport in the United Kingdom and in many other European countries, but there is little prospect that it can, by the end of this century, supplant association football as Europe's dominant sport. It must, therefore, negotiate its place in the 'space of sports', in which the NBA's quintessential 'Americanness' can be both an advantage for those trying to break away from the restrictions of a 'parent' sports culture and at the same time induce some resistance among those who see it as imposed, alien and inauthentic. Sometimes, the same human subject will feel the gravitational pull of competing sports, or see them as part of a mood-sensitive smorgasbord, or set them both aside for another cultural pursuit. In order to stimulate potential and capitalize on current interest, the NBA has begun playing regular season games outside the United States, the first ever in Europe in early March 2011 in London between the New Jersey Nets and the Toronto Raptors in basketball's 2012 Olympic venue, the O2 Arena (formally known as the Millennium Dome and for the purposes of the Olympics called the North Greenwich Arena). A similar proposal that each EPL club should play at least one game per year outside the United States has been rejected by a majority of its clubs and opposed by UEFA, but NBA practice and EPL prospect signal a tentative move towards the globalization of national sports competition in competitive as well as mediated terms.

Michael Veseth (2005) applies the pejorative term 'Globaloney' (first coined in the 1940s) to specious grand assertions of the destruction of local variations by aggressive global, predominantly American capitalism, especially in its popular cultural form. In rejecting the familiar use of Michael Jordan as a symbol of triumphant Americanization and globalization, he suggests, after considering how basketball and the NBA take local forms in new territories and then feed back into its primary sports context in the United States, that perhaps the 'NBA has been globalized *by* the rest of the world, and that in the process, American professional sports have become much more like spectator sports in the rest of the world' (Veseth 2005: 76, emphasis in the original). Ironically, perhaps, Veseth's approach to the concept of globalization is rather too US centric and so tends to conflate Americanization and globalization (Miller *et al.* 2001), but he clearly recognizes the limitations of a mechanical, linear approach to it. This point is reinforced further when the focus shifts to a sport that means little in the United States but was once dominated by Europe and is now firmly controlled by the Indian subcontinent – cricket.

The Indian Premier League: a redirection of flows?

As discussed above, the narrative of globalization tends to be entwined with that of Americanization and certainly a directional flow from the West to East or the 'Global North' to 'South'. This familiar story was certainly evident in cricket, with its close formative ties to British (specifically English) imperialism and colonialism (Farred 2004). As Peter Corrigan (2001: 232–3), drawing on the work of Keith Sandiford (1994), has observed,

> Cricket was one way through which imperial links were forged, maintained and preserved between England and the rather extensive patches of the world it colonized ... Playing the game marked one as a participant in the Empire, but was also an opportunity to show that one existed differently as, say, 'Australian' ...
>
> [A]n important function of cricket in the imperial era was the transmission of certain English cultural values to the colonies, both to remind the colonizers of who they were (or, rather, who they were supposed to be) and to display to the colonized what they were. Assimilation of these values was to a degree a way in which certain sections of the colonized could access some of the spoils of the imperial adventure for themselves.

Thus, cricket, despite the English imperial impulse to disseminate and diffuse the superiority of its 'gentlemen', could not be consistently and permanently secured in this way. Hilary Beckles (2001: 243) has observed in the Caribbean context that '[d]espite attempts by white colonial elites to monopolize and racially segregate the game, the popular demand for open access provided it with a radical, democratizing mandate'. The best-known analysis of this capacity of cricket both to draw from and challenge the colonial legacy is C. L. R. James's (1993) classic *Beyond a Boundary*, a sophisticated and highly personal account of how the sports field appeals as a place temporarily separated from politics but is always subject not just to its intrusion but is thoroughly permeated by the political. James was critical of the commercialization of cricket where it impinged on the nobler aspects of the game, but his death in 1989 (aged eighty-eight) meant that he did not witness a later stage in cricket's development when, after one-day cricket threatened the position of the more sedate five-day game and the Packer Revolution made the sport more lively and colourful for television (Barnett 1990), the power of India asserted itself, to be followed by its embrace of an even shorter, more spectacular, television friendly form – Twenty20 (see Chapter 2) as presented in the IPL and its (short-lived) rival the Indian Cricket League (ICL).

The rising power of the Indian subcontinent in cricket stems from a combination of factors – most notably the economic development of India since the mid-twentieth century and the growth in leisure consumption and broadcast media access of its huge population; the investment in cricket by local capital, especially from the media and entertainment sectors, and its intimate connection to its (mostly) illegal gambling industry; the extant and stimulated (both external and internal) popularity of the game that has seen it crowd out rival sports; and the belated cooperation and 'caucusing' among subcontinental representatives in the International Cricket Council with fragile, if not volatile, relationships (Haigh 2010; *Indian Express* 2011; Majumdar 2004; Malcolm, Gemmell and Mehta 2010; Williams 2003). The media are especially important in this context because exercising power over sport means not just receiving broadcasts sent from other regions but wresting control over production and integrating sport broadcasts across media sites and forms, including current affairs programmes, talkback radio stations, websites, colour magazines and both general news and sports pages.

In Chapter 2 it was argued that Western media corporations, notably News Corp, have established global media sport operations by licensing coverage of major Western sports competitions to which they have acquired broadcasting rights in other territories and, where necessary, establishing partnerships with local media. The IPL, as a major sports competition of the Board of Control for Cricket in India (BCCI), has directionally reversed this arrangement by selling in 2008 its inaugural ten-year global broadcast rights to a Consortium of Sony Entertainment Television (India) (a subsidiary of the Japan-owned Sony Pictures Entertainment, which is part of the Sony Corporation that acquired the US-based, Coca Cola–owned Columbia Pictures in 1989) and the Singapore-based World Sport Group (WSG) (which markets sport, manages sport events and athletes, and produces made-for-television sports programmes) for US$1.026 billion. Perhaps inevitably given the history of manoeuvring of various parties involved in the IPL, a subsequent dispute led to cancellation and legal action over WSG's rights (Engineer and Gollapudi 2010) and the suspension on grounds of impropriety of its founding chairman and commissioner of the IPL, Lalit Modi (Bal 2010).

IPL, whose Indian-city-based franchises are all India owned (with Lachlan Murdoch, son of Rupert, an investor in the Rajasthan Royals), has a range of international and Indian sponsors of the competition and its franchises (including title sponsor property Indian developer DFL, UK-based telecommunications company Vodafone and US-based soft drink company Pepsi Cola). Thus, while IPL is not an 'enclosed' Indian competition, it is clearly Indian controlled, with the BCCI exerting its local authority to eradicate the ICL, established by local company Zee Entertainment Enterprises (a subsidiary of the US-based Turner Group) and, as discussed below, hiring local and international players (while effectively banning those from Pakistan) in a contra flow of the earlier international cricket labour market that saw subcontinental players move along a more familiar path to the previously more lucrative setting of English County Cricket. As Mehta, Gemmell and Malcolm (2009: 701) argue in drawing on the work of Michael Curtin (2007) on film and television in China,

> In analysing India's rise as the centre of world cricket, it is possible to draw a parallel from theoretical frameworks in studies of the media and globalization, and in particular, the work of Michael Curtin's notion of what he calls 'media capitals'. At the heart of debates over media capitalism are concerns over location – centres with concentration of resources and their spheres of circulation which lead to concerns over culture, identity and power. Curtin's 'media capitals' are geographic centres which transcend national boundaries and become global. These are places where resources, talent and production processes concentrate

based on the inherent logic of capitalism: the accumulation of capital. Creative talent migrates towards 'media capitals' and the ruthless logic of efficiency fuels perpetual circuits of expansion. There is a socio-cultural dimension to this. For the logic of capitalist expansion to work, it needs to address local variations such as language, cultural issues, identities, communal imaginaries, etc., but primarily this is a process central to capitalism.

Mumbai, the media capital of India, is the headquarters of Sony Entertainment Television (India) and the BCCI, as well as Bollywood, which supplies both some of the IPL franchise co-owners (such as the actors Shah Rukh Khan and Shilpa Shetty, co-owners of the Kolkata Knight Riders and the Rajasthan Royals, respectively) and of the flamboyant presentational aesthetic of match entertainment. The raw expression of twenty-first century global cricketing capitalism and its accommodation with localism is evident in its latest iteration of the new international division of cultural labour (Miller *et al.* 2001) through the annual player auction. Each franchise bids (under a notional but apparently circumvented salary cap of US$9 million), drawing from a nominated list of players (350 in 2011) from around the world (except, for transparently but officially unacknowledged political reasons, neighbouring Pakistan), in various tiers and categories. It is not, though, a completely open market, with no more than ten foreign players permitted per squad, no more than four of whom can be chosen in a starting team and a minimum of eight local players and of two players aged under twenty-two in each squad. Local players are also favoured by gaining comparatively higher values than some better performed foreigners (Bhogle 2011; A. Wilson 2011) for essentially nationalist reasons – as Boria Majumdar (2011) explains:

> It was inevitable that the five Indian stars – Yuvraj Singh, Zaheer Khan, Gautam Gambhir, Yusuf Pathan and Rohit Sharma – would command the highest bids at the auction. This is simply not because they are the best players available, but also because an Indian name is still preferred to lead an outfit and they are essential names to have on the roster to enlist sponsors for the next three seasons. More than foreigners, Indian names remain the tried and tested option as far as the market is concerned and this resulted in huge sums being spent on these stars. In fact, Rajasthan Royals, champions of season 1, found it impossible to find a lead sponsor in year two because they lacked an Indian face. [Australians] Shane Warne and Shane Watson weren't enough for the marketers.

Although other factors are involved in the player auction – such as some nations requiring their players for international duties (B. Wilson 2011) – it is apparent that the market appeal of Indian players is such that if the game in that country has, as argued by Boria Majumdar (2007: 93), indeed, undergone a transition from 'nationalist romance to postcolonial sport' and that 'the frenzied nationalism stimulated by cricket' is 'at best a facade, a romantic escape', its institutional base remains firmly organized on nationalist lines. Gideon Haigh (2010: 196–7) acerbically comments in criticizing 'the contention that the IPL somehow leads to the sunny uplands of a post-nationalist cricket utopia' that 'the IPL is nationalism's ultimate triumph: a global tournament in which the same nation always wins'. But if India is always the winner in symbolic, economic or sporting terms, the riches generated by the IPL may be elusive for many of its player participants. Harsha Bhogle (2011) has noted the undervaluing of players from Bangladesh as a reflection of a resilient colonialism still evident among South Asia elites, while there are very substantial disparities in the values of the contracts gained by IPL players. Thus, for example, in the Darwinian competition of the player auction in 2011, Gautam Gambhir of the Kolkata Knight Riders received a contract worth US$2.4 million, while Jonathan Vandiar of South Africa received US$20,000. While there is no doubt a large gulf in their accomplishments, that one player receives less than one per cent of the other's remuneration indicates, even within the structured labour market of the IPL, the kind of hypermarket-based reward system advocated under the rubric of neoliberalism – and with the same distortions of its meritocratic framework.

In the light of such structurally induced material inequalities among both teammates and competitors, and the heavy promotion of status conscious, conspicuous consumption for spectators (Rowe and Gilmour 2008), Jack Williams (2003: 104–5) regards the ascendancy of South Asia in cricket flowing from its advancement of commercialization of the game not as a sign of de-Westernization but of the ultimate triumph of a globalized Western capitalism:

> This Asian drive for the greater commercialization of international cricket can be seen as part of the late-twentieth-century globalization of sport and of globalization in general ... Fast food, credit cards, and jeans, very much the icons of globalization, are American cultural artefacts, and while the internet can be regarded as a resource for a decentralized global economy, the American corporation Microsoft dominates computer software. The enhanced commercialization of international cricket has been stimulated largely by the revenue to be gained from satellite television and sponsorship, and can be seen as an imitation of the American model of sports presentation, with sports events packaged to maximise their television appeal.

For Williams, the postcolonial paradox of 'Asian-led' commercialization of international cricket is an expression of 'Western cultural imperialism' that discomfits the West (specifically England, the home and moral guardian of the game), which had, after first commercializing the game – a process much advanced in the 1970s by Australia (Cashman 2010) – resisted a full embrace of American-style *razzmatazz* because of a residual cultural conservatism (here, again, the relevance of Raymond Williams's typology of cultural forms is highly relevant). Therefore, a certain disarticulation between economic practices and sporting values is evident, but so, too, is the brute size and strength of the Indian market (itself, as noted, created by an enthusiasm for the game that is not matched in the West). Thus, the loss of political economic power in cricket by the West has created the conditions for a lament that the game is degraded – a position that can be readily reinforced by betting-related corruption and match-fixing, and by threats to withdraw from tours during disputes that would severely compromise the finances of other cricketing nations (see Chapter 6). Mike Marqusee (2010) has described the IPL as the 'dark side of the neoliberal dream' in a new entrepreneurialist India shielded from criticism by presenting its internal detractors as reactionary and its external critics as 'neocolonial', but which has exposed 'the true cost of unleashing the private sector'. However, he acknowledges that the English and Wales Cricket Board (ECB) had shown no less an enthusiasm for rapid, unprincipled capital accumulation through its involvement in the highly lucrative Twenty20 international matches in the Caribbean proposed by Allen Stanford, who was charged in 2009 with running a pyramid scheme (Haigh 2010). The 'Post-Westernization of World Cricket' (Rumford 2007) or the role of cricket in the 'Rise of the Non-West' (Gupta 2004) occurring under globalization are not, then, straightforward incidences of historical turn-taking and resistance. If cricket is a lead indicator of the rise of the Asia-Pacific in the twenty-first century and of the reversal of previous capital flows and lines of political authority, it has become so not by forging an entirely new path based on distinct Eastern cultural values (although non-Western cultural elements are obviously evident) but by turning the political economic weaponry perfected by cricket's formerly dominant colonial powers against them in what is clearly felt by many in India to be a delicious historical irony.

Mega media sports events in new places

In the earlier discussion the main concern has been with nation-based sports competitions and their control and mediated circulation, especially through television. These are vital to the globalization of sport, but so also are major events at greater intervals involving a bidding process and enormous investments by hosts. In Chapter 6 I will discuss the Beijing 2008 Olympics and the 2010 South Africa World Cup in terms of being sought and awarded as new host sites, interpreted as epochal changes in the global circulation of major sports events (South Africa having already hosted other World Cups in rugby union and cricket but becoming the first African country to host the world's largest sports event). In this immediate context I will address briefly the significance of awarding these major sport events outside their conventional orbit in terms of global media sport development. Since the revival of the Summer Olympics in 1896 by French aristocrat Baron Pierre de Coubertin the Games have mainly clustered in Europe and North America (the Winter Olympics even more so, but their specific climatic requirements means that they are more globally restricted in technical terms). A European city has hosted (including London 2012) the Summer Games on sixteen occasions (in eleven nations), and a North American one on six (the United States four of these, with one each to Canada and Mexico) and once in Australia. By contrast, the vast Asian continent has hosted the Games only three times, and South America will hold the Summer Games for the first time in Rio de Janeiro, Brazil in 2018. This skewing of the Games towards the West (Hill 1992) has been periodically countered by strategic inclusion of new Olympic hosts, notably as part of Japan's post–Second World War rehabilitation (1964), South Korea's economic and political emergence (1988), China's opening up to the world as an economic power to rival the United States (2008) (Rowe 2012) as well as Brazil's rise as one of the booming 'BRIC' countries (along with India, Russia and China). The pattern of the FIFA World Cup since its inception in 1930 and hosting by Uruguay has been considerably different in that it has reflected the prominent role of South America, which has been awarded it on five occasions (including Brazil 2014, a further confirmation of that country's newfound economic status) and also given its rotational system across the major confederations. Europe has been awarded the World Cup on eleven occasions, North America three times, Africa once and Asia twice. Of particular interest regarding the latter is the hosting of the 2022 World Cup in Qatar, described by its bid ambassador, the celebrated footballer Zinedine Zidane, as 'a victory for the Arab world' (FIFA 2010c).

The controversial choice of Qatar was justified by FIFA on grounds of its location in the growing Middle East football market and, although the smallest country to host the World Cup since the first one in Uruguay in 1930, its wealth presents a sharp contrast to that of the 2010 host, South Africa:

> Summer temperatures which can soar to above 50 degrees Celsius and a concern about lack of infrastructure did not deter FIFA Thursday from awarding the 2022 World Cup to the tiny Gulf state of Qatar.

> The Middle East has never before hosted a major global sporting event and analysts said Qatar's win would do much to boost the region's global profile.

> FIFA were likely to have been swayed by Qatar's hefty financial prowess with money no object for the world's largest exporter of liquefied natural gas.

> The country's economy, forecast to grow by 15.5 percent this year, is expected to soar by a staggering 21 percent in 2011, allowing Qatar to pour as much cash as necessary into preparations for 2022. (Doherty 2010)

Thus, the most significant global flow with regard to Qatar 2022 is that of energy, alongside the television images to be broadcast by Qatar-based Al-Jazeera Sport, which won the Middle East and North Africa rights for the 2014–22 World Cups. However, as is noted below, most of the proceeds of the media rights sale, which includes cable, satellite, terrestrial, mobile and online across twenty-three territories (Mann 2011), will not remain with Qatar:

> Revenue in the Middle East from football pay TV broadcast rights is expected to rise 30 percent to $550m over the next twelve years as a result of Qatar's successful bid to stage the World Cup in 2022, according to a new study.

> However, the bulk of the broadcasting revenue – believed to be as high as 90 percent – will not go to Qatar, but will go to FIFA …

> The growth in revenue from broadcasting rights was forecast by consultants Grant Thornton in a study commissioned by the Qatar 2022 bid team.

> 'Given the central location of Qatar, 82 percent of the world's time zones would receive Qatar 2022 games live in prime time, with a potential match day peak audience of 3.2 billion viewers,' the report added.

Middle East TV audiences for the FIFA World Cup have grown almost 350 percent since 1986, the Grant Thornton report said and FIFA's own evaluation of Qatar's bid revealed that television penetration in the Gulf state has risen from 67 percent to 94 percent in the last eight years.

Qatar has also claimed that football is the most-watched TV programme in the country, with 77 percent of men and 64 percent of women tuning into matches. (Football Marketing 2010)

It is apparent that, despite increased interest in football in the Middle East, winning the World Cup hosting rights in 2022 is not beneficial to Qatar in a strict accounting sense, given the enormous cost of building carbon neutral, air conditioned stadia, accommodation and so on (FIFA 2010d). The pivotal appeal is enhancement of global profile and reputation. As Chapter 6 indicates, in the sphere of global media sport the management of image and profile can be a hazardous enterprise and its outcomes as unpredictable as the very sport contests that distinguish sport from other cultural forms.

6

Tactical Manoeuvres, Public Relations Disasters and the Global Sport Scandal

Publicity: the good, the bad and the spaces between

Sport, from its inception in modernity, has been intimately connected to international relations and trade. It has been especially effective in this regard because, despite being suffused with politics and significantly commodified, sport somehow still manages to present itself and to be seen by many as somehow above and beyond the mundane world of political and economic conduct. Developing international relationships through sport – so-called sport diplomacy – is viewed as a reasonably safe, benign way of making friends and managing conflicts (Levermore and Budd 2004). There are several historical examples, ranging from the so-called ping-pong diplomacy that brought the United States and Communist China into contact in the early 1970s (Xu 2008) to the attempted use of the Olympics to improve relations between North and South Korea (Merkel 2008). When, for example, in 2006 Australia left the Oceania Football Confederation for the larger Asian Football Confederation, the non-sporting justification was that of 'football diplomacy':

> Sport … provides a common point of conversation between societies. Sport fans undoubtedly follow their teams passionately, but they also tend to share an appreciation for the game and its players that often crosses national and cultural boundaries, illustrated by the immense popularity of Australian cricketers Adam Gilchrist and Steve Waugh in India. Whether in football stadiums in Asia or Australia, or via media coverage of the sport, football will provide a much broader and more grass-roots engagement which has largely been absent in the past. Given the centrality of sport in the Australian psyche, the development of a sporting relationship with regional neighbours as enthusiastic about their sport as Australians could transform local perceptions – and preconceptions – of what individual Asian societies are really like. (Bubalo 2005: 6–7)

On occasions, nations may cooperate in introducing sports boycotts in the interests of political change, as in the case of apartheid-era South Africa and, more recently, in the isolation of Zimbabwe in sports such as cricket (although there can also be political bloc and unilateral boycotts, as in the case of the 1980 and 1984 Olympics). Sport may also function as a vehicle for national chauvinism, aggression and violence towards other nations, or at least as an opportunity for hostile stereotypes in the press, as in the case of encounters between the England football team and those from Germany or Argentina (Poulton 2004) or between the United States and nations with which it is in conflict (Miller *et al.* 2001). This chapter, though, will not attempt to cover comprehensively the political uses and abuses of sport in the international sphere but instead will concentrate on the global politics of hosting sports mega events. Such events are particularly important because they are also inherently 'media events' (Dayan and Katz 1992) whose very rationale depends on extensive, favourable global media coverage. Their profound mediatization is most conspicuous when they go wrong and rebound on the country that has spent billions of dollars in staging them with the intention of enhancing the global image of host cities and nations. These scandals of nation, though, do not monopolize communicative zones of negative publicity, as both sports and athletes are regularly brought into disrepute. For example, corruption within sport (sometimes linked to the bidding process for mega events) and the crimes and misdemeanours of athletes (many involving widely circulated salacious details) are also capable of producing extraordinary levels of media coverage without a sports mega event in sight. In investigating these various modes of sporting scandal, their place in global media sport will be assessed, with a particular emphasis on the power to control and explode carefully cultivated images.

Images of sport and nation

Bidding to host a sports mega event, despite the substantial risks and staggering costs, remains a compelling goal for cities and nations that range from the most affluent to the still developing (as noted in Chapter 5). For example, the most common estimate of the cost to South Africa of hosting the 2010 World Cup of Association Football is US$3.5 billion (with FIFA gaining an equivalent amount as broadcast and marketing revenue). The justification for this expenditure is grandiose indeed, but the outcome is uncertain. As one commentator (among many) has noted,

> Danny Jordaan, head of the 2010 World Cup Local Organising Committee described the world's largest sporting event as a 'rebranding of South Africa'.
>
> 700 million people were watching on TV and millions more were reading online or talking about it via social media. With this in mind, national and local governments (through their taxpayers) forked out billions of Rands on much-needed infrastructure spending, as well as the construction of mega stadia that now threaten to become 'white elephants' ...
>
> [I]ndustry stakeholders claim it is not necessarily traffic during the tournament but the long-term investment in the South African brand that is key.
>
> When asked whether he believed South Africa's brand expectations were met by the World Cup, Marc Hershowitz, formerly of the University of Cape Town Unilever Institute of Strategic Marketing, says, 'FIFA commissioned a six wave study of South African residents post World Cup and the findings were glowing. The study showed a marked upswing in national confidence – both local and abroad ... of the 75% of all visitors who toured South Africa for the first time, 83% stated their intention to return and a staggering 94% expressed they would gladly recommend South Africa to friends and family' ...

Whether the World Cup showed global business that South Africa can tackle crime and rally resources to achieve its goals; or whether it was merely a cover up of socio-economic weaknesses that will persist long after June–July 2010, will be a key factor when transnational corporations weigh-up South Africa's stability for their investment. (Schneider 2010a)

Thus, suggestions that this large sum of money could be better spent on social services and other infrastructure, or that newly built stadia would become 'white elephants' after the event had finished, were subordinated to the goals of the national rebranding of South Africa as an attractive, safe place for international tourists and as a profitable location for foreign direct investment and the raising of national morale and self-esteem (Schneider 2010b). As is represented in the 2009 film *Invictus*, the recently elected president of the Republic of South Africa, Nelson Mandela, had previously used the country's hosting of the 1995 World Cup of Rugby Union for reasons of national cohesion and international prestige. Both events were successful in this respect, particularly in that they succeeded in avoiding major controversies or sudden, negative occurrences (such as a terrorist attack or violence towards international visitors). This risk calculation is especially pressing given that all mega sports events attract large numbers of foreign journalists whose brief includes much more than coverage of sport contests and which correspondingly concentrate global attention on a nation for a brief period of time, but with possible long-lasting consequences. Thus, for example, there was considerable sensitivity about not just the incidence but also the media coverage of violent crime during the World Cup (given that South African cities and townships have some of the highest violence and homicide rates in the world), which in turn led to additional costs of saturation policing and security. As David Smith (2010) noted as the World Cup ended,

Sceptics predicted the World Cup would be a boom time for criminals in South Africa. In fact, the football appears to have led to a dramatic fall in violent offences.

A report by ADT, a private security firm, said crime was down by 70% in western Johannesburg, while the east of the city saw a 60% decline in the past month.

No official police figures are yet available, but the findings support anecdotal evidence that the World Cup has reduced crime.

Only 100 people have been found guilty of offences related to the tournament in special courts, where staff have spent many hours idle. There have been no murders or stabbings despite international fears about the event.

It also appears that more conventional crimes, such as house break-ins, have dropped because of visible policing, ADT said …

Facing unprecedented global attention, South Africa dedicated more than 40,000 police officers to World Cup security. But many have been paid overtime, which will be unsustainable in the long term …

South Africa has one of the world's highest crime rates with an average of 50 murders per day. There have been some high profile incidents during the

World Cup, with hotel staff arrested for stealing and foreign journalists targeted by muggers. Portuguese journalist Antonio Fimoes had a gun held to his head by robbers who broke into his hotel room.

Punishments have also been swift and decisive and, some argue, too harsh to be sustainable. A man who stole a mobile phone from an Argentinian fan was jailed for five years – prompting an appeal from the victim for leniency.

The extraordinary level of security for the duration of the event, as noted in the quotation above, cannot be sustained, leading to concerns that crime would return to its previous levels after the event – the main hope, of course, being that if it contributed to the alleviation of poverty, crime would fall as a consequence. But irrespective of the final outcome, it is clear that impression and media management are at the heart of hosting global media sports events (as argued in Chapter 5 with regard to Qatar's unlikely hosting of the 2022 FIFA World Cup). This issue was particularly prominent during Beijing's/China's hosting of the 2008 Summer Olympics. There had been considerable unease about awarding the Games to China in the light of its human rights record, with the 1989 Tiananmen Square massacre of demonstrators agitating for greater political democracy still in vivid memory. This unease was one reason why Beijing lost out to Sydney to host the 2000 Olympics:

> Western governments, politicians, and major media outlets strongly opposed Beijing's bid. An article in the *Los Angeles Times* argued that China's human rights record should disqualify it. The *Daily News of Los Angeles* ran a piece that chided, 'Olympics in China is a human wrong, not a human right', and the *New York Times* wrote, 'The city in question is Beijing in the year 2000, but the answer is Berlin 1936. The history of the modern Olympics is too short and the world is too small to forget murder'. The same article argued that 'denying Beijing [is] in the best interests of humanity'. (Xu 2008: 235–6)

This opposition still remained when the Beijing bid was successful in 2001. Thus, the IOC insisted that a principal justification for awarding the Olympics to a one-party, centralist state was that it would encourage greater openness and tolerance of free expression. Indeed, a loosening of China's control over the foreign press was presented as a condition for the Games being held there (Smith 2008).

As is now well known, however, China garnered bad publicity of global proportions before the Olympics had even commenced. A key risk of hosting a mega sport event is not only that media coverage may be adverse but also that the event presents an extraordinary opportunity for organized interest and protest groups to harness the intense attention given to the host location for their own political purposes. Sports mega events are inevitably involved in what has been described as a global or transnational civil society. John Keane (2003: 8) argues that the former concept should be approached with some scepticism but proposes a Weberian ideal type of what it 'properly refers to' as a term rather than as an empirical fact:

> A dynamic non-governmental system of interconnected socio-economic institutions that straddle the whole earth, and that have complex effects that are

felt in its four corners ... These non-governmental institutions and actors tend to pluralise power and to problematise violence; consequently, their peaceful or 'civil' effects are felt everywhere, here and there, far and wide, to and from local areas, through wider regions, to the planetary level itself.

The key point here is that beyond the formal apparatus of the state (although the state is obviously involved in various ways), movements that agitate for change cannot be contained within borders and have ramifications across multiple contexts. This is not the place to unpick the distinction between the 'global' and 'the transnational' or between 'civil society' and what Ulrich Beck (2000: 11) regards as 'the various autonomous logics of globalization – the logics of ecology, culture, economics, politics and civil society – [which] exist side by side and cannot be reduced or collapsed into one another'. Rather, it is to make the obvious, but nonetheless important, analytical observation that if even matters that are not prominent in the dominant theatres of politics and media can break out of their confines onto the world stage, an event such as the Olympics that is designed to involve all the places of the earth is particularly well suited to 'channel' a range of issues across global/transnational civil society (Horne and Whannel 2011). Inviting the world to watch a sports event is an exercise in global branding by the host that involves something analogous to the Gramscian notions of wars of position and movement in an expanded conception of politics as deployed by Stuart Hall (1987: 20):

So one of the most important things that Gramsci has done for us is to give us a *profoundly expanded conception* of what politics itself is like, and thus also of power and authority. We cannot, after Gramsci, go back to the notion of mistaking electoral politics, or party politics in a narrow sense, or even the occupancy of state power, as constituting the ground of modern politics itself. Gramsci understands that politics is a much expanded field; that, especially in societies of our kind, the sites on which power is constituted will be enormously varied. We are living through the proliferation of the sites of power and antagonism in modern society. The transition to this new phase is decisive for Gramsci. It puts directly on the political agenda the questions of moral and intellectual leadership, the educative and formative role of the state, the 'trenches and fortifications' of civil society, the crucial issue of the consent of the masses and the creation of a new type or level of 'civilisation', a new culture. It draws the decisive line between the formula of 'Permanent Revolution' and the 'formula of civil hegemony'. It is the cutting-edge between the 'war of movement' and the 'war of position': the point where Gramsci's world meets ours.

The above-mentioned 'point', in two senses of the word, is that 'modern politics' is not only played out across global civil society in a relentless process of manoeuvring and tactical resistance (as Gramsci 1971 saw it) but emanates from a range of positions and across wildly different terrains – including, notably, that of sport (see Rowe 2004b for a consideration of Gramsci's contribution to the theories of sport, despite his lack of concern with it). In the case of South Africa's hosting of the 2010 World Cup, this meant trying to overcome the doleful legacy of apartheid and widespread perceptions of the country as violent and poverty stricken. The Beijing 2008 Olympics, however, were seen by China as a signal both to its own population (indeed, Wolfram Manzenreiter (2010: 42) argues, although not altogether convincingly, that 'the Chinese government were overwhelmingly addressing domestic concerns and the need of educating the Chinese for the challenges of globalization and immediate encounters with the West') and to the world at large that it had 'arrived' as a major global economic and political power and that this prowess could be demonstrated by sporting success, logistical efficiency and grand urban design (Xu 2008), including of its signature Olympic venues such as the Bird's Nest and the Water Cube.

As noted in Chapter 5, the Summer Olympics had been held previously in Asia only in Tokyo (1964) and Seoul (1988), with the former seeking restoration to the international community and economy after the Second World War (Collins 2007; Tagsold 2009) and the latter using the Olympics as a sign of advancing modernity and as means of gaining a political advantage over its hostile neighbour, North Korea (Larson and Park 1993; Manheim 1990). Beijing in 2008, though, was different from earlier East Asian Summer Olympics in some respects, in that, although also representative of the 'Oriental other' that had been historically 'exocitized', colonized and marginalized by the West, it was now a rising power outside the US sphere of influence (Rowe 2012). As a country controlled by a Communist Party that was 'guiding' its capitalist development, China is regarded with considerable suspicion, although it should be recalled that political democracy was underdeveloped in post-war Japan (and its emperor only narrowly avoided indictment as a war criminal), while South Korea was awarded the Olympics while under military rule. But China in the early twenty-first century is on the ascendant, maintains something of its own 'empire' by strict and often oppressive means and also staged the Games in a period where the media sphere made information and ideas much more portable, and its own communicative borders more permeable, than at any previous Games in the region (including, with regard to digital media, even the 1998 Nagano Winter Olympics – Rowe 2012).

In the lead up to the 2008 Beijing Olympics, Lee Humphreys and Christopher Finlay (2008: 302) pondered the implications of this new media environment on contending narratives, particularly from within China at the time of the Games:

> While the High-Tech theme of the Olympics may connote Chinese technological progressivism and innovation, the increased adoption and prevalence of advanced information technology, including mobile technology, may provide opportunities for such a narrative to be hijacked and for counternarratives to emerge. Camera and video mobile phones provide a means of sousveillance through which everyday citizens can monitor, record, and disseminate official acts and behaviors of abuse or negligence. No doubt Western media, if their early framing is an indication, will be hungry for Olympic scandals involving the athletes, the events, or the host city and country during the 2008 Games.

Drawing on the ideas of Mann, Nolan and Wellman (2003), Humphreys and Finlay argue that 'sousveillance' (citizens watching authorities from below) is facilitated by new information and communications technologies and not just the usually emphasized surveillance (the authorities watching the citizenry from above). This is an important development which also possesses the possibility of globally circulating captured images and information of phenomena that authorities would prefer to suppress rather than suffer embarrassment or, worse, *opprobrium* (the most prominent case of the moment being WikiLeaks). However, such political interventions are confined neither to the time and place of the Games nor to 'catching out' the authorities conducting 'official acts and behaviours of abuse or negligence'. Instead, civil society actors can both capture themselves 'in the act' of protest and circulate a mediated record of them around the world and/or offer themselves to the world's media as ready-made 'news items'. Such was the case several months before the Beijing Games began on an auspicious date for the Chinese (8/8/08). As Monroe Price (2008) has argued, the Olympics constitute a platform over which there is substantial competition from many quarters – state-based, commercial, civic, sport-centred, civil–political and so on – to communicate their preferred messages. One of two case studies that he uses to show 'civil society mobilizing to use the Olympics platform to gain global attention and change China's behaviour' (Monroe Price 2008: 100) is the creation (by a US-based academic, Eric Reeves) of 'the accusatory concept of the "Genocide Olympics" as a way of altering China's dealings with Sudan' (Monroe Price 2008: 102) and, in particular, its Darfur region. This powerful rhetorical strategy in combining two shockingly contrasting words was effective, he argues, in recruiting prominent athletes and Hollywood celebrities to its cause and in putting pressure on corporations and nations, especially China and Sudan among the latter, to shift their ground and act on the humanitarian crisis in the Darfur region. While this 'seizure' of the Olympic platform was notable, the spectacular protests against China's treatment of Tibet during the Torch Relay garnered enormous media attention and revealed the power not just of words but of instant moving and still images in an age of global networked media.

Described as a 'Journey of Harmony', the Torch Relay followed a path from Mount Olympus in Ancient Greece to Beijing. As Humphreys and Finlay (2008: 294) note, the major Olympic sponsor and China's largest manufacturer of personal computers, Lenovo, designed (with, as befits the aforementioned 'high-tech' Olympic theme, the China Aerospace Science and Industry Group) the Beijing Olympic Torch so that the flame would remain alight under difficult atmospheric conditions, especially when it reached the world's highest mountain, Qomolangma (also known as Mount Everest) abutting Tibet. However, this direct association with the highly controversial passage of the Torch Relay through Tibet 'makes the company vulnerable to international criticism directed at China's political agenda' (Humphreys and Finlay 2008: 295). Sensitivity within the global company to bad publicity arising from this link to Tibet was, though, overwhelmed by the Torch Relay's triggering of mass protests in favour of Tibetan autonomy and opposing China's suppression of it. These protests were given additional impetus by representatives of *Reporters Sans Frontières* (Reporters without Borders), who 'gatecrashed' the conventional live global television broadcast of the flame-lighting ceremony at Ancient Olympia on 24 March 2008, displaying the Olympic rings made from handcuffs on a black flag during a speech by Liu Qi, president of the Beijing Organizing Committee for the Olympic Games (BOCOG).

This action encouraged various 'celebrities' and many less prominent protestors onto the streets, especially in Western Europe and North America, calling variously for a boycott of the Beijing Games, attempting to prevent the flame from passing, demanding freedom/autonomy for Tibet and making other criticisms of the Chinese government's policies on human rights, both domestic and international (Horne and Whannel 2010).

In these wars of movement, manoeuvre and position – which can also be described as 'semiotic "guerrilla warfare"' (Eco 1976: 150), an unfolding event like the Torch Relay is of global consequence as a positioned, scheduled opportunity for celebration or dissent and as both a routine and unpredictable news item. The most ambitious Torch Relay since the first staged exclusively in Europe for the 1936 Berlin Olympics (itself the most controversial of all Modern Olympics), its journey of 137,000 kilometres through twenty countries (following in part the historic Silk Road connecting China to its traditional trading countries) took it through international spaces that were difficult for the Olympic hosts to control, before entering Chinese sovereign territory (though conspicuously disputed in the case of Tibet and also in the Xinjiang Uyghur Autonomous Region). The 'sacred flame's' accompanying Chinese attendants dressed in track suits, as the most conspicuous representatives of the hosts in places outside Chinese jurisdiction, thus became controversial in themselves in embodying for some critics in leading newspapers such as the *Times* (of London) the unacceptable face of Chinese military authoritarianism:

> China's blue-clad flame attendants, whose aggressive methods of safeguarding the Olympic torch have provoked international outcry, are paramilitary police from a force spun off from the country's army.

> The squad of 30 young men from the police academy that turns out the cream of the paramilitary security force has the job at home of ensuring riot control, domestic stability and the protection of diplomats.

> Questions are now being asked as to who authorised their presence as the torch was carried through London. The Conservatives demanded clarification from the Government last night.

> The guards' task for the torch relay is to ensure the flame is never extinguished – although it was put out three times in Paris – and now increasingly to prevent protesters demonstrating against Chinese rule in Tibet from interfering with it.

> The security men entered Britain on visitors' visas but the Home Office would not reveal whether they had disclosed on the application form for whom they worked ...

> Less than a year ago these mysterious 'men in blue' were elite students from China's Armed Police Academy and were selected amid great fanfare to form the grandly titled Sacred Flame Protection Unit.

> In China, tens of thousands of their paramilitary colleagues have been deployed across Tibetan areas to restore order during riots, even opening fire when the anti-Chinese demonstrations have threatened to run out of control again. (Macartney and Ford 2008)

This kind of bad publicity in the Western media was a major departure from the conception of the Torch Relay as a 'feel-good' publicity opportunity for the 2008 Olympics and its Beijing hosts. For a period in April 2008 the Torch Relay protests were the most prominent news stories of the day in print, broadcast and online media, both professional and 'user generated'. Rowdy demonstrations in London, Paris and San Francisco led to tight security and, for example, a drastic shortening of its route in Delhi. It also provoked counter-demonstrations by Chinese nationalists (claimed by opponents to have been organized by the Chinese government rather than as 'spontaneous' expressions of diasporic sentiment), so that by the time the torch reached Canberra, Australia, on 24 April 2008, it became necessary for the authorities (who insisted that the flame attendants play a low-key role) not just to keep demonstrators from the Torch but also from each other (Rowe and McKay 2012).

But once the flame entered Asia and, especially, mainland China, there was much less controversy (having 'sidestepped' Taiwan after a disagreement over its designation by the People's Republic of China's as 'Taipei China' – Collins 2008: 203) either in terms of incidence or reportage, although the (truncated) leg of the relay on the Tibetan plateau reignited a diminishing global media interest in the subject. The familiar rhythm of a massive 'spike' in media coverage on a subject followed by its rapid 'exhaustion' (although with the possibility of subsequent mediated intensities) was in this case exacerbated by the appalling tragedy of the Sichuan earthquake on 12 May (only nine days after the flame had left Macau for mainland China). This 'natural' disaster immediately turned global media attention towards the rescue effort, which compared favourably with the torpid, paranoid response of the Myanmar government to a cyclone and tsunami ten days earlier. Humanitarian sympathy over this natural disaster in this instance countered the earlier humanitarian critique, although it was subsequently mitigated by revelations emanating from the local population that the negligent or corrupt undermining of earthquake zone building codes had caused a profoundly 'unnatural' level of fatalities, especially in public buildings such as schools (BBC 2008). Hosting the 2008 Olympics, then, had obviously attracted broader media interest towards China and had, as is usual (and, indeed, is avidly desired by their hosts), encouraged a focus not just on the Games but also on the context in which they are held. But, as Horne and Whannel (2010: 767–8) argue with reference, in particular, to Ulrich Beck's (1992) concept of the 'risk society', the volatility and complexity of global/ transnational civil society create the conditions for the conduct of a wide-ranging politics that is difficult to subdue and direct by formal organizations hoping to rely on a simple sender–message receiver paradigm:

> In the age of risk society where 'subpolitics' – motivated by ethical considerations, a decentered network form of organization and a pluralistic tactical focus – are more evident than institutionalized politics, global social movements seek to develop new worlds and new sport and thus contribute to global civil society. For authorities, including sports mega-event organizers, risk society raises questions about the calculation of spectacle and the need for enhanced impression management. In this context the Beijing Games and other Olympic Games will

remain a field of contestation 'in which conflicting discourses, constituted by different regimes of truth produced by various interest groups, vie for global attention'. (De Kloet, Chong and Liu 2008: 9)

Connecting Beck's analysis to Daniel Dayan's return to the aforementioned conceptual framework of the 'media event' (Dayan and Katz 1992) in the light of the Olympics in a 'New China', they see the Olympic flame as a metaphor for an eternal, global political struggle surrounding mega sport events and their sociopolitical uses and abuses:

> Just like the Olympic flame (as opposed to the torch) the global critical consciousness about social justice, social equity and social development cannot be extinguished when events come to an end. Sports mega-events 'have become strategic venues' [Dayan, 2008: 397] in political, as well as economic and sporting, terms. (Horne and Whannel 2010: 768)

The 2008 Beijing Olympics constituted a striking but by no means unique instance of the chaotic politics of the global media sports event. Beijing could be read as an epochal Olympics, an especially vivid exercise illuminating the ramifications of a change in the world order when 'the age of Western colonialism and imperialism is not that far behind us' and confronts the 'touted' prospect 'of a new age of Eastern imperialism and the rise of the "China threat"' (Brownell 2008: 185). Sport scholars, therefore, have analysed Beijing 2008 closely in seeking to define the significance of that Games in particular and of mega sport events in general, paying special attention to their global mediation (see, for example, several contributions to special issues of the journals *The International Journal of the History of Sport* (Luo and Richeri 2010) and *Sport in Society* (Martinez 2010)).

A successful Olympic bid, with its mandatory claims of advancing sport in the world and of the world that produces sport, can then be projected through the global media as a 'genocide Olympics' or as complicit in a new imperialism. However, for heuristic reasons I have focused on the risks to national reputation of hosting a major sports event, rather than the rewards (now routinely described as the legacy) or the strategic balance between them. In the case of Beijing 2008, it was demonstrated that a very noisy controversy erupted in the year of the Games in relation to China and human rights (concerns that had always attended Chinese bids but which really gained 'traction' by means of the global Torch Relay vehicle) but which was quietened to a degree by the appalling coincidence of an earthquake in the host country (Rowe, Gilmour and Petzold 2010). After that, there were some negative stories, such as that the Beijing Games were rather joyless and public space over-controlled, like the following comments by British journalist Marina Hyde (2008) directed towards readers from the next summer Olympics host city/country:

> For all their slick management and the great sporting display, it should be said that China's Games have been spectacularly, creepily humourless. There has been not one iota of good natured fun-poking in the national media, not a single comedy montage on the 18 state TV channels dedicated to reverential coverage of China's big moment. Nothing has been allowed to interfere with the official line.

The effect is oddly static, as though the people's joy is being handed to them like a stone tablet, instead of being a democratised, roots-up explosion.

Nonetheless, the media sport spectacle reasserted its prime position in the communicative order. This is a conventional occurrence because when the sports action takes place, and especially after the Opening Ceremony, the specialist sports media (as opposed to their colleagues in the general press) come to the fore, and only a major, unanticipated event (such as the terrorist attack at the 1972 Munich Games) can subordinate the sports competition. Here also, the 'global media' splinter into competing regional and national camps, foregrounding their own teams and athletes, and specific national interests, with customized commentary and coverage (de Moragas Spa, Rivenburgh and Larson 1995). Media coverage, therefore, varies by temporal, spatial and social context. Thus, as Raymond Boyle (2010: 1843) observes, coverage of the Beijing Olympics can be split into three phases: 'Pre-Games China' in which '[t]he run up to the Games saw both the domestic and international politics of China and the ways in which the Chinese wanted to present themselves to the world scrutinized'. Most of this news coverage, he observes, was critical of China, but this treatment changed in the next phase, 'Opening Up: The Games'. Here, the crucial global media event of '[t]he Opening Ceremony was universally admired in the media', and the success of the British team and awareness that London was to host the Olympics in 2012 shaped the coverage in that country:

> [O]nce the Olympics were under way, the stories of British success dominated the media coverage of Beijing 2008 in the UK media. In the process it reminded us that while this mega-event takes place on a global scale, they are inflected and made sense of through domestic and national frames of reference ...
>
> As is often the case, once the attention turned to sport, it was the traditional sporting narratives of success and failure, heroes and villains and triumph over adversity that took centre stage ... The majority of stories were framed by the growing success in medal terms of the British team and what this might mean for the country in the build-up to London 2012. (Boyle 2010: 1844–5)

Thus, China faded from view somewhat except as the ground on which the sports were taking place and as a point of comparison for the next Games for which Britain would be responsible. In the third phase, 'Post-Games China', there was little critical media reflection according to Boyle:

> Once over, reflections on the games were overwhelmingly positive from within the UK media, no doubt enhanced by the British success in the Games. Domestic media sports chatter soon returned to issues of funding and the allocation of the lottery monies so closely associated with fuelling Britain's successful Games ...
>
> The Games did put China centre stage for a while and heightened awareness among the UK public to the changes taking place in that country. With regard to China and Chinese issues, coverage of that country in the UK media has however returned to being relatively minimal. The legacy impact on UK public opinion of the games regarding the perception that China has changed will depend in

part on what China does next in terms of its relationship with the wider global community. (Boyle 2010: 1845–6)

Important here is a consideration of a temporary, stimulatory effect on media coverage and public discourse concerning host cities and nations. It is difficult to isolate the 'Olympic effect' on knowledge and attitudes of those who encounter the host nation through the spectacle of the Games and other major sports events, while readings are conditioned in various ways by historical relationships between peoples and the preoccupations of nations and of subgroups within them (see various contributions to de Moragas Spa *et al.* 1995; Luo and Richeri 2010) as well as of transnational diasporic cohorts and of those who display multiple identities and affiliations. It can only be proposed that any entry into the world of global media sport through mega event hosting – and, indeed, by less ambitious means – is a highly uncertain exercise in attempted image management and communicative control in the face of sundry variables, not least the ability of diverse interest groups within transnational civil society to 'seize the platform' and retain a hold on it for specified purposes (Price 2008). But it is not only host cities and nations exposed in this way – international sports organizations confront their own global politics of positional warfare and are equally scrutinized by media searching for flaws and sensitive to the interests of their own audience constituencies.

Sports organizations and tainted images

In Chapter 2 it was argued that, as sport modernized, its organizational framework became increasingly professional and, indeed, corporate in nature. This meant increased expectations of accountability, transparency and responsibility that represented a considerable departure from the community-based and then neo-feudal arrangements that preceded them under the regime of amateur sport. As the twentieth century progressed, and the industrialization of sport intensified, international sports organizations like the IOC and FIFA assumed ever greater levels of responsibility for arranging and developing international sport, attracting and distributing growing sums of money from sponsors and television, handling the relationships between sport and national governments and managing the global reputation of sport in terms of ethical practices and responsiveness to sports practitioners and followers. However, the Empire-like dimensions of major sport structures, and the consequent distance between everyday sport fan and high-powered sport executive, have created considerable suspicion, and even hostility, of the former towards the latter. International sports organizations are expected to be more democratic in nature than, say, multinational corporations run by boards of directors and blocs of shareholders because they have been set up not to make money for their owners but to handle the 'precious', commonly owned popular cultural resource that is international sport. At the same time, they must balance the interests of stakeholders, including the competing interests of their constituent international membership. It is here, as well as among the elite ranks of salaried employees, that temptations and opportunities for corruption and malpractice are manifest in an environment where multibillion contracts are awarded and decisions of great moment are made – not least of which are broadcast agreements and host city/country selections for mega events.

International sports organizations have become global brands and also resemble nation states in their influence while remaining closely tied to global civil society. It is not surprising, therefore, that they have attracted the interest of the investigative media and of critical sport scholars, who have unearthed and/ or extensively covered several governance scandals in areas such as financial corruption and the management of protocols concerning performance-enhancing drugs. With regard to the latter, for example, Bernat Lopez (2010: 10) has argued,

> The leaderships of IOC, IAAF [International Association of Athletics Federations], FINA [Fédération Internationale de Natation] and UCI [Union Cycliste Internationale], to name only the most important international sports governing bodies, have quite often been accused of adopting a lukewarm and ambiguous stance towards doping ...

> The most famous example of this supposed lack of wholeheartedness concerning anti-doping is the controversy generated by the words of then-President of the IOC, Juan Antonio Samaranch, who in late July 1998 (at the height of the Festina scandal in the Tour de France) publicly pleaded for an overhaul of the list of prohibited substances on the grounds that those which could not be proven to be dangerous for athletes' health should be removed from the list ... The anti-doping campaign considered this stance 'a public capitulation to the drug cheats' (Parisotto, 2004: 40). In a similar vein it has also been argued that Avery Brundage, the President of the IOC between 1952 and 1972, 'was never as concerned about doping as he was about professionalism ... drugs never seemed [to Brundage] quite the image of evil that Mammon did'. (Guttmann 1984: 123, quoted in Dimeo 2007: 100)

As Lopez notes, though, there is some variation in attitudes towards 'doping' and, indeed, to amateurism within the IOC, but there is no such room for manoeuvre over taking bribes and other forms of financial corruption. In recent times there has been a specific concentration on mega events, especially after the bribery scandal concerning the 2002 Winter Olympics in Salt Lake City, which was publicly revealed only because an IOC insider, Marc Hodler, disclosed that inducements were offered and accepted to encourage IOC member votes for the subsequently successful Salt Lake City bid (Jennings and Sambrook 2000). Under the long presidency (1980–2001) of the late Juan Antonio Samaranch, the IOC became an increasingly wealthy organization, securing very substantial sponsorship and broadcast rights funding and assiduously exploiting the intellectual property rights associated with the 'five rings'. This powerful position necessarily demanded greater scrutiny of the IOC, although Samaranch's past as a Falangist and Spanish minister for sport under the dictatorship of General Franco perhaps ensured that scandal was never too far from the IOC for those who believed that his personal history and conduct disqualified him from the presidency (Simson and Jennings 1992). In any case, there is much that requires investigating in the affairs of the IOC and FIFA given their global status as organizations with membership, respectively, of 205 national committees and 208 national associations, both of which outnumber the 192 member states of the United Nations (given the lack of precise global fit between sovereign nations and sporting nations).

The bidding process for the summer Olympics and the FIFA World Cup involve all the world's nations as bidders and/or members as well as a substantial proportion of the world's population as media spectators. Hence, the bidding and awarding processes are substantial news stories in their own right, often involving heads of state and celebrities as bid 'ambassadors'. In 2005, for example, then British Prime Minister Tony Blair flew from London to Singapore for last-minute lobbying for the London Olympic bid and then returned two days later to Scotland to host the G8 Summit (BBC 2005). Other leaders in attendance at Singapore included Jacques Chirac, then president of France, then Russian Prime Minister Mikhail Fradkov, Senator Hillary Clinton and King Juan Carlos of Spain in support, respectively, of the Paris, Moscow, New York and Madrid bids. All did more than lend their moral support given the requirement, directly and indirectly, to devote public funds and other resources to bidding for and hosting major sports events. Under these circumstances, there is considerable sensitivity to nations' involvement in any 'tainted' process and an expectation that, as with the sports contests themselves, they should not be 'fixed'.

The British investigative journalist Andrew Jennings has, for several years, accused the IOC and FIFA of being ridden with corruption and in several books, newspaper articles and television documentaries has made substantial accusations against both organizations. On his website, 'Transparency in Sport', Jennings (2010a) is highly critical of sports governance. For example, in an article entitled 'Kickbacks & Match-Fixing: An Everyday Story of Olympic Handball' he reports,

> The officials of one of the most popular Olympic sports meet in Rome next weekend for an acrimonious special congress that could end in a walkout by European federations.
>
> Handball, which achieved the third highest television viewing figures for the Beijing Games and is played by 20 million people worldwide, is now tainted by allegations of match-fixing, contract kick-backs and lavish life-styles for top officials.
>
> Nonetheless the besieged International Handball Federation president, Egypt's Hassan Moustafa, is determined to celebrate a decade in power by persuading an 'extraordinary' congress to give him more power – and control of the federation's finances.
>
> A report in the German news magazine *Der Spiegel* in late January this year alleged that Moustafa took a 600,000 Euros kickback after signing a contract giving handball's TV rights to the French Sportfive marketing agency.

The money was channelled through a company set up by Moustafa that offered to exploit his 'good relations' with sports organisations for the exclusive benefit of Sportfive.

That contract has now expired and Moustafa has signed a new one that runs until 2013 with the same executive – but who has now moved to the UFA agency. There's whispers around the corridors of the IHF that this deal wasn't any cleaner than the previous one. (Jennings 2010b)

Many such articles 'breaking' and covering alleged and confirmed scandals in sports governance appear on Jennings's website. It would be misleading to conclude that this type of investigative journalism characterizes more than a small proportion of media sports coverage. Most of this output (as is by no means unknown in other reporting rounds, such as business, travel and technology) consists of routine description, commentary, gossip, speculation and so on and does very little to challenge the principal structures, practices and ethics of contemporary sport, preferring instead to keep its promotional engine turning over (Boyle *et al.* 2010; Schultz-Jorgensen 2005). Thus, as I have previously argued at length (e.g., Rowe 2007) most global media sport discourse is routine, uncritical and self-referential, but there is always the possibility that sport-related controversies will erupt in the public sphere, either through scandals integral to sports institutions (see, for example, investigative journalist Declan Hill's (2010) work on match-fixing and organized crime in association football) or by attachment to, or extrapolation from, sport-related scandals into wider sociocultural issues, especially those concerning class, race, ethnicity, gender and sexuality (see the discussion below of scandals and sportspeople).

Apart from investigative journalism, transnational civil society organizations and think tanks are active in sport, such as the Franco-Belgian Sport et Citoyenneté (Sport and Citizenship) (2010), 'an independent association that aims to stimulate the study and debate of sport's role in society, and promote its basic values', and which, among other concerns it attributes to its genesis, are that '[m]en and nations remain unable to solve conflicts. The lack of awareness towards the major issues that our society is facing (environment, poverty, all kind of injustices …) is worrying. Image and medias' [sic] power is not really under control'. Such organizations are not only concerned with what might be rotten within the institution of sport but also with the negative and positive impact that it can have on the world at large. Similarly, the goals of the Denmark-based Play the Game (2010a) (an organization that is also closely connected to Andrew Jennings's exposé work) describes itself as follows:

Play the Game aims to strengthen the basic ethical values of sport and encourage democracy, transparency and freedom of expression in world sport.

This is achieved by

- Creating awareness of the role of sport in society at a local, national and international level
- Drawing a many-sided picture of sport and supporting the right of the individual to choose and influence his or her own daily sporting activities

- Ensuring a free, independent, open and fact-based debate on the current situation and future development of sport
- Providing journalists, researchers and political leaders with both the inspiration and the tools to explore the cultural, political, social and economic aspects of sport
- Creating networks across national and professional boundaries in order to meet the challenges of a globalized sports and media world. (Play the Game 2010b)

It is notable here that the remit of Play the Game is global by necessity because sport and media are, themselves, global. It is instructive that its goals imply that sports organizations cannot be relied upon to 'strengthen the basic ethical values of sport and encourage democracy, transparency and freedom of expression in world sport'. Of course, no institution should be exempt from external scrutiny or can be trusted implicitly to operate in appropriate ways, but the activities of watchdog organizations like Play the Game display considerable scepticism, if not suspicion, towards the public accounts that major sports organizations give of their scrupulous attention to their mission statements. Getting 'inside' global sport organizations and beyond their public pronouncements is no easy task, and some academics, such as John Sugden and Alan Tomlinson (1999b), have used both the methods and prose style of journalists in this task (as well as more conventional academic approaches, such as Sugden and Tomlinson 1998). For example, their account of the 1998 contest for the FIFA presidency between Sepp Blatter and Lennart Johansson contains passages that are redolent of journalistic modes of address, such as the following:

> That night we prowled the lobbies of the FIFA hotels [in Paris], trying to find delegates who could explain how a couple of dozen votes promised to Johansson had been prized away and ended up in Blatter's favour.

> By the early hours, the dishing out of $50,000 in envelopes by FIFA officials was still a pervasive theme – but another, more shocking, story had emerged. The previous evening, it was rumoured, a private jet had arrived in Paris. This was definitely not Prince Faisal. Nor was it the Kuwaitis, who had made it clear that they didn't want to be a part of whatever was going on.

> But it was a sheikh with more bank accounts than camels. His burnouses, so said the grapevine, patrolled the FIFA hotels looking for African delegates, who were then made the most sophisticated of offers. This was an offer you couldn't refuse – because nobody could ever prove you had accepted. On the table, delegates were told, was $2 million to be shared between the Africans if Blatter won. Nobody had to promise to vote for him and they could back Johansson if they wished. But the offer was there, and this, the dirtiest of dirty tricks, might have cost Johansson the presidency. (Sugden and Tomlinson 1999a: 21)

Allegations of this type made by journalists, non-government organizations and academics create a picture that resembles the genre of fictional crime drama but seem so only because, perhaps, sports romantics find it difficult to come to terms with endemic corruption within an institution that derives much of its appeal by claiming a strategic symbolic distance from the blemished quotidian world of material conflict. The fantasy of transcendent sport isn't necessarily accepted *in toto* – as noted in Chapter 4 there is considerable unease among sports fans of the corrupting effect of money and power – but the 'shock' of recurrent sporting scandals depends substantially on denial and selective memory loss among those who would prefer matters to be otherwise, the capacity of those responsible to cover up transgressions and, where that is not possible, to isolate them as aberrations or dismissed as having been already addressed and corrected. In this rhythmic pattern of revelation, outrage and temporary redress the news and, especially, the sports media have been largely complicit, often lacking the will or the appropriate strategic allocation of resources consistently to apply themselves to the fourth-estate watchdog role in what still tends to be regarded as the 'soft' focus area of sport (Rowe 2007a).

The spectacular eruptions of scandals around sports organizations tend to rely on continuing investigative and reporting work outside the mainstream media (even where formal legal processes are in train, as in the case of the general lack of mainstream media interest in court proceedings surrounding FIFA's awarding of broadcast marketing rights). Matters of probity do periodically receive high-priority media treatment, such as when aligning with news cycles about the awarding of host city/country mega event venues. For example, as the final selection of hosts for the 2018 and 2022 FIFA World Cups approached in early December 2010, greater media scrutiny was given to the bidding process, and some news organizations engaged in 'entrapment' exercises that exposed alleged bribery and corruption. Less than a month before the decision was announced in Lausanne after final bid presentations and a vote of the FIFA Executive Committee, two of its members, Amos Adamu from Nigeria and Reynald Temarii, President of the Oceania Football Confederation, were fined and banned from voting in the ballot and suspended from football activity for three years and one year, respectively, after FIFA's Ethics Committee found that they had sought money in exchange for their votes (the charges were denied by both of the accused). In addition, Ismael Bhamjee (Botswana), Amadou Diakite (Mali), Ahongalu Fusimalohi (Tonga) and Slim Aloulou (Tunisia) received suspensions of varying lengths and were fined after being 'found to have broken rules on general conduct and loyalty and of failing to report evidence of misconduct in relation to the case' (BBC 2010f). However, these disciplinary actions were not the outcome of FIFA discovering this misconduct but only followed a story in the British newspaper, *The Sunday Times*, which filmed the two FIFA executive members appearing to trade their votes with two reporters pretending to be lobbyists for a company consortium supporting the 2022 US World Cup bid.

This relatively rare case of mainstream investigative journalism in sport was followed on the eve of the decision by the FIFA Executive Committee by a BBC 'Panorama' programme, 'FIFA's Dirty Secrets', in which Andrew Jennings made further allegations of malpractice within FIFA, in particular concerning secret payments to FIFA executive members by the failed marketing company International Sport and Leisure (ISL):

> Three of the Fifa executive committee members [Issa Hayatou (Cameroon); Nicolás Léoz (Paraguay, Head of the South American Football Federation) Ricardo Teixeira (Brazil)], who will decide the fate of the 2018 World Cup were tonight accused of taking bribes in a corruption scandal involving around $100m (£64.2m) of secret payments. The BBC's Panorama documentary, the timing of which had been branded 'unpatriotic' by bid executives before broadcast and 'frustrating' by the prime minister, David Cameron, also contained fresh allegations against the Concacaf president, Jack Warner, concerning a ticketing scandal linked to the 2010 World Cup.
>
> Warner and the three votes he controls are seen as key to England's hopes of progressing beyond the first round and Prince William, David Beckham and Cameron – the bid's 'three lions', as the chief executive, Andy Anson, called them – will be called upon to try to limit the damage. Cameron will arrive in Zurich tomorrow and is expected to meet Warner, who has been scathing in his criticism of the BBC documentary.
>
> Critics of the timing of the programme tonight insisted that the strength and topicality of the new allegations did not justify broadcasting it three days before the vote – particularly as the claims had nothing to do with the bidding process.
>
> England 2018 also condemned the programme, calling it 'an embarrassment' to the BBC. They said in a statement: 'We stand by our previous position that the BBC's Panorama did nothing more than rake over a series of historical allegations none of which are relevant to the current bidding process. It should be seen as an embarrassment to the BBC' ...
>
> On the back of the *Sunday Times* investigation that led to the suspension of six Fifa officials but created a climate of suspicion among the electorate, the Panorama allegations are likely to lead to further hostility against the British media. (Gibson 2010a)

Of particular interest with regard to the *Sunday Times* and 'Panorama' affairs, apart from the substantive, troubling (if not outrageous) issues of corruption in world sport (see, for example, Andersen 2010), is what they reveal about the global politics of FIFA and its relationship with the media. The 'cheerleader' role of the news media in sport comes to the fore here, with both news organizations having to defend the negative impact that they might have on the England bid for the 2010 World Cup, with the Director General of the BBC, Mark Thompson, required to defend the timing and broadcast of the 'Panorama' programme from accusations of being 'unpatriotic' by the bid team and 'frustrating' by the British prime minister. Perhaps, though, the discomfort of those supporting the British bid for the 2018 World Cup concerning consequent antagonism toward Britain among FIFA members and victimization of the bid was, indeed, justified according to various media reports, such as the following:

> The controversial Fifa executive committee member Jack Warner today broke his silence on the contested 2018 World Cup vote when he said voting for

England would have been 'the ultimate insult' to Fifa in the wake of British media allegations of corruption.

England 2018 insiders claim Warner, pivotal to their chances of success and wooed by David Beckham and successive prime ministers, promised the three votes under his control to England before voting for Russia. But the Concacaf president said the revelations in the Sunday Times and Panorama were the reason England polled only two of the 22 votes available and were knocked out in the first round ...

'Suffice it to say the Fifa exco as a body could not have voted for England having been insulted by their media in the worst possible way at the same time. To do so would have been the ultimate insult [to Fifa]', said Warner.

It is understood the Fifa president Sepp Blatter raised the issue of the 'evil' media coverage of Fifa just hours before the vote and England's rivals, including the Russian prime minister Vladimir Putin and influential Spanish ex-co member Angel María Villar Llona, played heavily on it ...

Some on England's bid team believe the revelatory media exposes, which they tried desperately to disassociate themselves from, were a factor but others believe that the issue became a convenient excuse for Fifa members to switch their votes for other reasons.

Japan's Junji Ogura said the investigations, which led to the suspension of six senior Fifa officials including two executive committee members in the case of the Sunday Times, had an impact.

'What I can say is that the reports definitely had an impact on the England bid. There's no mistake about that,' said Ogura, heavily courted by England but believed to have backed Russia.

Ogura said his colleagues were angry at the Sunday Times sting on Nigeria's Amos Adamu and Tahiti's Reynald Temarii. 'The African members of the executive committee were furious over the Sunday Times report,' Ogura said.

'They even suggested suing the paper at the executive committee meeting. The people being accused were from Africa and Oceania, not Europe or Asia, and some felt racism was behind it'. (Gibson 2010b)

The politics of FIFA media coverage emerge here, with two of its executive media members (one of whom has been the subject of persistent allegations of misconduct, although not only by the British press) openly describing critical media coverage as a factor in voting and the president reportedly discussing 'the evils of the media' just prior to the decision. The byzantine global politics of FIFA itself is further revealed in the clear disparity between the promise and the delivery of votes, the claim that concern over British media coverage was a smokescreen for a bid that was already lost to Russia and the additional, familiar allegation that the criticism of, especially, African members by Western media was grounded in racism (Sugden and Tomlinson (1999a: 15) note the history of racialized readings of such critiques of FIFA in recalling how '[a] senior London soccer reporter alleged, in those days when few frowned at such language, that success [under former President Jão Havelange] came partly through "small brown envelopes going into large black hands"'). It is clear that the media sphere is a major battleground where different interest groups seek to gain a strategic advantage over others, but it follows that when there is no longer a prospect of gaining such an advantage – as here, where a bid to host a mega sport event has ended in the humiliating failure of only two votes, one of which is from the country's own representative – then media discourse can also shift. Hence, once the England bid had been lost there were several open public criticisms of FIFA's governance from within its football authorities, including a member of the board that had condemned the BBC's broadcast of allegations questioning the integrity of the bid process itself:

> The BBC was right to broadcast last week's Panorama programme, which alleged bribe-taking by three named senior Fifa executive committee members, according to Paul Elliott, the former Chelsea defender who served on the five-man board of England's 2018 World Cup bid.
>
> The bid team, led by the chief executive Andy Anson and the chief of staff Simon Greenberg, disparaged the programme before it was broadcast, tried to persuade the BBC not to air it three days before Fifa's decision on host countries for 2018 and 2022, and issued a vitriolic statement about it immediately after it was broadcast.
>
> Before the programme went out, the bid team wrote a letter to all Fifa's executive committee members, signed by the bid's chairman Geoff Thompson and international president David Dein, pleading with them not to 'judge negatively' England's bid because of the British media's investigations. 'As a member of the football family we naturally feel solidarity with you and your colleagues,' the letter said.
>
> The statement after the broadcast, officially from the England 2018 bid, said the programme 'did nothing but rake over a series of historical allegations ... It should be seen as an embarrassment to the BBC'.
>
> Elliott told the Guardian that 'in hindsight' the programme had powerful evidence of possible corruption and it was in the public interest for the BBC to show it. He said the timing had been difficult, and he had seen it as a setback because he was still hoping England would be chosen.
>
> Having seen how Fifa conducted the process – he and other bid members now believe the World Cup was heading for Russia from an early stage – and the 'disrespect' he believes the executive committee members showed to defeated bid teams, Elliott has changed his view. (Conn 2010b)

Such inconsistencies are inevitably produced on the shifting ground where, despite emphasis on the technical quality of the host bids and major developmental considerations for the sport, it is apparent that the outcome will be determined by internecine politics and, on the basis of evidence adduced by media organizations and 'whistle-blowers', a degree of malfeasance. Thirteen years after Blatter's election to the FIFA presidency, the organization was besieged by controversy over fresh allegations of corruption surrounding

Qatar's winning of the rights to host the 2022 World Cup; the suspension of key Executive Committee members Mohamed bin Hammam and Jack Warner, and other officials by FIFA's Ethics Committee, for alleged corruption surrounding the former's campaign to replace Blatter in the 2011 presidency elections (including the putatively mandatory cash in brown envelopes); and accusations of Blatter's own corrupt practice and/or inaction in eradicating corruption and unethical behaviour within FIFA. The Ethics Committee cleared Blatter to stand unopposed for another term as president, which he won, in classic 'banana republic' style, by 183–0 out of the 203 votes cast. In order to deal with FIFA's organizational problems, Blatter then announced the formation of a FIFA Solutions Committee including opera singer Plácido Domingo, former US Secretary of State Henry Kissinger and former Dutch footballer and current sport philanthropist Johan Cruyff (Andersen 2011). It can be safely anticipated that the formation of this 'Council of Wisdom' and the re-election of Blatter until 2015 will not put an end to FIFA's escalating cycle of scandal.

Sports organizations from club level upwards are likely to be implicated in periodic scandals given the combination of secrecy, sur/sousveillance and wealth that characterizes global sport. I have concentrated on the upper-level machinations of the IOC and FIFA here because these are the most global of sport organizations, but by their nature they reach down to the smaller, more local sports operations which form their foundation. Mega event bidding and securing high office and influence present many temptations for scandalous behaviour, but there are sundry other areas where 'killings' can be made through money laundering, match-fixing, betting scams and other abuses of the labyrinthine apparatus of sport. In 2010, for example, the aforementioned IPL was 'hit by allegations of massive corruption, money laundering and tax evasion, as well as secret deals to hide teams' real owners and even links to India's criminal underworld' (Lal 2010), including the expulsion and prosecution of its founder, Lalit Modi, and threatened expulsion (not carried out) of two of its franchises, the Rajasthan Royals and Kings XI Punjab, for undeclared ownership structure changes (Haigh 2010). The vast sums involved in establishing and running the IPL, which now has an estimated brand value of over US$4 billion, and its vulnerability to betting-related corruption, have already created several major scandals in its short life. Nonetheless, for all the attention that organizational sport scandals generate, they generally involve administrators and officials who are not the primary focus of sports followers. The riches that produced these scandals also created the celebrity sportspeople who actually practise sport on the field of play and who are routinely scrutinized by the media and their audiences. It is to the frequent scandals of varying seriousness and type with sports stars at their centre that I now turn.

Scandalous sport celebrity

As this chapter was being prepared, a 'sports story' broke in Melbourne, Australia. It was an important time in the state of Victoria, as a new government assumed power and the former premier resigned and as the WikiLeaks controversy raged on. But the most prominent story of the day in the city's journal of record, *The Age*, concerned a football club, although in a sport – Australian rules football – that was out of season. It involved a scandal of sex, sport and revenge:

> ST KILDA Football Club was under extraordinary attack in cyberspace last night, with naked photographs of several of its star players going viral on the internet, despite a court order intended to stop their publication.
>
> The club was rocked yesterday when a teenage girl posted the explicit photographs of captain Nick Riewoldt and Nick Dal Santo on her Facebook account.
>
> The 17-year-old was the subject of an AFL investigation this year when she said she fell pregnant to a separate St Kilda player when she was a schoolgirl.
>
> Last night, a Federal Court judge ordered that the teenager and Facebook remove the images. Facebook closed the teenager's account shortly after 8pm, but she responded at about 9pm by posting a link on Twitter to the pictures.
>
> That link was removed at about 9.20pm, but by then the images had gone viral and were widely available elsewhere on the web.
>
> At 9.50pm, she pointed on Twitter to a friend's Facebook account, which featured the Riewoldt photograph and was last night rapidly gaining 'friends'. But it, too, was shut down shortly after 10.30pm.
>
> One of the photographs shows Riewoldt posing naked next to teammate Zac Dawson, who is wearing jeans and is holding out what appears to be a condom packet. The other shows Dal Santo in a more explicit pose.
>
> 'Merry Christmas courtesy of the St Kilda schoolgirl' is written across the photographs …
>
> The teenager said she received nearly 3000 friend requests on Facebook in the space of an hour yesterday. (Millar and Sexton 2010)

This is not a sport story focused on the field of play but about the social institution of sport in which athletes, administrators and followers are involved in a series of interweaving primary, secondary and tangential relationships. It involves a complaint to a sport organization that, according to the complainant, was not satisfactorily handled, and it also raised questions of the law, duty of care, celebrity, gender, sexual conduct, privacy and age that would be of some interest to people who have little or no concern with sport in general and Australian rules football in particular. An especially prominent aspect of the story – and here there was an implied connection to WikiLeaks – is the capacity of the Internet to enable anyone to produce texts and images accessible to anyone in the world with access to it (until they were taken down, although their 'imprint' remains in various online spaces). It emphasizes the 'levelling' power of social media, whereby a young woman in a weak position can herself become something of a media celebrity through association with sport celebrities and the ready use of such platforms as Facebook, Formspring, Twitter and Ustream:

> Whatever was done to the young woman earlier in the year, what has happened lately is significant. It has been a possibility for months but the reality was still sudden and shocking. Gone are the days when a football club can ignore trouble, when an aggrieved young woman, rightly or not, can be relied upon to simply go away.
>
> Gone too are the days when such a woman had no means or method to convey her displeasure. When she might be more worried about blows to her reputation than a star footballer to his. If anything has become clear in this exchange it is the speed with which a powerless woman has become powerful and a powerful footballer powerless. She has not taken her story to the media, the media has flocked to her.
>
> Ultimately it might prove to be not in the interests of neither Riewoldt and Dal Santo, the intended targets, nor of the woman. By mid-afternoon yesterday, she was boasting of the 29 radio and four TV interviews she had done and teasing thousands of followers with a threat to publish more pictures. It seemed like she had started something that she didn't know how to stop – nobody does. It's unlikely to be the last time somebody has to try. (Silkstone 2010)

This was by no means the end of the story, with the 'St Kilda schoolgirl' subsequently releasing a video of a player manager in her hotel room in his underwear, alleging that he had taken cocaine and that they'd had a sexual relationship, appearing on the leading television current affairs show 'Sixty Minutes' to discuss it, threatening to release more video material of footballers taking illicit drugs and encouraging the assault of a woman in the street and declaring that she was writing a book on the subject (La Canna 2011), while new revelations, retractions and media appearances by the various parties continued to attract extensive media attention (Penberthy 2011). This is, then, a story about the established media's (both general and sports) agenda being set for them by 'user-generated content' and a shifting of the line between journalist and source (Allan 2006). It does not mean that major news organizations are no longer important, as the widespread dissemination of the story clearly relied on them 'picking up and running with it' and connecting the 'amateur' communicator with the large, attentive audiences of professional newsmakers. This case also reveals the idiosyncratic nature of media globalization, whereby of all the major stories of the day across the world, one that is very local becomes the principal object of attention for the media at the site where it is produced but is at the same time made available to a global audience that could absorb the story if it was so disposed. As was pointed out in Chapter 3, something analogous occurs with the global circulation of television sport, with compelling content in one country circulated as marginal media material in others. But online and social media create new lines of communication that are much more likely to be encountered serendipitously and also are typically not the packaged and sold products of media corporations, with their professional aesthetic conventions and values, and predictable timescale and scheduling.

This is a much messier media world than once existed and is here addressed with regard to the phenomenon of global sport scandal. As with all that is global, these 'play' differently according to context, being of lesser or greater concern according to their proximity to the sport and the global standing of their protagonists. Thus, on a sliding scale of 'globality', the St Kilda scandal is global only in a technical sense, while the biggest of recent years is at the other end of the global media spectrum – that of Tiger Woods (discussed in greater detail further on). Somewhere in between would be another recent 'sex scandal' involving the prominent retired Australian cricketer, commentator and professional card player Shane Warne, which was given additional prominence through the involvement of a well-known British film actress, Elizabeth Hurley (Elser 2011). In exploring the 'natural history' of the global media sport scandal it is necessary to acknowledge such generic parallels and differences.

In the previous section there was a focus on sports organizations and financial scandals of various kinds. Although these either directly or indirectly involved leading sports administrators who are well known and perhaps even household names, such scandals tend to be 'abstract' in that they generally involve backroom dealing within complex organizations. In the case of leading, active sportspeople, however, there is a much richer library of easily recognizable images, and, indeed, may be in full view and real time during a sports contest. For example, when the *News of the World*, the now-closed British Sunday newspaper notorious for its 'stings' (and a Murdoch-media stable mate of the *Sunday Times*, which broke one of the above-discussed FIFA corruption stories with a sting of its own) entrapped a subject in a 'spot-fixing' scandal (mentioned in Chapter 1), it was able to juxtapose the caught-on-camera statements of the 'fixer' and his receipt of large quantities of bank notes with his predicted actions of Pakistani cricketers on the field of televised play. As *The New York Times* (a newspaper not noted for its cricket coverage but which registered the story's broad significance for global sport) reported,

> Spot-fixing refers to a form of corruption that has plagued cricket, soccer and other sports in Europe, particularly Britain, the former colonial power in what is now Pakistan. Instead of bribing players to fix matches outright, considered too risky for the Asian betting syndicates involved, the schemes often rely on fixing details of play that – while not necessarily affecting a game's outcome – can attract millions of dollars of bets across Asia.

> *News of the World*, one of the tabloids owned by Rupert Murdoch's News Corporation media conglomerate, ran its top Sunday story under a banner headline that read: 'Caught!'

> The paper said that an undercover reporter posing as a wealthy businessman planning to bet on the Lord's game [between England and Pakistan] had paid the equivalent of more than [US]$230,000 to a London-based 'fixer' who claimed to have seven members of the Pakistan team 'in his pocket' and four who had specifically agreed to join in the scheme.

> On its Web site the newspaper accompanied its story with a video showing the man suspected of being the fixer, Mazhar Majid, 35, sitting in a London hotel

room with stacked bundles of British pound sterling notes on a table. Scotland Yard said it had arrested Mr. Majid on suspicion of fraud before interviewing the cricketers.

The video appears to show Mr. Majid telling the undercover reporter details of exactly when during Thursday and Friday's match at Lord's, Pakistan's bowlers – cricket's equivalent of baseball pitchers – would deliver three 'no balls', cricket terminology that refers to balls ruled foul by umpires because the bowler's front foot falls beyond a chalk line on the 22-yard pitch at the moment of delivery.

As the game developed, the no-balls were delivered by the Pakistani team's star fast bowlers, Mohammed Asif and the teenager Mohammed Amir, at exactly the moments in the game specified by Mr. Majid in his video exchange with the News of the World reporter.

'I'm telling you, if you play this right, you're going to make a lot of money, believe me', Mr. Majid told the undercover team, according to the newspaper. (Burns 2010)

In explaining some of the rules of cricket for a predominantly US audience and using baseball as its point of reference, *The New York Times* demonstrates how sports scandals resonate around the world, connecting common practices such as betting, sports governance issues, global media corporations (here the Rupert Murdoch–controlled News Corp) and the universal concern among sports fans that competitive sport may not be all that it seems. Another US publication, *The Atlantic*, referenced baseball's most famous 'fixing' controversy, the so-called Black Sox Scandal of 1919 in which several Chicago White Sox players were banned for 'throwing' the World Series. By invoking the apocryphal story of the young fan's anguished appeal to 'Shoeless' Joe Jackson, 'Say It Ain't So, Joe!' (Nathan 2003), both history and affect were conveyed in marking a familiar fan *cris de coeur*: 'If ever a country needed sporting heroes, it is Pakistan today. "Say it ain't so" must be ringing from the lips of schoolchildren from Karachi to Lahore' (Tierney 2010). The disgrace of the athlete here relates directly to privileging their own material interests over the emotional investments of sports fans – a classic recipe for sport scandal.

'Taking a dive', as it is called in boxing, is, though, only one manifestation of scandal. Another form involves violent or abusive conduct on the field of play, the most famous recent example of which was the sending off for violent conduct of the French captain Zinedine Zidane (who is of Algerian heritage) during the 2006 FIFA World Cup final (which France subsequently lost). His 'off the ball' head butting of Italian opponent Marco Materazzi in front of a massive live TV audience (although the incident was initially missed by the main cameras following the play) prompted saturation media coverage concerned, above all, with what Materazzi had said to provoke it. Newspapers hired multilingual lip readers in order to ascertain whether, as was suspected, racial abuse had been used and, in particular, whether Zidane had been called 'the son of a terrorist whore' (Denham and Desormeaux 2008; Rowe 2010a). This controversy cannot be discussed here in detail, but of particular note in the current context is the worldwide debate that it provoked not only about whether Zidane's actions should be condoned or condemned but also of the incidence of racism in world sport. The case reveals – as also occurred in early 2008 when the Indian cricketer Harbhajan Singh was accused of racially abusing the Australian Andrew Symonds (one of whose biological parents is Afro-Caribbean) by calling him a 'monkey' during a test match in Sydney (Rowe 2012) – the manner in which on-field conflicts can become full-blown sport scandals that bring to the surface social tensions. In the case of Zidane, these involved the history of French–Algerian relations, the 'racialization' of Islam in the twenty-first century (Zidane is a self-described non-practising Muslim) and discrimination against people of colour in Western-dominated sport (Jiwani 2008; *New Formations* 2007). Similarly, the Singh case raised questions of postcolonial resistance to cricket's traditional domination by the Anglo-sphere (now largely supplanted, as noted in Chapter 5, by the Indian subcontinent) as well as racism among people of colour. In this sense, global media sport scandals stimulate civil society debates revolving around social power relations within sport, their manifestation in the wider world and, in turn, the reproduction of and resistance to dominant power relations that frame the institution of sport in the first place.

Such debates are ongoing, but scandals have the effect of drawing them into sharp relief and providing them with an instantaneous world stage. They also often frequently take place off the field, as with the NFL's 'burgeoning scandal over the treatment of Ines Sainz, a sports reporter for TV Azteca of Mexico, during a weekend practice', after which she complained that 'she was bombarded with catcalls' and subjected 'to boorish antics at the Jets' New Jersey training facility, to the extent of feeling the need to "cover my ears"' (Armstrong and Goldiner 2010). Or in the aforementioned case of the leading Australian swimmer Stephanie Rice's tweeting '[s]uck on that faggots' when the Australian rugby union team defeated South Africa's in an exciting finale (White 2010b). Both incidents provided a focus for public debates on sexism in the workplace and homophobia in general discourse in which the sport was at first central but ultimately the pretext for wide-ranging discussions of the subjects in the United States and Australia, respectively, and which were also available to be picked up in other places in the world.

More difficult to appraise in political terms, though, are personal scandals involving sport celebrities, probably the most prominent of which has concerned the serial infidelities of golfer Tiger Woods. After a domestic confrontation with his wife and car accident in late 2009, the world's richest sportsmen's carefully cultivated image was progressively dismantled (Davie, King and Leonard 2010) and, remarkably, led to his scandal being voted by the US news organizations comprising the membership of the Associated Press (AP) news agency as its 2010 'Sports Story of the Year' (Cohen 2010). The Woods affair sparked considerable discussion of such issues as masculinity, fidelity, celebrity and 'race', some of which were more directly related to sport than others, like the place of women in the lives of leading sportsmen and the long-standing anxiety that they distract men and drain them of their vitality (Rowe 2010b). However, much of the media coverage was prurient, salacious and even comic, with several websites devoted to Tiger Woods jokes.

This is not an unusual phenomenon when sport scandals are predominantly about sexual peccadilloes, as occurred in the case of English footballers David Beckham, Ashley Cole, Wayne Rooney, John Terry and sundry others, with the first two doubly newsworthy given the *dramatis personae* via their marriages to well-known pop singers. The aforementioned cricketer Shane Warne, who has gained notoriety regarding his seemingly compulsive suggestive texting, appeared to conduct a flirtatious 'courtship' with actor Elizabeth Hurley (Davidson 2010) in the public realm of Twitter before, and once again, the tabloid *News of the World* provided photographic and other documentary evidence of their liaison. Questions of collusion between publicity-seeking sports celebrities and the tabloid media, however, render problematic whether these are in fact scandals at all but, rather, ritual forms of media exposé from which both parties benefit. Here, as noted in earlier chapters, the combination of legacy and new media provides manifold opportunities for these seemingly tangential aspects of global media sports culture (from the viewpoints of sports purists) to become the most prominent 'sports stories' of the moment.

Fair and foul play

The global media sports cultural complex can be regarded as an 'engine' of scandal given the enormous material resources that it generates and handles, and the inevitable gap that lies between its persistent high-flown romanticism and the ruthlessness of its means-end schema. Media sport scandals run the full gamut of transgressions in such areas as gambling, violence, sexual assault, racism, cheating and fraud (see, for example, Finley, Finley and Fountain 2008). They also extend to ancillary areas, such as the global Nike campaigns dedicated to improving working conditions and labour rights for the factory workers producing their sport and leisure goods in developing countries (see, for example, Oxfam Australia 2011), which can themselves generate scandals by means of media coverage of repressive and exploitative practices, and demonstrations and boycotts in Western countries (Miller *et al.* 2001). Media sport scandals also expose the power of the gender order in sport. Because men tend to be in dominant positions within sport and the wider society, they have further to fall from grace within the structure of scandal. Thus, the same forces that work to discount sportswomen as heroic figures also operate to neglect them as the central figures brought down by sport scandals. In most cases, women's roles in sport scandals tend to be as victims of men's bad behaviour (and from which they may seek redress, as in the famous early 1990s case of the ill-treatment of sports journalist Lisa Olson – Kane and Disch 1993) or as catalysts of it (Rowe 2010b). On rare occasions, though, women are at the centre of the sports scandal as active agents – perhaps most notoriously in the instance of Tonya Harding's participation in a conspiracy in 1994 to break the legs of her Olympic figure skating rival Nancy Kerrigan (Baughman 1995). This type of transgression, though, can be placed in the service of sexual/gender stereotyping of the 'monstrous-feminine' (Creed 1993), the nightmare figure whose unthinkable badness is 'against nature', thereby reinforcing images of women as innately passive, maternal and subordinate.

The terms 'sport scandal' and 'media scandal', it should be noted, tend to be used rather loosely, and sometimes describe the gravity of the offence that has been revealed, and on other occasions to the method by which it has been revealed and in other cases both. An element of surprise and attempted suppression is usually implied, but this is not always so in a structural sense. That is, much of what passes for scandal is, as noted, quite routine and predictable, such as the above-mentioned infidelities of celebrity sportsmen. To be scandalized in such cases, it is necessary to know who the sportsperson is, care about their extra-(sporting)curricular activities and to believe in the integrity of their cultivated public image and persona. None of these components of scandal can be assumed to be operative 'before the fact', and their nature and reception are highly variable across value systems and global contexts.

The subject matter may be more serious, such as in the case of NFL quarterback Michael Vick's involvement in a dog-fighting ring, for which he was sent to prison (Macur 2007). For those who are not NFL followers, many will have only come to know of Vick through media coverage of the scandal, which only became a major news story because a prominent sportsman was involved. It is likely that many would regard this as a scandal of animal abuse rather than a sport scandal *per se*, while NFL followers would find it difficult to disentangle these elements given their attachment to the sport and (mediated) knowledge of the perpetrator. What constitutes a sport scandal, then, is often a question of the strength of its connection both to sport and to sports audiences. Violence on the field of play or corruption in sports organizations are, above all, sports scandals, but the connection, especially 'causal', to sport in a technical sense can be otherwise tenuous. For example, are all the transgressions of sportspeople – dangerous driving, shoplifting, alcohol and illicit drug abuse, domestic violence and so on – sport scandals by definition or only incidentally so? It is on this question that debates surrounding them often hinge, with some arguments that sport has crucially formed or influenced the transgressor, while others emphasize their incidence in the wider population, and the extra-sporting factors involved, and that the publicity attached to the sport star magnifies and exaggerates the connection between sport and criminal behaviour (see, for example, Benedict 1997; Jamieson and Orr 2009). It is a key task of the critical social science of sport to engage with these matters of sport, media and power, one aspect of which is to explain the emergence and significance of media sport scandals. As James Lull and Stephen Hinerman (1997: 9) note,

> Managers of modern news media actively try to turn stories into scandals. To call a story a scandal is to give it a bizarre kind of journalistic appeal and integrity ('This must *really* be something!'). Not every controversial story qualifies. Certain criteria must be met to achieve scandal status.

Lull and Hinerman go on to propose ten criteria separating scandal from non-scandal and argue that '[a] scandal does not materialize until events are shaped into narrative form and those narratives are made accessible to a consuming public, who interpret and use the symbolic resources scandals provide for their own purposes ... The scandal, thus, is produced not only by the media, but by audiences' (Lull and Hinerman 1997: 16). Thus, it is important not to reify the global media sport scandal – even where it is technically global, in the sense that it may be accessed anywhere in the world with the right media technology, it is only activated in the context of highly variable audience relations. John Urry (2003: 113–14) emphasizes this 'complexity of scandal' in arguing that '[t]he late-twentieth-century emergence of a "mediated power" criss-crossing the globe produced distinctly new forms of mediated scandals'. Drawing, as do Lull and Hinerman, on the influential perspective of John Thompson (1995, 1997, 2000), he argues that accelerated contemporary communication and the enhanced permeability of individual societies mean that '[s]candals thus involve complex sets of events that are unpredictable *and* irreversible. They run out of control once there is exposure, because of the mobility and speed of the processes of exposure, visualization and recirculation' (Urry 2003: 116). I have touched in various ways in this chapter on how media sport scandals can flare up and 'go global' but also the ways in which they may 'splutter out' or fail to register in unreceptive contexts (as is also the case with the 'sister' concept of moral panics – see Critcher 2003). Nonetheless, they remain, through the archive of popular and media memory, available to be reactivated and repurposed, able to be combined into new patterns and narratives, and given new significance and visibility.

Sport – itself increasingly difficult to pin down as a distinct cultural form – operates as both a vehicle and focus for myriad discourses within the mediated global public sphere. Its remarkable popularity, portability and plasticity mean that sport is always available to be invoked and mobilized for many different purposes. Hence, for example, the enduring and in some ways bewildering, risky appeal of hosting mega sports events that are the subject both of grandiose claims of universal benefit and the focus for multiple internal and external criticism. It is these constantly shifting tensions surrounding the purposes and pleasures of sport – and, through the media, its tentacular insinuation into everyday consciousness and experience – that compel the closest, most searching attention. Under these circumstances, it can be difficult to distinguish journalistic/academic scrutiny and media voyeurism. There are many pleasures and horrors of the gaze in tracking global media sport, but it is undeniable that a critical analytical understanding of it returns the gaze to the world that has made it and of which we are all citizens.

7

Departure Lounge Note

Convulsions, continuities and campaigns

The cult of the global

Globalization is a word and concept that has entered everyday and academic discourse with remarkable speed since the 1980s. As Malcolm Waters (2001: 2) has noted, 'the word "global" is over 400 years old', but it only began to be used processually as 'globalization' rather than adjectivally in the 1960s (mostly in economics) and only then in limited circles. It is remarkable that as recently as February 1994 'the catalogue of the US Library of Congress contained only 34 publications with the term [globalization] or one of its derivatives in the title. By February 2000 this number had risen to 284. None of these was published before 1987' (Waters 2001). When in March 2011 I checked the Library of Congress' Online Catalogue for the title keyword 'globalization' alone (i.e. without derivatives), there were 5,200. This assessment only took place in the literary sphere, but globalization and its derivatives is now in every domain where humans communicate with each other – an exact-wording Google search for 'globalization' on the same day produced almost 28 million results. It is not particularly original to observe that the idea of the global has proliferated as an exemplification of itself, flowing across increasingly permeable boundaries and eroding differences – here conceptual and discursive – in all the spaces that it enters. But, inevitably, with all this pervasiveness comes both the elaboration and loss of meaning. If interrogating, deconstructing and reconstructing globalization have become something of an industry among academe and the 'punditariat', its buzzword status has also meant that it can be invoked, with wild imprecision, in virtually any discursive context – including the virtual. Globalization is prone to be used in a manner that forecloses debate in specific conversational settings, cutting off opportunities for action in the name of mysterious forces that render them futile as always, everywhere to be overridden by mere mention of the global. Or in a banal, totalizing way to describe a common state of affairs that ignores or underplays contextual variations and countervailing pressures. When coupled with media and sport – which have their own processual usages as 'mediatization' and 'sportification' – the tendency towards crude globalism is exacerbated.

The incontestable growth and development of the media apparatus around the world, and its inevitable impact on what it mediates, create a misleading conflation of communicative technological capability, textual circulation and audience interpretation. This is especially the case when the experience of Western media sport and of its media sport analysis – the *milieu* of this author – is extrapolated to every corner of the earth (Rowe and Gilmour 2008). Sport, as one the most prominent and popular forms of media content, is implicated in this depiction of a world at one with itself, especially when the size of the global media audience is emphasized during mega sports events. In this book I have highlighted the importance of the global media sport nexus but not, it is hoped, in a totalizing way that exaggerates its cohesion and completeness. The plural emphasis on flows is a recognition of its dynamism, on forms its complexity and on futures its uncertainty. In this chapter's title I have added three other elements in the global media sports cultural complex: the continuities that draw into sharper relief what has changed and is currently undergoing change; the convulsions that signal rapid, sometimes dramatic shifts in the familiar or even the traditional; and the campaigns that give political focus to the sociocultural issues at stake in this domain. The aim is to avoid (however inadequately) two contrasting forms of intellectual banality – the over-extension of 'mega trends' that produces theoretical intelligibility but empirical implausibility or the over-emphasis on particularity that duly recognizes empirical complexity at the expense of any prospect of plausible theoretical explanation. In the following (mercifully) brief concluding passages to this book it is intended to draw out these questions a little further and to propose some useful pathways for research and scholarship on global media sport that will do justice to it as a field of pleasure, sociality and cultural politics.

It is important to acknowledge that globalization is not the only or even the primary force in contemporary society and culture, but it is integral to it. As John Tomlinson (1999) argues in his influential book *Globalization and Culture*, all manner of extravagant, transformative claims are made on behalf of globalization, but at the heart of it are the modes of 'connectivity' that disturb various received notions of territory and identity. The difficulty, though, is to ascertain whether globalization is an effect of the outcome of a process or of a series of intersecting processes or in some overarching way causal or determinative. This is the problem that leads John Urry (2003: 96) to resist 'defining "globalization" as a single, clear and unambiguous entity', a position which (he notes that he) shares with Bob Jessop (2000: 339) in interpreting it as 'the complex resultant of many different processes rather than as a distinctive process in its own right'. Jessop mentions sport as one of a series of 'functional subsystems' that are both globally interdependent and distinctive:

> Globalization has both structural and strategic moments. Structurally, it involves the processes whereby increasing global interdependence is created among actions, organizations and institutions within (but not necessarily across) different functional subsystems (economy, law, politics, education, science, sport etc.). These processes occur on various spatial scales, operate differently in each functional subsystem, involve complex and tangled causal hierarchies rather than a simple, unilinear, bottom-up or top-down movement, and often display an eccentric 'nesting' of the different scales of social organization. This implies in turn, of course, that globalization is liable to uneven development in spatio-temporal terms. Nonetheless, globalization can be said to increase insofar as the co-variation of relevant activities is spatially more extensive and/or occurs more rapidly. (Jessop 2000: 339–40)

Here, Jessop invokes the processes of 'time-space distantiation' (Giddens 1981: 90; spelt as 'distanciation') that chronologically and spatially 'stretches' societies and 'time-space compression' that, via the capitalist motor of history, speeds them up and appears to 'shrink' space 'to a "global village" of telecommunications' (Harvey 1989: 240). As can be discerned from earlier discussions in this book, the global mega media sport event manifests as a perfect – if by nature untypical – instance of these processes at work. But such spectacular instances of globally mediated sport do not explain in themselves how different processes are 'organized within certain emergent, irreversible global outcomes that move backwards and forwards between the more localized and more global levels' (Urry 2003: 96). For Urry, the global might be seen in performative terms, as something that is necessarily elusive and constantly made and remade through signification, rather than available to be grasped independently of its own construction. As was hinted above regarding the comparatively late and restricted circulation of globalization as word and concept until the past decade, trying to come to terms with globalization requires a critically reflexive and flexible intellectual engagement with an analytical object that is both external and internal to the analyst. Interrogating globalization is part search for the macrovariables that produce 'irreversible global outcomes', part sceptical challenge to the very terms and tools that create a global 'mirage' that seems to disappear in the haze at the precise moment when it seems close at hand. The secrets of the global, including its relationship to media and sport, can never be unlocked, therefore, by seductively mechanical models of 'over-determination' in any – even the last – instance. In an earlier work (Miller *et al.* 2001: 4) I and colleagues treated globalization as part of

> five simultaneous, uneven, interconnected processes which characterize the present moment in sport: Globalization, Governmentalization, Americanization, Televisualization, and Commodification (GGATaC). They are in turn governed by a New International Division of Cultural Labour (NICL). Hence the paradox ... that the processes nominated by GGATaC operate in both complementary and contradictory ways. It is not appropriate to view globalization as always already a homogenizing force ... Yet many components of globalization are common across sites, leading to the acceptance of certain governing rules, media norms, and economic tendencies. (Miller *et al.* 2001: 4)

Living and operating with paradox, contradiction and complexity may be a little frustrating, but they are essential elements of a tenable analytical approach to global media sport. To take a conspicuous example, it is often claimed that the coming of globalization means the end of nation states as we have known them (Beck 2000), although many theorists regard predictions of their demise as premature (e.g. Held 1991). As I argued in Chapter 2, the rise of the nation state, media and sport was more or less coterminous in modernity, and so it is impossible to consider globalization and the nation–media–sport triad in isolation from each other. Although the nation state as legal entity and the nation as sociocultural formation are not identical, their relationship remains pivotal – for example, as discussed, with regard to media regulation (although weakened in the digital age) and international sport event hosting. The ripple effect of the decline of nations in media sport would be profound indeed but, as I have registered at various points in this book, international sport competition and global sports television have both been deeply dependent on the prominence and integrity of nations as sources of the necessary affect and identity that invest many of the most prominent sports contests (even those, like Grand Slam tennis tournaments, that are between individual competitors, not national representatives) with meaning-laden competitive tension. Nations are not only integral to the governance and organization of major sport, then, but they also organize them in visual and aural presentational terms that are essential to the dynamic spectacle of media sport. It is difficult to imagine any international tournament or contest in team sports without players bearing national insignia and spectators draped in national colours and voicing support in nationally significant ways. Major sports contests contained within nations are no less opportunities for national display – as, for example, in the patriotic flag waving evident in every Super Bowl and especially in times of conflict and war (Falcous and Silk 2005). It is for such reasons that I have been sceptical about propositions that globalization is bringing about the demise of the sporting nation. Hence, at a time when, perhaps, the globalization literary industry was at its most effervescent, I produced an article (Rowe 2003) that was both auto-critique and scholarly field provocation. It is useful in this closing chapter to revisit the questions that animated 'Sport and the Repudiation of the Global' and the dialogue that it stimulated with leading sport scholars David Andrews and George Ritzer (2007), whose 'The Grobal in the Sporting Glocal' was a friendly but critical response to it.

Global, local, glocal and grobal

In brief, I raised in the article the question of 'whether sport, despite appearances and, especially, the spectacular instances of global mega media sports events like the Olympics and the football World Cup (not forgetting the more routine forms of mediatized sport circulated around the globe), may be constitutively unsuited to carriage of the project of globalization in its fullest sense' (Rowe 2003: 281). In suggesting this possibility I sought to go beyond the orthodoxy of cultural nationalist resistance and 'glocal' adaptations under an unevenly achieved globalization, indicating 'more radically, that the social institution of sport is so deeply dependent on the production of difference that it repudiates the possibility of comprehensive globalization while seeming to foreshadow its inevitable establishment' (Rowe 2003: 281–2). The particular form of globalization at issue here is cultural, although a modified argument might have been made for other forms, political, technological, economic and so on. In very brief summary, my conclusion is that national culture is so central to the sporting formation that globalization, interpreted as the process via which 'the relationship between sport and *national* identity is self-evidently unravelling to reveal an increasingly global sporting culture' (Bairner 2001), is incapable of what is so often claimed for it – the progressive dismantlement of nations under the sign of the global and, in the final analysis, the erasure of distinctive local cultures, including those surrounding sport. If this is a challenge to the harder edge of globalization as homogenization, rather than to more qualified and cautious perspectives, it is precisely because the rhetorical uses of the concept of globalization, not least within prevailing discourses of the coming of global sport, as Bairner (2001: 6) puts it, are as frequently posited by both optimistic and pessimistic commentators (among which I would count myself in some recorded and unrecorded utterances) as 'inevitable and all-consuming'. Bairner (2001: 176) concludes his book with approving reference to Maguire's (1994, 1999) application of the 'diminishing contrasts, increasing varieties' formulation (off which Chapter 2 'riffed'), without wishing

> to deny the extent to which global capitalism has affected the ways in which sport is played, administered, packaged, and watched throughout the world. This has clearly compressed the distance between the sporting nations of the world both physically and metaphorically. Indeed, as far as the most popular sports are concerned we can actually recognize the emergence and consolidation of a global sporting political economy involving the sale of merchandise, sponsorship, labor migration, and so on. (Bairner 2001: 176)

For Bairner, sport and globalization are 'accomplices' in preserving national identity in the face of 'supranationalist tendencies', bringing national identities to the fore at the very moment that sport is at its most global – the Olympics and the World Cup. But there are still uncertainties about the ways in which the global and the local can be theorized in relational terms. In their response to my article Andrews and Ritzer (2007: 136) argue that

> [it] falsely polarizes globalization and localization in a manner that implicitly privileges, perhaps even romanticizes, the local ...

> Rather than articulating the global and the local as polarities upon the globalization continuum (an approach which virtually necessitates the privileging of one pole over the other), it is important to view the 'complementary and interpenetrative' relations linking homogenization and heterogenization, universalism and particularism, sameness and difference, and the global and the local; the global being complicit in the 'creation and incorporation' of the local, and *vice versa*. (Robertson 1995)

Instead of positing the global against the local, Andrews and Ritzer (2007: 137) prefer to use one established neologism (the glocal/glocalization) alongside another of Ritzer's (the grobal/grobalization):

> assumption that virtually no 'areas and phenomena throughout the world are unaffected by globalization' (Ritzer 2004: xiii). This implies the declining, or even disappearing, relevance of the local and the need to reconceptualise virtually everything we think of as local as glocal. Rather than viewing the core tension as existing being between the global and the local, and certainly as evidenced within the sporting realm, our contention is that the *local* has been so effected [sic] by the *global*, that it has become, at all intents and purposes, *glocal* (Ritzer 2004: xiii, xi). Thus, the processual and empirical continuum through which we conceptualize

globalization is bounded by *grobalization* ('the imperialistic ambitions of nations, corporations, organizations, and the like and their desire, indeed need, to impose themselves on various geographic areas') and *glocalization* ('the interpenetration of the global and the local, resulting in unique outcomes in different geographic areas'): the *grobal* and the *glocal*. (Ritzer 2006: 337–8)

In providing concrete examples of this dual model, they then offer 'four suggestive sporting scenarios' that display 'the necessary, but never guaranteed, interpenetrative relationship between the grobal and the glocal' (Andrews and Ritzer 2007: 137): 'indigenous incorporation', 'corporate re-constitution', 'universal differentiation' and 'dichotomous agency'. Thus, Andrews and Ritzer present what they see as a hard-headed analysis that emphasizes conventional notions of political, economic and cultural imperialism under late modernism attached to the project of globalization at the expense of more 'decentred' postmodern-influenced romanticizations of the peripheral that, for them, amount to an unfortunate drift towards the aforementioned 'globaloney'.

This debate has brought to the surface important matters that require continuous, critically reflexive analysis. Andrews and Ritzer are quite right to critique residual romanticization of the local, not only because it cannot be assumed that sociocultural structures and practices in relatively insulated environments are inherently superior (Miller *et al.* 2001) but also, as has been shown throughout this book, it is increasingly difficult to establish the boundaries of the local that is being romanticized. That homogenization and heterogenization are forces in constant interplay means that, as represented by the concept of glocalization, '[c]ulturally, as well as socially, economically and politically, the contemporary world can be characterized as involving dialectics of sameness and difference' (Inglis and Hughson 2003: 224). These dialectics are played out in diverse ways in wide-ranging debates surrounding cosmopolitanism, mobilities, hybridity, 'liquid modernity' and so on (Bauman 2000; Creswell 2006; Harindranath 2006; Urry 2007), although several contributions to it counsel caution that the spatial and ideational horizons of much of the world's population are empirically much more restricted than many theorists allow (Savage, Bagnall and Longhurst 2004; Turner and Khonder 2010). In seeking to understand this cultural complexity in sport, it is also, as Andrews and Ritzer argue, important not to downplay the 'transnational strategizing' (Andrews and Ritzer 2007: 141) of News Corp, Nike, FIFA or the IOC by which they are 'able to seamlessly operate within the language of the sporting glocal, simultaneously, in multiple locations' (Andrews and Ritzer 2007: 145). Each of the sporting scenarios they present 'exhibit – in varying ways and to varying intensities – the necessary, but never guaranteed, interpenetrative nature of the relationship between the sporting grobal and the sporting glocal' (Andrews and Ritzer 2007: 148). Thus, by both 'problematizing the very possibility of the local within conditions of intensive and extensive globalization (leading to the concept of the glocal), and simultaneously reinscribing the importance of the global (through the concept of the grobal)' their schema, they contend, 'represents a more useful and insightful model for examining the contemporary sporting popular' (Andrews and Ritzer 2007: 148–9).

While, as should be obvious from the previous comments, the grobal–glocal schema of Andrews and Ritzer has much to commend it, it is in my view limited by its implicit assumption of the 'triumph' of the grobal. Thus, it tends to attach the grobal exclusively to the 'imperialistic ambitions of nations, corporations, organizations and the like' and associates the glocal with either the strategic adaptation of (mostly Western, capitalist) products, practices and so on to local environments or the strategic negotiation and modification of them by local actors. As I have argued in this book, these are crucial factors, but it is an almost exclusively action-response model that takes little apparent account of those factors that are in various respects chaotic, blind, non-linear, unpredictable, unconscious and unintended (Urry 2003). The analytical account that I have offered of the global media sports cultural complex conceives it as profoundly influenced not only by the major organizations motivated by capital, governmental authority and ideological power but also by much more diffuse, informal and elusive pleasures, identities and collective meanings. Andrews and Ritzer's schema gives primacy to the former which, having destroyed 'to all intents and purposes' the possibility of the local, would seem only to need to agree to favourable terms with it. This is because, despite their *caveat* that the interpenetration of the relationship between the sporting grobal and sporting glocal is 'never guaranteed', it is difficult to see how it could be otherwise within their model given its rather etiolated conception of the local component of the glocal.

The sceptical-rationalist approach of Andrews and Ritzer has analytical virtue, but it ironically echoes the stern admonitions of false consciousness delivered by some Marxists to adherents of disapproved forms of popular culture (Rowe 1995). Their criticism, for example, of the campaign against News Corp by the South Sydney Rabbitohs in gaining reinstatement to Australia's National Rugby League ('What on the surface appears to be a "glocal alternative" may in fact have become an example of the grobalization of cultural processes and practices that exudes the *nothingness* associated with grobality', Rowe 1995: 147) and of anti-Glazer (the club's American owners) Manchester United fans (for having 'fallen foul of fetishizing the sporting glocal, by not acknowledging the grobal relations complicit in the structure and experience of contemporary sport forms', Rowe 1995: 148) is not only a little harsh on those concerned but also tends towards the tautological in arguing that globality and nothingness will get them in the end. There is no doubt that such localist movements do display a certain narrowness of vision, parochialism and naivety, but characteristics of this kind are not only common aspects of mobilizing rhetorics but also of sport fandom itself. So it could be argued that if all sporting affiliation, activism and fandom were to be held so strictly to account, then almost any sport-related affect would be found wanting. Because sports culture is so suffused with myths of belonging and identity, it is rather improbable that they can be avoided in popular campaigning around sport – indeed, they invest popular politics with a rhetorical power that would surely be absent in baldly 'acknowledging the grobal relations complicit in the structure and experience of contemporary sport forms'.

South Sydney's reinstatement to the National Rugby League (NRL) and subsequent retention was, in fact, achieved despite the High Court of Australia ultimately finding in favour of News Limited (News Corp's Australian subsidiary) on appeal (Davies 2003). The 'grobal' was, no doubt, registered with its subsequent ownership by Australian–New Zealand Hollywood actor Russell Crowe, a long-term fan and Sydney resident, and in the continuing involvement of News Corp in the NRL (both as broadcaster and, until its planned exit in 2011, as co-owner). However, the campaign was successful in its own terms and the club still retains a strongly local (especially indigenous Australian) character without, of course, ever being able to return to a 'pure' localism given, among other changes, the urban gentrification of parts of its locale. In the case of Manchester United, as was discussed in Chapter 2, it is at the time of writing still owned by the Glazers, with the highly localist breakaway semi-professional club FC United of Manchester continuing to play in a much lower league. If, as has been proposed, a member-based ownership for Manchester United transpires, it would be less grobal while inevitably remaining substantially so as part of the deeply commercial EPL. In other words, the stern test of the local set by Andrews and Ritzer for all those who invoke the local in professional sport is certain to be failed (as, no doubt, was my own test for sport's 'carriage of the project of globalization in its fullest sense', Rowe 2003: 281). But, as argued throughout this book, the age of pre-modernist folk sport is irrevocably lost, while, following Williams (1977), still being present in residual cultural form as part of contemporary sport's constitutive mythological structure. The dual neologisms of sporting grobal/glocal would seem best to apply to the specific contact zone where transnational organizations and national/local organizations meet (e.g. club takeovers, international broadcast rights contracts or new branches and competitions of overseas sports in non-originary territories), with the global and the local remaining as ideal typical constructions that embrace, more comprehensively and loosely, the flows, forms and futures evident across the whole global media sports cultural complex.

I have explored and elaborated on this debate over the global, local, glocal and grobal in sport in some detail in order to demonstrate that the field of global media sport retains its intellectual vitality and broad, deep relevance across society and culture. My provocation concerning sport's repudiation of the global, in eliciting Andrews and Ritzer's critique of 'a concern for narrower and more specific elements such as the actor, the local and even the glocal' (Andrews and Ritzer 2007: 149), reveals how this field of inquiry can advance through vigorous but constructive debate. It would be hoped that other researchers and scholars in this field can take it further, not least by those outside the Anglo-sphere, in critically analysing global/local forces in sport and the range of histories, political economic processes and sociocultural dynamics that produce global media sport in both its standardized and distinctive forms. This discussion has also suggested ways in which interventions might be made in the global cultural politics of media sport.

A cultural politics of global media sport

In this book it is hoped that rich possibilities have been glimpsed concerning not only ways of researching global media sport but also of translating that critical knowledge into some beneficial impact on the object of analysis and its sociocultural milieu. The concept that I have foregrounded in this respect has been cultural citizenship in contending that, as sport has globalized, its social, cultural and political importance in both national and transnational contexts has been enhanced. Gerard Delanty (2002: 64) connects cultural citizenship succinctly to 'common experiences, learning processes and discourses of empowerment. The power to name, create meaning, construct personal biographies and narratives by gaining control over the flow of information, goods and cultural processes is an important dimension of citizenship as an active process'. Apart from some 'control over the flow' of culture, it is also important not to be bypassed and marginalized by flows controlled by others. In this regard, mediated sport relates directly to the politics of inclusion and exclusion that condition the rights of 'global citizens' to participate, where they so choose, in significant sports events and rituals that signify active membership in communal life. Some brief indicative examples can be mentioned here in proposing areas where the cultural politics of sport can be usefully practised.

One key area that I have emphasized has been free access to televised sport of demonstrable cultural significance. As we have seen, within nations it has been necessary for citizens to mobilize to prevent the siphoning of key national sports events onto exclusive subscription platforms, while the same vigilance is necessary with regard to global media sport events. Communication and media technology innovations have, furthermore, caused disturbances in relationships between sports organizations, media companies, telecommunications corporations, viewers and sport fans, and it is necessary for current laws and regulations in media sport to keep up with these changes in order to preserve and, as necessary, extend the rights of cultural citizenship pertaining to them. Decisions on funding priorities of governments in sport are open to informed, vigorous debate, as is sport's role in international development aid. In cases where the importation of slickly marketed sports brands has marginalized local sports, where there is exploitation of a local and foreign sports labour force and corrupt conduct by sports organizations and personnel, there are many opportunities to exert pressure for appropriate action from national and supranational authorities. The global commercial exploitation of sport has, it has been noted, sometimes led to the relative disempowerment of sports fans and their consequent organization and cooperation to prevent or reverse alienation from their own cultural experience, including assuming greater ownership and control of the clubs that they support. Grass-roots, voluntary fan and other non-government organizations can also be effective, with the assistance of government, media and sports bodies, to counter prejudice and discrimination within sport in such vital areas as racism, sexism and homophobia. In particular, preventing the use of sport as a vehicle for fomenting conflict is an important task for fan groups as, more proactively, is the use of sport as an agent of peace and intercultural dialogue in zones of conflict (Sugden 2010).

Because of the frequent failure of the sport and general news media to discharge their 'fourth-estate' watchdog role in the sphere of sport and society, there is a simultaneous need for demanding mainstream media users and inquisitive citizen journalists. It is also important to scrutinize, and intervene in, regimes of representation in media sport, not least those involving the routine stereotyping that disparages and degrades athletes and fans alike (Birrell and McDonald 2000). In their collection on sports media and identity, Hundley and Billings (2010) use:

> concrete examples from mediasport to further the contention that the portrayal of identity – whether it involves gender, sexuality, nationality, race, disability, or fan affiliation, is a part of a grand negotiation between those who enact, produce, consume and institutionalize sport and the mechanisms that rise from it … The way in which mediasport is represented and consumed can speak volumes about whom and what a society strives to be; the negotiation of identity plays an integral role in this process as well. (Billings and Hundley 2010: 12–13)

This is an area that I have touched on only lightly in this book, not as a judgement of its importance but of focus – that is, by emphasizing the flows, forms and futures of global media sport I have concentrated on its (mobile) scaffolding rather than its detailed interior design in each of its zones and sites. The intention has been to help create an analytical structure for authors and readers to apply their own stress tests, searching out weaknesses, challenging assumptions and conclusions, exposing inconsistencies and filling in gaps. There are many subjects that have not been given the kind of detailed attention that they demand. For example, there has been much greater emphasis on men's than women's sport (or at least male-dominated sport) and on men rather than women *in* sport (the concerns of such work as Creedon 1994; Hargreaves 1994; Messner 2002; Pfister and Hartmann-Tews 2003; Scraton and Flintoff 2002). Also, the primary focus has been on sports (even those that have been highly modified, such as Twenty20 cricket) that are fairly traditional, orthodox and established professional sports, rather than those, such as so-called lifestyle or extreme sports, that are a developing – and by no means negligible – feature of the media sports cultural complex (see, for example, Kusz 2007; Rinehart and Sydnor 2003; Robinson 2008; Wheaton 2004). The mitigating argument advanced in countering this reasonable charge is that this analysis has largely followed where the power in global media sport historically, currently and for the foreseeable future lies. A compendious work would do more in this area – but this is not a compendium, and as author I would – not too self-servingly, it is hoped – point to an *oeuvre* that engages in greater scope and depth with the critical reading of media sport texts and interrogation of their ideologies of dominance.

The subject of global media sport is so large, diverse and mutable, and the task so daunting, as to call into being a critical global media sport scholarship that at present resembles (in a laboured genuflection to the poetry of Yeats) a slouching rough beast whose hour has come at last. By this I mean that a highly promising aspect of the maturation of this research field is the fuller participation of those from the spaces once known as the periphery whose media sport contexts have been talked *about*, largely in ignorant extrapolation, by those at its imperial intellectual core. To pluck one example among myriad potential ones, Sumei Wang (2009: 370) argues that

> the case of baseball in Taiwan illustrates a complicated interpenetration of colonialism, class, ethnicity, and nationalism. The meaning of baseball in Taiwan is therefore unique. Baseball in Taiwan is a good example in showing that some practices introduced from abroad are actively sought out and welcomed, indeed loved by members of the host population and are culturally enriching. All global flows do not fit into the category of oppressive imperialist imposition, in which the host culture figures as passive recipient or victim. A globalised world is not necessarily a homogenizing world or a world where all existing orders are being replaced. In fact, people often appropriate and domesticate foreign imports to fit their needs.

> The story of baseball in Taiwan demonstrates how a foreign sport can take on different meanings when it circulates into different places. The spreading popularity of baseball does not represent a circulation of a fixed message from its country of origin, the United States, to the rest areas, such as Japan, Korea, and Taiwan. New meanings and experiences of baseball are created along with local traditions and social structures. (Sumei Wang 2009: 370)

My lay and scholarly knowledge of Taiwanese baseball is slight to the point of negligible; yet Wang's knowledge of its historical, political and sociocultural dimensions, when coupled with a flexible theory of globalization (honed in Lancaster via Taipei), is an effective illustration of how critical work in this area can illuminate not only the 'functional subsystem' of sport (as Jessop describes it above) but also its place and role within both individual societies and the world at large. This globalization of global media sport research is crucial to a field dominated by Western, mostly white scholars and their concerns (McDonald 2010; Rowe and Gilmour 2008). All researchers and scholars in this field, though, irrespective of their orientation and origin, can be confident that their subject will continue, voluntarily or by default, to feature in the lives of many (if not most) of the people of the earth. They will also have discovered that, as with a live mediated sport event, the object of their gaze is changing in front and beneath them, and it is ill advised to look away for too long.

References

Allan, S. (2006), *Online News: Television and the Internet*, Maidenhead, UK: Open University Press.

Andersen, J. S. (2010), 'The Magicians of Sport: How the Greatest Corruption Scandal in World Sport Vanished before We Knew It Existed', *Play the Game*, 19 October. Available at http://www.playthegame.org/knowledge-bank/articles/the-magicians-of-sport-how-the-greatest-corruption-scandal-in-world-sport-vanished-before-we-knew-i.html [accessed 21 January 2011].

Andersen, J. S. (2011), 'The Titanic Challenge of Joseph S. Blatter', *Play the Game*, 6 June. Available at http://www.playthegame.org/news/detailed/the-titanic-challenge-of-joseph-s-blatter-5177.html [accessed 12 June 2011].

Andrews, D. L. (1996), 'Deconstructing Michael Jordan: Reconstructing Postindustrial America', *Sociology of Sport Journal*, 13(4): 315–18.

Andrews, D. L. (2006), *Sport–Commerce–Culture: Essays on Sport in Late Capitalist America*, New York: Peter Lang.

Andrews, D. L. and Jackson, S. J. (eds) (2001), *Sport Stars: The Cultural Politics of Sporting Celebrity*, London and New York: Routledge.

Andrews, D. L. and Ritzer, G. (2007), 'The Grobal in the Sporting Glocal', *Global Networks*, 7(2): 135–53.

Ang, I. and Pothen, P. (2009), 'Between Promise and Practice: Web 2.0, Intercultural Dialogue and Digital Scholarship', *Fibreculture*, 14. Available at http://journal.fibreculture.org/issue14/issue14_ang_pothen.html [accessed 12 March 2011].

Anheier, H. and Isar, Y. R. (eds) (2010), *Cultural Expression, Creativity and Innovation*, London: Sage.

Appadurai, A. (1996), *Modernity at Large: Cultural Dimensions of Globalization*, Minneapolis, MN: Cultural Dimensions of Globalization.

Appadurai, A. (ed.) (2001), *Globalization*, Durham, NC: Duke University Press.

Armstrong, K. and Goldiner, D. (2010), 'NFL Looking into Reporter Ines Sainz's Claims of Sexually Suggestive Comments Made by New York Jets', *New York Daily News*, 13 September. Available at http://www.nydailynews.com/sports/football/jets/2010/09/12/2010-09-12_nfl_looking_into_reporter_ines_sainz_claims_of_sexually_suggestive_comments_mad.html [accessed 3 January 2011].

Asian Football Confederation (AFC) (2010), 'Surging J-League Crowds Give KFA Food for Thought', 26 July. Available at http://cms.the-afc.com/en/features/29893-surging-j-league-crowds-give-kfa-food-for-thought [accessed 17 January 2011].

Associated Press (AP) (2010), 'Roger Federer Backs Shorter Season', 9 November. Available at http://sports.espn.go.com/sports/tennis/news/story?id=5783753 [accessed 6 March 2011].

Australian Football League (AFL) (2010), 'International Broadcast Partners: Television'. Available at http://www.afl.com.au/international%20broadcast%20partners/tabid/14533/default.aspx [accessed 13 November 2010].

Australian Government, Department of Broadband, Communications and the Digital Economy (2009), 'Sport on Television – Review of the Anti-Siphoning Scheme in the Contemporary Digital Environment Discussion Paper', August. Available at http://www.dbcde.gov.au/television/antisiphoning_and_antihoarding/sport_on_television__review_of_the_anti-siphoning_scheme_discussion_paper [accessed 9 March 2011].

Australian Government, Department of Broadband, Communications and the Digital Economy (2010a), 'Sport on Television – A Review of the Anti-Siphoning Scheme in the Contemporary Digital Environment', November. Available at http://www.dbcde.gov.au/television/antisiphoning_and_antihoarding/sport_on_television__review_of_the_anti-siphoning_scheme_discussion_paper [accessed 9 March 2011].

Australian Government, Department of Broadband, Communications and the Digital Economy (2010b), 'Code of Practice for Sports News Reporting (Text, Photography and Data)'. Available at http://www.dbcde.gov.au/__data/assets/pdf_file/0019/127324/Code_of_Practice_Sports_News_Reporting_MARCH_2010.pdf [accessed 13 December 2010].

Bairner, A. (2001), *Sport, Nationalism, and Globalization: European and North American Perspectives*, Albany, NY: State University of New York Press.

Baker, A. and Boyd, T. (eds) (1997), *Out of Bounds: Sports, Media, and the Politics of Identity*, Bloomington, IN: Indiana University Press.

Bal, S. (2010), 'Lalit's Last Hurrah', ESPN *Cricinfo*, 25 April. Available at http://www.espncricinfo.com/magazine/content/story/457324.html [accessed 28 February 2011].

Bale, J. (1993), *Sport, Space and the City*, London and New York: Routledge.

Bale, J. (1998), 'Virtual Fandoms: Futurescapes of Football', in A. Brown (ed.), *Fanatics! Power, Identity and Fandom in Football*, London: Routledge, pp. 265–77.

Bale, J. and Cronin, M. (eds) (2003), *Sport and Postcolonialism*, Oxford, London and New York: Berg.

Barnett, S. (1990), *Games and Sets: The Changing Face of Sport on Television*, London: British Film Institute.

Baughman, C. (1995), *Women on Ice: Feminist Essays on the Tonya Harding/Nancy Kerrigan Spectacle*, New York: Routledge.

Bauman, Z. (2000), *Liquid Modernity*, Cambridge: Polity.

BBC World Service (2010), *World Football*, 29 May. Available at http://www.bbc.co.uk/programmes/p002vsyx [accessed 18 January 2011].

Beck, U. (1992), *Risk Society: Towards a New Modernity*, London: Sage.

Beck, U. (2000), *What Is Globalization?* Cambridge: Polity.

Beckles, H. (2001), 'Brian Lara: (Con)testing the Caribbean Imagination', in D. L. Andrews and S. J. Jackson (eds), *Sport Stars: The Cultural Politics of Sporting Celebrity*, London and New York: Routledge, pp. 243–56.

Beech, J., Horsman, S. and Magraw, J. (2008), 'The Circumstances in Which English Football Clubs Become Insolvent', Centre for the International Business of Sport Working Paper Series – No. 4. Available at http://www.coventry.ac.uk/researchnet/external/content/1/c4/53/26/v1215786928/user/CIBS%20WP04_edit.pdf [accessed 15 January 2011].

Benedict, J. (1997), *Public Heroes, Private Felons: Athletes and Crimes against Women*, Boston, MA: Northeastern University Press.

Bernstein, A. and Blain, N. (eds) (2003), *Sport, Media, Culture: Global and Local Dimensions*, London: Frank Cass.

Bhogle, H. (2011), 'Decoding the Auction', ESPN Cricinfo, 14 January. Available at http://www.espncricinfo.com/magazine/content/story/496593.html [accessed 28 February 2011].

Billings, A. and Hundley, H. L. (2010), 'Examining Identity in Sports Media', in H. L. Hundley and A. C. Billings (eds), *Examining Identity in Sports Media*, Thousand Oaks, CA: Sage, pp. 1–15.

Birrell, S. and McDonald, M. G. (eds) (2000), *Reading Sport: Critical Essays on Power and Representation*, Boston, MA: Northeastern University Press.

Blainey, G. (2010), *A Game of Our Own: The Origins of Australian Football*, second edition, Melbourne: Black Ink.

Bloomfield, S. (2010), *Africa United: Soccer, Passion, Politics, and the First World Cup in Africa*, Edinburgh: Canongate.

Bourdieu, P. (1978), 'Sport and Social Class', *Social Science Information*, 17(6): 819–40.

Bourdieu, P. (1984), *Distinction: A Social Critique of the Judgement of Taste*, London: Routledge and Kegan Paul.

Bowen, W. G. and Levin, S. A. (2003), *Reclaiming the Game: College Sports and Educational Values*, Princeton, NJ: Princeton University Press.

Boyle, R. (2006), *Sports Journalism: Context and Issues*, London: Sage.

Boyle, R. (2010), Contribution to L. Qing (ed.), 'Encoding the Olympics – Visual Hegemony? Discussion and Interpretation on Intercultural Communication in the Beijing Olympic Games', *The International Journal of the History of Sport*, 27(9/10): 1843–6.

Boyle, R. and Haynes, R. (2004), *Football in the New Media Age*, London: Routledge.

Boyle, R. and Haynes, R. (2009), *Power Play: Sport, the Media & Popular Culture*, second edition, Edinburgh: Edinburgh University Press.

Boyle, R. and Whannel, G. (2010a), 'Editorial: Sport and the New Media', *Convergence*, 16(3): 259–62.

Boyle, R. and Whannel, G. (eds) (2010b), 'Sport and the New Media', Special Issue, *Convergence*, 16(3).

Boyle, R., Rowe, D. and Whannel, G. (2010), '"Delight in Trivial Controversy?" Questions for Sports Journalism', in S. Allan (ed.), *Routledge Companion to News and Journalism Studies*, London: Routledge, pp. 245–55.

British Broadcasting Corporation (BBC) (2005), 'Blair Beats Drum for London Bid'. Available at http://news.bbc.co.uk/sport2/hi/other_sports/olympics_2012/4645817.stm [accessed 31 December 2010].

British Broadcasting Corporation (2008), 'China Anger over "Shoddy Schools"', 15 May. Available at http://news.bbc.co.uk/2/hi/asia-pacific/7400524.stm [accessed 29 December 2010].

British Broadcasting Corporation (2010a), 'Liverpool Remain Confident Takeover Will Be Completed', 10 October. Available at http://news.bbc.co.uk/sport2/hi/football/teams/l/liverpool/9077048.stm [accessed 10 October 2010].

British Broadcasting Corporation (2010b), 'Manchester United Reports Pre-Tax Loss of £80m', 8 October. Available at http://www.bbc.co.uk/news/business-11499023 [accessed 11 October 2010].

British Broadcasting Corporation (2010c), 'Cricket World Shocked at Test "Betting Scam"', 29 August. Available at http://www.bbc.co.uk/news/uk-11123605 [accessed 7 March 2011].

British Broadcasting Corporation (2010d), 'Spot Betting: How Does It Work?', 31 August. Available at http://www.bbc.co.uk/news/uk-11137067 [accessed 20 October 2010].

British Broadcasting Corporation (2010e), 'London's O2 Arena to Host NBA Regular Season Matches', 9 August. Available at http://news.bbc.co.uk/sport2/hi/other_sports/basketball/8898864.stm [accessed 4 November 2010].

British Broadcasting Corporation (2010f), 'Fifa Bans Adamu and Temarii over World Cup Vote Claims', 18 November. Available at http://news.bbc.co.uk/sport2/hi/football/9203378.stm [accessed 16 March 2011].

British Broadcasting Corporation (2011), 'Coach Andy Flower Bemoans England Schedule', 4 February. Available at http://newsrss.bbc.co.uk/sport1/hi/cricket/england/9387335.stm [accessed 7 March 2011].

Brooker, W. and Jermyn, D. (eds) (2003), *The Audience Studies Reader*, New York and Oxford: Routledge.

Brookes, R. (2002), *Representing Sport*, London: Arnold.

Brown, A. (ed.) (1998a), *Fanatics! Power, Identity and Fandom in Football*, London: Routledge.

Brown, A. (1998b), 'United We Stand: Some Problems with Fan Democracy', in A. Brown (ed.), *Fanatics! Power, Identity and Fandom in Football*, London: Routledge, pp. 50–67.

Brownell, S. (2008), *Beijing's Games: What the Olympics Mean to China*, Lanham, MD: Rowman and Littlefield.

Bruns, A. (2008), *Blogs, Wikipedia, Second Life, and Beyond: From Production to Produsage*, New York: Peter Lang.

Bryant, J. and Cummins, R. G. (2010), 'The Effects of Outcome of Mediated and Live Sporting Events on Sport Fans' Self- and Social Identities', in H. L. Hundley and A. C. Billings (eds), *Examining Identity in Sports Media*, Thousand Oaks, CA: Sage, pp. 217–38.

Bubalo, A. (2005), *Football Diplomacy*, Policy Brief, Sydney: Lowy Institute for International Policy.

Burns, J. F. (2010), 'Cricket Scandal Rocks Pakistan', *The New York Times*, 29 August. Available at http://www.nytimes.com/2010/08/30/world/europe/30cricket.html [accessed 2 January 2011].

Buteau, M. and Fixmer, A. (2011), 'Fox Says Super Bowl Was Most-Watched Program in U.S. Television History', Bloomberg, 8 February. Available at http://www.bloomberg.com/news/2011-02-07/green-bay-s-win-ties-1987-giants-broncos-super-bowl-for-highest-tv-rating.html [accessed 9 February 2011].

Calhoun, C. J. (1997), *Nationalism*, Maidenhead and Minneapolis, MN: Open University Press and University of Minnesota Press.

Callow, J. (2010), 'Forbes Rates Manchester United Top of World Sport's Rich List', *The Guardian*, 22 July. Available at http://www.guardian.co.uk/football/2010/jul/22/manchester-united-forbes-rich-list [accessed 20 October 2010].

Canning, S. (2009), 'Senate Inquiry to Decide Who Owns Sports Match Footage', *The Australian*, 16 March. Available at http://www.theaustralian.news.com.au/business/story/0,28124,25190559-36418,00.html [accessed 13 December 2010].

Carrington, B. (2010), *Race, Sport and Politics: The Sporting Black Diaspora*, London: Sage.

Carrington, B. and McDonald, I. (eds) (2001), '*Race*', *Sport and British Society*, London and New York: Routledge.

Casey, M. (2011), 'AFC Insist It's Satisfied with Asian Cup Crowds Despite Dismal Attendance at Several Matches', The Canadian Press, 15 January. Available at http://www.google.com/hostednews/canadianpress/article/ALeqM5hxe4 NNrnmloOE93LCdb1Fiv1c_TA?docId=5649547 [accessed 17 January 2011].

Cashman, R. (2010), *Paradise of Sport: A History of Australian Sport*, revised edition, Sydney: Walla Walla.

Castells, M. (1996), *The Informational City*, Oxford: Blackwell.

Castells, M. (1998), *The Information Age: Economy, Society and Culture Volume 1: The Rise of Network Society*, Oxford: Blackwell.

Caudwell, J. (ed.) (2006), *Sport, Sexualities and Queer/Theory*, London and New York: Routledge.

Chandler, J. M. (1988), *Television and National Sport: The United States and Britain*, Urbana, IL: University of Illinois Press.

Clarke, J. and Critcher, C. (1985), *The Devil Makes Work: Leisure in Capitalist Britain*, London: Macmillan.

Coakley, J., Hallinan, C., Jackson, S. and Mewett, P. (2009), *Sports in Society: Issues and Controversies in Australia and New Zealand*, Sydney: McGraw Hill.

Cohen, R. (2010), 'Tiger Woods Scandal Voted AP Sports Story of Year', *The Huffington Post*, 16 December. Available at http://www.huffingtonpost.com/2010/12/16/tiger-woods-scandal-story-of-year_n_797900.html [accessed 3 January 2011].

Collins, S. (2007), ' "Samurai" Politics: Japanese Cultural Identity in Global Sport – The Olympic Games as a Representational Strategy', *International Journal of the History of Sport*, 24(3): 357–74.

Collins, S. (2008), 'The Fragility of Asian National Identity in the Olympic Games', in M. E Price and D. Dayan (eds), *Owning the Olympics: Narratives of the New China*, Ann Arbor, MI: The University of Michigan Press, pp. 185–209.

Conn, D. (2010a), 'AFC Wimbledon and Ebbsfleet Have Different Reasons for FA Cup Hope', Guardian: The Sport Blog, 5 November. Available at http://www.guardian.co.uk/football/blog/2010/nov/05/afc-wimbledon-ebbsfleet-united-fa-cup [accessed 20 December 2010].

Conn, D. (2010b), 'BBC Correct to Air Fifa Exposé, Says Paul Elliott of 2018 Bid Team', *The Guardian*, 8 December. Available at http://www.guardian.co.uk/football/2010/dec/08/england-2018-bid-bbc-statement [accessed 2 January 2011].

Conn, D. (2010c), 'Premier League Clubs Owe 56% of Europe's Debt', *The Guardian*, 23 February. Available at http://www.guardian.co.uk/football/2010/feb/23/premier-league-clubs-europe-debt [accessed 15 January 2011].

Corrigan, P. (2001), 'Imran Khan: The Road from Cricket to Politics', in D. L. Andrews and S. J. Jackson (eds), *Sport Stars: The Cultural Politics of Sporting Celebrity*, London and New York: Routledge, pp. 231–42.

Couldry, N. (2008), 'Mediatization or Mediation? Alternative Understandings of the Emergent Space of Digital Storytelling', *New Media & Society*, 10(3): 373–91.

Crawford, G. (2004), *Consuming Sport: Fans, Sport and Culture*, London and New York: Routledge.

Creed, B. (1993), *The Monstrous-Feminine: Film, Feminism, Psychoanalysis*, London: Routledge.

Creedon, P. J. (ed.) (1994), *Women, Media and Sport: Challenging Gender Values*, Thousand Oaks, CA: Sage.

Cresswell, T. (2006), *On the Move: Mobility in the Modern Western World*, London: Routledge.

Critcher, C. (2003), *Moral Panics and the Media*, Buckingham, UK: Open University Press.

Curran, J. (ed.) (2010), *Media and Society*, fifth edition, London: Bloomsbury.

Curtin, M. (2007), *Playing to the World's Biggest Audience: The Globalization of Chinese Film and TV*, Berkeley, CA: University of California Press.

Darby, P. Akindes, G. and Irwin, M. (2007), 'Football Academies and the Migration of African Football Labor to Europe', *Journal of Sport and Social Issues*, 31(2): 143–61.

Davidson, H. (2010), 'Shane Warne and Liz Hurley Have Been Flirting on Twitter for Over Three Months', news.com.au, 13 December. Available at http://www.news.com.au/entertainment/celebrity/shane-warne-and-liz-hurley-have-been-flirting-on-twitter-for-over-three-months/story-e6frfmqi-1225970191739 [accessed 3 January 2011].

Davie, W. R., King, C. R. and Leonard, D. J. (2010), 'A Media Look at Tiger Woods – Two Views', *Journal of Sports Media*, 5(2): 107–16.

Davies, C. (2003), 'News Ltd v South Sydney District Rugby League Football Club Limited: The High Court Decision', *James Cook University Law Review*, 10: 116–28.

Dawson, B. (2010), 'The NBA Sets Its Eyes on India', *Box Score News – Ottawa*, 20 October. Available at http://boxscorenews.com/the-nba-sets-its-eyes-on-india-p5570-68.htm [accessed 21 January 2011].

Dayan, D. (2008), 'Beyond Media Events: Disenchantment, Derailment, Disruption', in M. E. Price and D. Dayan (eds), *Owning the Olympics: Narratives of the New China*, Ann Arbor, MI: The University of Michigan Press, pp. 391–401.

Dayan, D. and Katz, E. (1992), *Media Events: The Live Broadcasting of History*, Cambridge, MA: Harvard University Press.

De Kloet, J., Chong, G. P. L. and Liu, W. (2008), 'The Beijing Olympics and the Art of Nation-State Maintenance', *China Aktuell*, 2: 5–35.

Delanty, G. (2002), 'Review Essay: Two Conceptions of Cultural Citizenship: A Review of Recent Literature on Culture and Citizenship', *The Global Review of Ethnopolitics*, 1(3): 60–6.

Delanty, G. and Kumar, K. (eds) (2006), *The Sage Handbook of Nations and Nationalism*, London: Sage.

de Moragas Spà, M., Rivenburgh, N. K. and Larson, J. F. (1995), *Television in the Olympics*, London: John Libbey.

Denham, B. and Desormeaux, M. (2008), 'Headlining the Head-Butt: Zinedine Zidane/Marco Materazzi Portrayals in Prominent English, Irish and Scottish Newspapers', *Media, Culture & Society*, 30(3): 375–92.

Dimeo, P. (2007), *A History of Drug Use in Sport 1876–1976. Beyond Good and Evil*, London: Routledge.

Doherty, R. E. (2010), 'Tiny Qatar Brings 2022 World Cup to Middle East', Reuters, 2 December. Available at http://www.reuters.com/article/2010/12/02/us-soccer-world-qatar-idUSTRE6B13V320101202 [accessed 14 March 2011].

Earth Times (2010), 'Taiwan Romances Real Madrid for Spot on Team's Asia Tour', 4 January. Available at http://www.earthtimes.org/articles/news/301959,taiwan-romances-real-madrid-for-spot-on-teams-asia-tour.html# [accessed 17 January 2011].

Eco, U. (1976), *A Theory of Semiotics*, Bloomington, IN: Indiana University Press.

Eco, U. (1986), 'Sports Chatter', in *Travels in Hyperreality* (trans. W. Weaver), New York: Harcourt Brace Jovanovich, 159–66.

Elias, N. and Dunning, E. (1986), *Quest for Excitement: Sport and Leisure in the Civilising Process*, Oxford: Basil Blackwell.

Elser, D. (2011), 'Ten Reasons Shane Warne and Liz Hurley Will Make It (and Ten Reasons They Won't)', News.com.au, 9 February. Available at http://www.news.com.au/entertainment/celebrity/ten-reasons-shane-warne-and-liz-hurley-will-or-wont-make-it-as-a-couple/story-e6frfmqi-1226002911788 [accessed 16 March 2011].

Engineer, T. and N. Gollapudi (2010), 'BCCI Cancels IPL Rights Deal with WSG', ESPN Cricinfo, June 30. Available at http://www.espncricinfo.com/india/content/story/465322.html [accessed 28 February 2011].

Ennis, D., Reuters (2009), 'UEFA Dismisses European Super League Plans', *The Independent*, Football section, 17 March. Available at http://www.independent.co.uk/sport/football/european/uefa-dismiss-european-super-league-plans-1646891.html [accessed 13 January 2011].

Espnstar.com (2010), Available at http://espn.go.com/ [accessed 12 March 2011].

Falcous, M. and Maguire, J. (2006), 'Imagining "America": The NBA and Local–Global Mediascapes', *International Review for the Sociology of Sport*, 41(1): 59–78.

Falcous, M. and Silk, M. (2005), 'Manufacturing Consent: Mediated Sporting Spectacle and the Cultural Politics of the "War on Terror"', *International Journal of Media & Cultural Politics*, 1(1): 59–65.

Farred, G. (2004), 'The Double Temporality of Lagaan: Cultural Struggle and Postcolonialism', *Journal of Sport and Social Issues*, 28: 93–114.

Farred, G. (2006), *Phantom Calls: Race and the Globalization of the NBA*, Chicago, IL: Prickly Paradigm Press.

Farred, G. (2008), *Long Distance Love: A Passion for Football*, Philadelphia, PA: Temple University Press.

Fédération Internationale de Basketball Amateur (FIBA) (2011), Available at http://www.fiba.com/pages/eng/fc/FIBA/quicFact/p/openNodeIDs/962/selNodeID/962/quicFacts.html [accessed 21 January 2011].

Fédération Internationale de Football Association (FIFA) (2004), 'Venglos: "Asia's Footballing Potential Is Boundless"', 15 September. Available at http://www.fifa.com/worldfootball/news/newsid=94178.html [accessed 17 January 2011].

Fédération Internationale de Football Association (2010a), 'FIFA Brand – Our Commitment', Zurich, Switzerland: FIFA. Available at http://www.fifa.com/aboutfifa/federation/mission.html [accessed 19 March 2010].

Fédération Internationale de Football Association (2010b), 'FIFA.com Attracts over a Quarter of a Billion Visits as the World Engages Online with the 2010 FIFA World Cup'. Available at http://www.fifa.com/worldcup/organisation/media/newsid=1273696/index.html#fifa+attracts+over+quarter+billion+visits+world+engages+online+with+2010+cup, 13 July [accessed 25 September 2010].

Fédération Internationale de Football Association (2010c), 'Zidane: A Victory for the Arab World', 2 December. Available at http://www.fifa.com/worldcup/qatar2022/news/newsid=1345137/index.html [accessed 14 March 2011].

Fédération Internationale de Football Association (2010d), '2022 FIFA World Cup Bid Evaluation Report: Qatar'. Available at http://www.fifa.com/mm/document/tournament/competition/01/33/74/56/b9qate.pdf [accessed 14 March 2011].

Fenton, B. and Blitz, R. (2011), 'BSkyB Faces Hit from "Landlady" Football Ruling', *Financial Times*, 3 February. Available at http://www.ft.com/cms/s/0/70111278-2f8d-11e0-834f-00144feabdc0.html#axzz1G59YRKuD [accessed 3 February 2011].

Finley, P., Finley, L. L. and Fountain, J. J. (2008), *Sports Scandals*, Westport, CT: Greenwood.

Fiske, J. (1987), *Television Culture*, London: Methuen.

Fiske, J. (1989), *Understanding Popular Culture*, London: Unwin Hyman.

Football Club United of Manchester (2010), Available at http://www.fc-utd.co.uk/home.php [accessed 3 November 2010].

Football Marketing (2010), 'Football TV Broadcast Revenue in Middle East to Rise 30% to $550m by World Cup 2022', arabianbusiness.com, 9 December. Available at http://www.football-marketing.com/2010/12/09/football-tv-broadcast-revenue-in-middle-east-to-rise-30-to-550m-by-world-cup-2022/# [accessed 14 March 2011].

The Football Supporters' Federation (2010), 'The Fans' Blueprint for the Future of the Beautiful Game'. Available at http://www.fsf.org.uk/fansblueprint.php [accessed 12 March 2011].

Frank, S. and Steets, S. (eds) (2010), *Stadium Worlds: Football, Space and the Built Environment*, London: Routledge.

FreeMyFC (2009), Available at http://freemyfc.com/ [accessed 12 March 2011].

Frith, S. (1978), *The Sociology of Rock*, London: Constable.

Gibson, O. (2010a), 'Panorama: Three Fifa World Cup Voters Accused of Taking Bribes', *The Guardian*, 29 November. Available at http://www.guardian.co.uk/football/2010/nov/29/panorama-fifa-world-cup-bribes [accessed 2 January 2011].

Gibson, O. (2010b), 'Fifa Vice-President Jack Warner Blames British Media for 2018 Defeat', *The Guardian*, 7 December. Available at http://www.guardian.co.uk/football/2010/dec/07/jack-warner-2018-world-cup-fifa [accessed 2 January 2011].

Gibson, O. (2011), 'FIFA and UEFA Lose in EU Court over UK's "Crown Jewels" Legislation', *The Guardian*, 17 February. Available at http://www.guardian.co.uk/football/2011/feb/17/fifa-uefa-television-legislation [accessed 9 March 2011].

Giddens, A. (1981), *A Contemporary Critique of Historical Materialism*, Volume 1, London: Macmillan.

Gilmour, C. and Rowe, D. (2010), 'Sport in Malaysia: National Imperatives and Western Seductions', *Modern Sports in Asia: A Cultural Perspective Workshop*, Asia Research Institute, National University of Singapore, April (unpublished paper).

Giulianotti, R. (1999), *Football: A Sociology of the Global Game*, Cambridge: Polity.

Giulianotti, R. and Robertson, R. (eds) (2007), *Globalization and Sport*, Oxford: Blackwell.

Giulianotti, R. and Robertson, R. (2009), *Globalization and Football*, London: Sage.

Goldlust, J. (1987), *Playing for Keeps: Sport, the Media and Society*, Melbourne: Longman Cheshire.

Gramsci, A. (1971), *Selections from the Prison Notebooks* (trans. Quintin Hoare and Geoffrey Nowell Smith), London: Lawrence and Wishart.

Gratton, C. and Henry, I. P. (eds) (2001), *Sport in the City: The Role of Sport in Economic and Social Regeneration*, London: Routledge.

Gray, J., Sandvoss, C. and Harrington, C. L. (eds) (2007), *Fandom: Identities and Communities in a Mediated World*, New York: NYU Press.

Grundy, P. and Shackelford, S. (2005), *Shattering the Glass: The Remarkable History of Women's Basketball*, New York: The New Press.

Guardian (2011), *Phone Hacking: How the Guardian Broke the Story*. London: Guardian Shorts.

Gupta, A. (2004), 'The Globalisation of Cricket: The Rise of the Non-West', *The International Journal of the History of Sport*, 21(2): 257–76.

Guttmann, A. (1978), *From Ritual to Record: The Nature of Modern Sports*, New York: Columbia University Press.

Guttmann, A. (1984), *The Games Must Go On: Avery Brundage and the Olympic Movement*, New York: Columbia University Press.

Haigh, G. (2010), *Sphere of Influence: Writings on Cricket and Its Discontents*, Melbourne: Victory.

Hall, S. (1987), 'Gramsci and Us', *Marxism Today*, June, pp. 16–21.

Hallinan, C. and Hughson, J. (eds) (2010), *The Containment of Soccer in Australia: Fencing Off the World Game*, London: Routledge.

Harcourt, T. (2010), 'Aussie Rules Goes Global', SmartCompany, 24 September. Available at http://www.smartcompany.com.au/gone-global/20100924-aussie-rules-goes-global.html [accessed 15 November 2010].

Hargreaves, J. (1986), *Sport, Power and Culture: A Social and Historical Analysis of Popular Sports in Britain*, Cambridge: Polity.

Hargreaves, J. (1994), *Sporting Females: Critical Issues in the History and Sociology of Women's Sports*, London: Routledge.

Harindranath, R. (2006), *Perspectives on Global Cultures*, Maidenhead, UK: Open University Press.

Harris, N. (2010), 'Premier League Nets £1.4bn TV Rights Bonanza', *The Independent*, 23 March. Available at http://www.independent.co.uk/sport/football/premier-league/premier-league-nets-16314bn-tv-rights-bonanza-1925462.html [accessed 3 November 2010].

Harvey, D. (1989), *The Condition of Postmodernity: An Inquiry into the Conditions of Cultural Change*, Oxford: Basil Blackwell.

Hassall, G. (2010), 'My View', *The Guide: The Sydney Morning Herald*, 8–14 November, p. 3.

Hawkey, I. (2009), 'Real President Calls for European Super League', *The Sunday Times*, 5 July. Available at http://www.timesonline.co.uk/tol/sport/football/european_football/article6637943.ece [accessed 4 November 2010].

Hay, R. (1994), 'British Football, Wogball or the World Game? Towards a Social History of Victorian Soccer', in J. O'Hara (ed.), *Ethnicity and Soccer in Australia*, Studies in Sports History Number 10, Campbelltown: Australian Society for Sports History, pp. 44–79.

Haynes, R. (1995), *The Football Imagination: The Rise of Football Fanzine Culture*, Aldershot, UK: Arena.

Held, D. (1991), 'Democracy, the Nation-State and the Global system', *Economy and Society*, 20(2): 138–72.

Hermes, J. (2005), *Re-Reading Popular Culture*, Oxford: Blackwell.

Hesmondhalgh, D. (2007), *The Cultural Industries*, second edition, London: Sage.

Hill, C. (1992), *Olympic Politics*, Manchester: Manchester University Press.

Hill, D. (2010), *The Fix: Soccer and Organized Crime*, Toronto, ON: McClelland & Stewart.

Hill, S. (1988), *The Tragedy of Technology: Human Liberation versus Domination in the Late Twentieth Century*, London: Pluto.

Hinch, T. and Higham, J. (2004), *Sport Tourism Development*, Clevedon: Channel View.

Hirst, P. Q. and Thompson, G. (2009), *Globalization in Question: The International Economy and the Possibilities of Governance*, revised second edition, Cambridge: Polity.

Hobsbawm, E. and Ranger. T. (eds) (1983), *The Invention of Tradition*, Cambridge: Cambridge University Press.

Holt, R. (1989), *Sport and the British: A Modern History*, Oxford: Oxford University Press.

Horne, D. (1964), *The Lucky Country: Australia in the Sixties*, Melbourne: Penguin.

Horne, J. (2006), *Sport in Consumer Culture*, Basingstoke, UK: Palgrave Macmillan.

Horne, J. (2007), 'The Four "Knowns" of Sports Mega-Events', *Leisure Studies*, 26(1): 81–9.

Horne, J. (2009), 'Sport in a Credit Crunched Consumer Culture', *Sociological Research Online*, 14 (2/3). Available at: http://www.socresonline.org.uk/14/2/7.html [accessed 23 August 2011].

Horne, J. and Manzenreiter, W. (eds) (2006), *Sports Mega-Events: Social Scientific Analyses of a Global Phenomenon*. Oxford: Blackwell.

Horne, J. and Whannel, G. (2010), 'The "Caged Torch Procession": Celebrities, Protesters and the 2008 Olympic Torch Relay in London, Paris and San Francisco', *Sport in Society*, Special Issue 'Documenting the Beijing Olympics' (edited by D. P. Martinez), 13(5): 760–70.

Horne, J. and Whannel, G. (2011), *Understanding the Olympics*. London and New York: Routledge.

Horsman, M. (1997), *Sky High: The Inside Story of BSkyB*, London: Orion.

Howe, J. (2009), *Crowdsourcing: Why the Power of the Crowd Is Driving the Future of Business*, New York: Crown Business.

Humphreys, A. and Grayson, K. (2008), 'The Intersecting Roles of Consumer and Producer: A Critical Perspective on Co-Production, Co-Creation and Prosumption', *Sociology Compass*, 2: 963–80.

Humphreys, L. and Finlay, C. J. (2008), 'New Technologies, New Narratives', in M. E. Price and D. Dayan (eds), *Owning the Olympics: Narratives of the New China*, Ann Arbor, MI: The University of Michigan Press, pp. 284–306.

Hundley, H. L. and Billings, A. C. (eds) (2010), *Examining Identity in Sports Media*, Thousand Oaks, CA: Sage.

Hutchins, B. (2011), 'The Acceleration of Media Sport Culture: Twitter, Telepresence and Online Messaging', *Information, Communication & Society*, 14(2): 237–57.

Hutchins, B. and Mikosza, J. (2010), 'The Web 2.0 Olympics: Athlete Blogging, Social Networking and Policy Contradictions at the 2008 Beijing Games', *Convergence*, 16(3): 279–97.

Hutchins, B. and Rowe, D. (2009a), 'From Broadcast Rationing to Digital Plenitude: The Changing Dynamics of the Media Sport Content Economy', *Television & New Media*, 10(4), 354–70.

Hutchins, B. and Rowe, D. (2009b), '"A Battle between Enraged Bulls": The 2009 Australian Senate Inquiry into Sports News and Digital Media', Record of the Communications Policy & Research Forum 2009, Sydney: Network Insight Institute, pp. 165–75. Available at http://www.networkinsight.org/verve/_resources/CPRF_2009_papers.pdf [accessed 20 November 2010].

Hutchins, B. and Rowe, D. (2010), 'Reconfiguring Media Sport for the Online World: An Inquiry into "Sports News and Digital Media"', *International Journal of Communication*, 4: 696–718.

Hutchins, B. and Rowe, D. (2012), *Sport Beyond Television: The Internet, Digital Media and the Rise of Networked Media Sport*, New York: Routledge (forthcoming).

Hutchins, B., Rowe, D. and Ruddock, A. (2009), '"It's Fantasy Football Made Real": Networked Media Sport, the Internet, and the Hybrid Reality of MyFootballClub', *Sociology of Sport Journal*, 26(1): 89–106.

Hyde, M. (2008), 'Olympics: London Can Take Heart from These Spectacularly Humourless Games', *The Guardian*, 23 August. Available at http://www.guardian.co.uk/sport/2008/aug/23/olympics20081 [accessed 16 March 2011].

The Independent (2011), 'Super Bowl 2011 Ads Expand into Social Media', 22 January. Available at http://www.independent.co.uk/arts-entertainment/tv/super-bowl-2011-ads-expand-into-social-media-2191378.html# [accessed 11 March 2011].

Indian Express (2011), 'Youths Staking Huge Bets on World Cup, Reveals Survey', 25 February. Available at http://www.indianexpress.com/news/Youths-staking-huge-bets-on-World-Cup--reveals-survey/754676/ [accessed 26 February 2011].

Inglis, D. and Hughson, J. (2003), *Confronting Culture: Sociological Vistas*, Cambridge: Polity.

Inglis, S. (2000), *Sightlines: A Stadium Odyssey*, London: Random House.

Inou, S. and Akinyosoye, C. (2010), 'Six Problems with African Football', *Afrikanet*, 15 October. Available at http://www.afrikanet.info/menu/diaspora/datum/2010/10/15/six-problems-with-african-football/?type=98&cHash=2c06107a6d [accessed 18 January 2011].

International Journal of Cultural Policy (2008), 'Sport and Cultural Policy in the Re-Imaged City', J. Hughson (ed.), 14(4): 355–477.

International Olympic Committee (IOC) (2010), *Olympic Charter*, Lausanne, Switzerland: IOC. Available at http://www.olympic.org/Documents/Olympic%20Charter/Charter_en_2010.pdf [accessed 5 March 2011].

Jackson, J. (2010), 'World Cup 2010: England Are "Paying Price of Foreign Premier League"', *The Guardian*, 8 July. Available at http://www.guardian.co.uk/football/2010/jul/08/jose-luis-astiazaran-la-liga-england [accessed 3 November 2010].

James, C. L. R. (1993), *Beyond a Boundary*, Durham, NC: Duke University Press.

Jamieson, L. M. and Orr, T. J. (2009), *Sport and Violence: A Critical Examination of Sport*, Oxford and Burlington, MA: Butterworth-Heinemann.

Jenkins, H. (2006a), *Convergence Culture: Where Old and New Media Collide*, New York: New York University Press.

Jenkins, H. (2006b), *Fans, Bloggers, and Gamers: Exploring Participatory Culture*, New York: New York University Press.

Jennings, A. (2006), *Foul! The Secret World of FIFA: Bribes, Vote-Rigging and Ticket Scandals*, London: Harper Collins.

Jennings, A. (2010a), *Transparency in Sport*. Available at http://www.transparency insport.org/ [accessed 31 December 2010].

Jennings, A. (2010b), 'Kickbacks & Match-Fixing: An Everyday Story of Olympic Handball'. Available at http://www.transparencyinsport.org/An_everyday_story_ of_Olympic_handball/an_everyday_story_of_olympic_handball.html [accessed 31 December 2010].

Jennings, A. and Sambrook, C. (2000), *The Great Olympic Swindle: When the World Wanted Its Games Back*, London: Simon and Schuster.

Jessop, B. (2000), 'The Crisis of the National Spatio-Temporal Fix and the Tendential Ecological Dominance of Globalizing Capitalism', *International Journal of Urban and Regional Research*, 24(2): 323–60.

Jiwani, Y. (2008), 'Sports as Civilizing Mission: Zinedine Zidane and the Infamous Head-Butt', *Topia: Canadian Journal of Cultural Studies*, 19: 11–33.

Johal, S. (2001), 'Playing Their Own Game: A South Asian Football Experience', in B. Carrington, B. and I. McDonald (eds), *'Race', Sport and British Society*, London and New York: Routledge, 153–69.

Johnson, L., Smith, R., Willis, H., Levine, A. and Haywood, K. (2011), *The Horizon Report 2011*, Austin, TX: The New Media Consortium. Available at http://www.nmc.org/pdf/2011-Horizon-Report.pdf [accessed 6 March 2011].

Josza, F. P., Jr. (2004), *Sports Capitalism: The Foreign Business of American Professional Leagues*, Burlington, VT: Ashgate.

Judd, B. A. (2005), 'Australian Football as Aboriginal Cultural Artefact', *The Canadian Journal of Native Studies*, XXV(1): 215–37.

Kane, M. and Disch, L. (1993), 'Sexual Violence and the Male Reproduction of Power in the Locker Room: A Case Study of the Lisa Olson "Incident"', *Sociology of Sport Journal*, 10(4): 331–52.

Katz, E. and Scannell, P. (eds) (2009), 'The End of Television? Its Impact on the World (So Far)', Special Issue, *The Annals of the American Academy of Political and Social Science Series*, 625(6): 235 pp.

Keane, J. (2003), *Global Civil Society?* Cambridge: Cambridge University Press.

Kenny, C. (2009), 'Revolution in a Box', *Foreign Policy*, November/December. Available at http://www.foreignpolicy.com/articles/2009/10/19/revolution_in_a_ box?page=full [accessed 20 November 2010].

King, A. (1998), *The End of the Terraces: The Transformation of English Football in the 1990s*, Leicester: Leicester University Press.

King, A. (2003), *The European Ritual: Football in the New Europe*, Aldershot, UK: Ashgate.

Klayman, B. (2008), 'Global Sports Market to Hit $141 Billion in 2012', Reuters, 16 June. Available at http://www.reuters.com/article/idUSN1738075220080618 [accessed 12 November 2010].

Klayman, B. (2010), 'NBA Signs Two TV Deals to Air Games in India', Reuters, 2 December. Available at http://www.reuters.com/article/idUSTRE6B14EH20101202 [accessed 21 January 2011].

Kusz, K. W. (2007), *Revolt of the White Athlete: Race, Media and the Emergence of Extreme Athletes in America*, New York: Peter Lang.

La Canna, X. (2011), 'I Have So Much Evidence This Time, Claims St Kilda Photo Scandal Girl', *Herald Sun/AAP*, 16 March. Available at http://www.heraldsun.com.au/news/victoria/i-have-so-much-evidence-this-time-says-st-kilda-photo-scandal-girl/story-e6frf7kx-1226022016598 [accessed 16 March 2011].

Lal, K. (2010), 'IPL Fights for Its Future Amid Scandals, Confusion', *Agence France Presse*, 2 November. Available at http://www.indiaeveryday.in/sports/fullnews-ipl-fights-for-its-future-amid-scandals-confusion-afp-1015-1938895.htm [accessed 2 January 2011].

Larson, J. F. and Park, H. S. (1993), *Global Television and the Politics of the Seoul Olympics*, Boulder, CO: Westview Press.

Laslett, P. (1965), *The World We Have Lost: England Before the Industrial Age*, London: Methuen.

Leonard, D. J. (ed.) (2009a), 'New Media and Global Sporting Cultures', Special Issue, *Sociology of Sport Journal*, 26(1): 183 pp.

Leonard, D. J. (2009b), 'New Media and Global Sporting Cultures: Moving Beyond the Clichés and Binaries', Editorial, Special Issue, *Sociology of Sport Journal*, 26(1): 1–16.

Levermore, R. and Budd, A. (2004), *Sport and International Relations: An Emerging Relationship*, London: Routledge.

Lewis, O. and Khadder, K. (2007), 'Israeli Soccer Club Puts Online Fans in Charge', Reuters, 23 October [accessed 20 December 2010].

López, B. (2010), 'Doping as Technology: A Re-Reading of the History of Performance-Enhancing Substance Use', *Centre for Cultural Research Occasional Paper Series*, 1(4), 1–17.

Lovesey, P. (1979), *The Official Centenary of the AAA*, London: Guinness Superlatives.

Lull, J. and Hinerman, S. (1997), 'The Search for Scandal', in J. Lull and S. Hinerman (eds), *Media Scandals: Morality and Desire in the Popular Culture Marketplace*, Cambridge: Polity and New York: Columbia University Press, pp. 1–33.

Luo, Q. and Richeri, G. (eds) (2010), *The International Journal of the History of Sport*, Special Issue, 'Encoding the Olympics – The Beijing Olympic Games and the Communication Impact Worldwide', 27(9/10).

Macartney, J. and Ford, R. (2008), 'Unmasked: Chinese Guardians of Olympic Torch', *The Times*, 9 April. Available at http://www.timesonline.co.uk/tol/news/world/asia/article3671368.ece [accessed 29 December 2010].

MacKenzie, D. and Wajcman, J. (eds) (1998), *The Social Shaping of Technology*, second edition, Buckingham, UK: Open University Press.

Macur, J. (2007), 'Vick Receives 23 Months and a Lecture', *The New York Times*, 11 December. Available at http://www.nytimes.com/2007/12/11/sports/football/11vick.html [accessed 3 January 2011].

Magee, J. and Sugden, J. (2002), '"The World at Their Feet": Professional Football and International Labour Migration', *Journal of Sport and Social Issues*, 26(4): 421–37.

Maguire, J. (1994), 'Sport, Identity Politics, and Globalization: Diminishing Contrasts and Increasing Varieties', *Sociology of Sport Journal*, 11(4): 398–427.

Maguire, J. (1999), *Global Sport: Identities, Societies, Civilizations*, Cambridge: Polity.

Majumdar, B. (2004), *Twenty-Two Yards to Freedom: A Social History of Indian Cricket*, New Delhi: Penguin-Viking.

Majumdar, B. (2007), 'Nationalist Romance to Postcolonial Sport: Cricket in 2006 India', *Sport in Society*, 10(1): 88–100.

Majumdar, B. (2011), 'Flying Start to IPL 4', *The Financial Express*, 16 January. Available at http://www.financialexpress.com/news/Flying-start-to-IPL-4/737926/ [accessed 28 February 2011].

Malcolm, D., Gemmell, J. and Mehta, N. (eds) (2010), *The Changing Face of Cricket: From Imperial to Global Game*, London: Routledge.

Manheim, J. B. (1990), 'Rites of Passage: The 1988 Seoul Olympics as Public Diplomacy', *Political Research Quarterly*, 43(2): 279–95.

Mann, C. (2011), 'Al Jazeera Sport Nets World Cup Rights', Advanced Television, 26 January. Available at http://www.advanced-television.tv/index.php/2011/01/26/al-jazeera-sport-nets-world-cup-rights/ [accessed 14 March 2011].

Mann, S. Nolan, J. and Wellman, B. (2003), 'Sousveillance: Inventing and Using Wearable Computing Devices for Data Collection in Surveillance Environments', *Surveillance and Society*, 1(3): 331–55.

Manzenreiter, W. (2010), 'The Beijing Games in the Western Imagination of China: The Weak Power of Soft Power', *Journal of Sport and Social Issues*, 34: 29–48.

Markovits, A. S. and Hellerman, S. L. (2001), *Offside: Soccer and American Exceptionalism*, Princeton, NJ: Princeton University Press.

Marqusee, M. (2010), 'IPL's Dark Side of Neoliberal Dream', *The Guardian*, 9 May. Available at http://www.guardian.co.uk/commentisfree/2010/may/09/india-cricket-ipl [accessed 28 February 2011].

Martin, C. R. and Reeves, J. L. (2010), 'The Whole World Isn't Watching (But We Thought They Were): The Super Bowl and U.S. Solipsism', in D. K. Wiggins (ed.), *Sport in America Volume II: From Colonial Leisure to Celebrity Figures and Globalization*, Champaign, IL: Human Kinetics.

Martinez, D. P. (2010), 'Documenting the Beijing Olympics', Special Issue, *Sport in Society*, 13(5): 745–918.

Mason, R. and Moore, M. (2009), 'Setanta Collapse Leaves Millions of Sports Fans in Dark', *Telegraph*, 24 June. Available at http://www.telegraph.co.uk/culture/tvandradio/5614557/Setanta-collapse-leaves-millions-of-sports-fans-in-dark.html [accessed 3 November 2010].

McChesney, R. W. (2008), *The Political Economy of Media: Enduring Issues, Emerging Dilemmas*, New York: Monthly Review Press.

McComb, D. G. (2004), *Sports in World History*, New York: Routledge.

McDonald, M. G. (2010), 'The Whiteness of Sport Media/Scholarship', in H. L. Hundley and A. C. Billings (eds), *Examining Identity in Sports Media*, Thousand Oaks, CA: Sage, pp. 153–72.

McKay, J. (1995), '"Just Do It": Corporate Sports Slogans and the Political Economy of Enlightened Racism', *Discourse: Studies in the Cultural Politics of Education*, 16(2): 191–201.

McKay, J., Lawrence, G., Miller T. and Rowe, D. (2001), 'Gender Equity, Hegemonic Masculinity and the Governmentalisation of Australian Amateur Sport', in T. Bennett and D. Carter (eds), *Culture in Australia: Policies, Publics and Programs*, Melbourne: Cambridge University Press, 232–50.

McQuire, S. (2010), 'Re-Thinking Media Events: Large Screens, Public Space, Broadcasting and Beyond', *New Media & Society*, 12(4): 567–82.

McVeigh, T. (2010), 'Rupert Murdoch's BSkyB Takeover Bid Must Be Challenged – Lord Puttnam', *The Guardian*, 19 September. Available at http://www.guardian.co.uk/media/2010/sep/19/bskyb-takeover-david-puttnam?INTCMP=ILCNETTXT3487 [accessed 9 March 2011].

Means, J. and Nauright, J. (2007), 'Going Global: The NBA Sets Its Sights on Africa', *International Journal of Sports Marketing & Sponsorship*, 9(1): 40–50.

Mehta, N., Gemmell, J. and Malcolm, D. (2009), '"Bombay Sport Exchange": Cricket, Globalization and the Future', *Sport in Society*, 12(4): 694–707.

Merkel, U. (2008), 'The Politics of Sport Diplomacy and Reunification in Divided Korea: One Nation, Two Countries and Three Flags', *International Review for the Sociology of Sport*, 43(3): 289–311.

Messner, M. A. (2002), *Taking the Field: Women, Men, and Sports*, Minneapolis, MN: University of Minnesota Press.

Messner, M. A. (2009), *It's All for the Kids: Gender, Families, and Youth Sports*, Berkeley, CA: University of California Press.

Millar, P. and Sexton, R. (2010), 'Naked Saints Go Viral', *The Age*, 21 December. Available at http://www.theage.com.au/afl/afl-news/naked-saints-go-viral-20101220-1934g.html [accessed 22 December 2010].

Miller, T. (2006), *Cultural Citizenship: Cosmopolitanism, Consumerism, and Television in a Neoliberal Age*, Philadelphia, PA: Temple University Press.

Miller, T. (2010), 'Soccer Conquers the World', *The Chronicle of Higher Education*, 30 May. Available at http://chronicle.com/article/Soccer-Conquers-the-World/65681/ [accessed 6 June 2010].

Miller, T., Lawrence, G., McKay, J. and Rowe, D. (2001), *Globalization and Sport: Playing the World*, London: Sage.

Miller, T., Rowe, D. and Lawrence, G. (2010), 'The New International Division of Cultural Labour and Sport', in J. Maguire and M. Falcous (eds), *Sport and Migration: Borders, Boundaries and Crossings*, London: Routledge, pp. 217–29.

Mills, J. and Dimeo, P. (2003), '"When Gold Is Fired It Shines"; Sport, the Imagination and the Body in Colonial and Postcolonial India', in J. Bale and M. Cronin, M. (eds), *Sport and Postcolonialism*, Oxford, London and New York: Berg, pp. 107–22.

Monroe, M. (2009), 'Veni, Vidi, Vici: How David Stern and the N.B.A. Conquered the World', *American Way*, 15 February. Available at http://www.americanwaymag.com/nba-david-stern-china-yao-ming-parker-jr [accessed 21 January 2011].

Montague, J. and FlorCruz, J. (2010), 'China Crisis: Soccer Rocked by Corruption Scandals', *CNN*, 24 May. Available at http://edition.cnn.com/2010/SPORT/football/05/11/football.china.corruption.scandal/index.html [accessed 17 January 2011].

Musembi, P. (2010), 'East Africa Misses Out on World Cup Fever', 28 May, newZimSituation.com. Available at http://newzimsituation.com/east-africa-misses-out-on-world-cup-fever-47687.htm [accessed 17 January 2011].

MyFootballClub (MFC) (2011), available at http://www.myfootballclub.co.uk/ [accessed 12 March 2011].

Nathan, D. A. (2003), *Saying It's So: A Cultural History of the Black Sox Scandal*, Champaign, IL: University of Illinois Press.

National Basketball Association (NBA) (2010), 'Live, Learn or Play'. Available at http://www.nba.com/nba_cares/mission/live_learn_play.html [accessed 21 January 2011].

New Formations (2007), 'Zidane's Melancholy', Special Issue, 62.

News Corporation (2010a), 'Annual Report 2010'. Available at http://www.newscorp.com/Report2010/AR2010.pdf [accessed 21 November. 2010].

News Corporation (2010b), 'Star Company Information'. Available at http://www.newscorp.com/management/startv.html [accessed 21 November 2010].

Nielsen (2008), 'The Final Tally – 4.7 Billion Tunes in to Beijing 2008 – More than Two in Three People Worldwide'. Available at http://blog.nielsen.com/nielsenwire/wp-content/uploads/2008/09/press_release3.pdf, 5 September [accessed 25 September 2010].

Nielsen, J. (2006), 'Participation Inequality: Encouraging More Users to Contribute', 9 October. Available at http://www.useit.com/alertbox/participation_inequality.html [accessed 12 March 2011].

Nunn, S. and Rosentraub, M. S. (1997), 'Sports Wars: Suburbs and Center Cities in a Zero-Sum Game, *Journal of Sport & Social Issues*, 21(1): 65–82.

Oates, T. and Polumbaum, J. (2004), 'Agile Big Man: The Flexible Marketing of Yao Ming', *Pacific Affairs*, 77(2): 187–210.

Oxfam Australia (2011), 'Nike: So What's the Problem with Nike?' Available at http://www.oxfam.org.au/explore/workers-rights/nike# [accessed 3 January 2011].

Parisotto, R. (2004), *Blood Sports: The Inside Dope on Drugs in Sport*, South Yarra, Melbourne: Hardie Grant.

Parliament of Australia Senate Standing Committee (2009), *The Reporting of Sports News and the Emergence of Digital Media*, The Senate Standing Committee on Environment, Communications and the Arts, Commonwealth of Australia, May. Available at http://www.aph.gov.au/SEnate/committee/eca_ctte/sports_news/report/index.htm [accessed 9 December 2010].

Penberthy, D. (2011), 'Dopey Old Men and a Deeply Troubled Schoolgirl', *The Punch*, 12 June. Available at http://www.thepunch.com.au/tags/st-kilda-schoolgirl/ [accessed 12 June 2011].

Pfister, G. and Hartmann-Tews, I. (2003), *Sport and Women: Social Issues in International Perspective*, London: Routledge.

Phillips, M. G. (2001), 'Diminishing Contrasts and Increasing Varieties: Globalisation Theory and "Reading" Amateurism in Australian Sport', *Sporting Traditions*, 18(1): 19–32.

Play the Game (2010a), Available at http://www.playthegame.org/home.html [accessed 31 December 2010].

Play the Game (2010b), 'Our Goals'. Available at http://www.playthegame.org/about-play-the-game/our-goals.html [accessed 31 December 2010].

Poli, R. (2010), 'Understanding Globalization through Football: The New International Division of Labour, Migratory Channels and Transnational Trade Circuits', *International Review for the Sociology of Sport*, 45(4): 491–506.

Poulton, E. (2004), 'Mediated Patriot Games: The Construction and Representation of National Identities in the British Television Production of Euro 96', *International Review for the Sociology of Sport*, 39(4): 437–55.

Price, M. E. (2008), 'On Seizing the Olympic Platform', in M. E. Price and D. Dayan (eds), *Owning the Olympics: Narratives of the New China*, Ann Arbor, MI: The University of Michigan Press, pp. 86–114.

Rader, B. J. (1984), *In Its Own Image: How Television Has Transformed Sports*, New York: Free Press.

Raney, A. A. (2006), 'Why We Watch and Enjoy Mediated Sports', in A. A. Raney and J. Bryant (eds), *Handbook of Sports and Media*, Mahwah, NJ: Lawrence Erlbaum, 313–29.

Raney, A. A. and Bryant, J. (eds) (2006), *Handbook of Sports and Media*, Mahwah, NJ: Lawrence Erlbaum.

Real, M. (2006), 'Sports Online: The Newest Player in Mediasport', in A. A. Raney and J. Bryant (eds), *Handbook of Sports and Media*, Mahwah, NJ: Lawrence Erlbaum, 171–84.

Reuters (2010), 'World Cup Finale Draws 700 Million Viewers'. Available at http://www.reuters.com/article/idUSTRE66C0ZV20100713, 13 July [accessed 25 September 2010].

Richardson, B. (2004), 'New Consumers and Football Fandom: The Role of Social Habitus in Consumer Behaviour', *Irish Journal of Management*, 25(1): 88–101.

Rinehart, R. E. and Sydnor, S. S. (eds) (2003), *To the Extreme: Alternative Sports, Inside and Out*, Albany, NY: State University of New York Press.

Ritzer, G. (2004), *The Globalization of Nothing*, Thousand Oaks, CA: Pine Forge Press.

Ritzer, G. (2006), 'Globalization and McDonaldization: Does It All Amount to ... Nothing?', in G. Ritzer (ed.), *McDonaldization: The Reader*, second edition, Thousand Oaks, CA: Pine Forge Press, 335–48.

Ritzer, G. and Jurgenson, N. (2010), 'Production, Consumption, Prosumption: The Nature of Capitalism in the Age of the Digital "Prosumer"', *Journal of Consumer Culture*, 10(1): 13–36.

Robertson, R. (1995), 'Glocalization: Time-Space and Homogeneity-Heterogeneity', in M. Featherstone, S. Lash and R. Robertson (eds), *Global Modernities*, London: Sage, pp. 25–44.

Robinson, D. C., Buck, E. B. and Cuthbert, M. (1991), *Music at the Margins: Popular Music and Global Cultural Diversity*, Newbury Park, CA: Sage.

Robinson, J. (2010), 'News Corp Notifies Brussels of BSkyB Takeover Bid', *The Guardian*, 3 November. Available at http://www.guardian.co.uk/media/2010/nov/03/news-corp-bskyb-takeover-europe [accessed 21 November 2010].

Robinson, V. (2008), *Everyday Masculinities and Extreme Sport: Male Identity and Rock Climbing*, Oxford: Berg.

Roche, M. (2000), *Mega-Events and Modernity: Olympics and Expos in the Growth of Global Culture*, London and New York: Routledge.

Rojek, C. (2010), *The Labour of Leisure: The Culture of Free Time*, London: Sage.

Rosentraub, M. S. (1999), *Major League Losers: The Real Cost of Sports and Who's Paying for It*, New York: Basic.

Rowe, D. (1995), *Popular Cultures: Rock Music, Sport and the Politics of Pleasure*, London: Sage.

Rowe, D. (1998), 'If You Film It, Will They Come? Sports on Film', *Journal of Sport & Social Issues*, 22(4): 350–9.

Rowe, D. (2001), 'Globalisation, Regionalisation and Australianisation in Music: Lessons from the Parallel Importing Debate', in T. Bennett and D. Carter (eds), *Culture in Australia: Policies, Publics and Programs*, Melbourne: Cambridge University Press, pp. 46–65.

Rowe, D. (2003), 'Sport and the Repudiation of the Global', *International Review for the Sociology of Sport*, 38(3): 281–94.

Rowe, D. (2004a), *Sport, Culture and the Media: The Unruly Trinity*, second edition, Maidenhead, UK: Open University Press.

Rowe, D. (2004b), 'Antonio Gramsci: Sport, Hegemony and the National-Popular', in R. Giulianotti (ed.), *Sport and Modern Social Theorists*, Basingstoke, UK: Macmillan, pp. 97–110.

Rowe, D. (2006), 'Watching Brief: Cultural Citizenship and Viewing Rights', in D. McArdle and R. Giulianotti (eds), *Sport, Civil Liberties and Human Rights*, London and New York: Routledge, pp. 93–110.

Rowe, D. (2007a), 'Sports Journalism: Still the "Toy Department" of the News Media?', *Journalism: Theory, Practice & Criticism*, 8(4): 385–405.

Rowe, D. (2007b), 'The Stuff of Dreams, or the Dream Stuffed? Rugby League, Media Empires, Sex Scandals, and Global Plays', *8th Annual Tom Brock Annual Lecture*. Sydney: Australian Society for Sports History. Available at http://www.la84foundation.org/SportsLibrary/TomBrock/TomBrockLecture8.pdf [accessed 8 March 2011].

Rowe, D. (2010a), 'Stages of the Global: Media, Sport, Racialization and the Last Temptation of Zinedine Zidane', *International Review for the Sociology of Sport*, 45(3): 355–71.

Rowe, D. (2010b), 'Attention La Femme! Intimate Relationships and Male Sports Performance', in L. K. Fuller (ed.), *Sexual Sports Rhetoric: Global and Universal Contexts*, New York: Peter Lang, 69–81.

Rowe, D. (2011a), 'Sports Media: Beyond Broadcasting, Beyond Sports, Beyond Societies?', in A. Billings (ed.), *Sports Media: Transformation, Integration, Consumption*, New York: Routledge, pp. 94–113.

Rowe, D. (2011b), 'Sport and Its Audiences', in V. Nightingale (ed.), *Handbook of Media Audiences*, Oxford: Blackwell, pp. 509–26.

Rowe, D. (2011c), 'The Televised Sport "Monkey" Trial: "Race" and the Politics of Postcolonial Cricket', *Sport in Society*, 14(6): 786–98.

Rowe, D. (2012), 'Image Projection and Gaze Reception: Mediating East Asia through the Summer Olympics', *International Journal of the History of Sport* (forthcoming).

Rowe, D. and Baker, S. A. (2011), 'Truly a Fan Experience'? The Cultural Politics of the Live Site', in R. Krøvel and T. Roksvold (eds), *Mediated Football Fan Culture*, Gothenburg, Sweden: Nordicom (forthcoming).

Rowe, D. and Gilmour, C. (2008), 'Contemporary Media Sport: De- or Re-Westernization?', *International Journal of Sport Communication*, 1(2): 177–94.

Rowe, D. and Gilmour, C. (2009), 'Global Sport: Where Wembley Way Meets Bollywood Boulevard', in A. Moran and M. Keane (eds), *Cultural Adaptation*, London: Routledge, pp. 171–82.

Rowe, D. and McKay, J. (2012), 'Torchlight Temptations: Hosting the Olympics and the Global Gaze', in J. Sugden and A. Tomlinson (eds), *Watching the Games: Politics, Power and Representation in the London Olympiad*, London: Routledge, pp. 122–37.

Rowe, D. and Stevenson, D. (2006), 'Sydney 2000: Sociality and Spatiality in Global Media Events', in A. Tomlinson and C. Young (eds), *National Identity and Global Sports Events: Culture, Politics, and Spectacle in the Olympics and the Football World Cup*, New York: State University of New York Press, pp. 197–214.

Rowe, D., Gilmour, C. and Petzold, T. (2010), 'Australia: Mediated Representation of Global Politics', *The International Journal of the History of Sport*, 27(9/10): 1510–33.

Rowe, D., Ruddock, A. and Hutchins, B. (2010), 'Cultures of Complaint: Online Fan Message Boards and Networked Digital Media Sport Communities', *Convergence: The International Journal of Research into New Media Technologies*, Special Issue on 'Sport in New Media Cultures', 16(3): 298–315.

Ruddock, A., Hutchins, B. and Rowe, D. (2010), 'Contradictions in Media Sport Culture: "MyFootballClub" and the Reinscription of Football Supporter Traditions through Online Media', *European Journal of Cultural Studies*, 13(3): 323–39.

Rugby League Four Nations (2010), *International Broadcast Information*, 12 October. Available at http://www.rlfournations.com/default.aspx?s=article-display&id=31187 [accessed 15 November 2010].

Rumford, C. (2007), 'More than a Game: Globalization and the Post-Westernization of World Cricket', *Global Networks*, 7(2): 202–14.

Ryan, B. (1992), *Making Capital from Culture: The Corporate Form of Capitalist Cultural Production*, Berlin and New York: Walter de Gruyter.

Samuel, E. (2009), 'More Like Super Flop: MSL in Such a Pathetic State It Badly Needs a Revamp', August 23, *The Sunday Star*, S53.

Sandiford, K. (1994), *Cricket and the Victorians*, Aldershot, UK: Scholar.

Sandvoss, C. (2003), *A Game of Two Halves: Football, Television, and Globalisation*, London: Routledge.

Sandvoss, C. (2005), *Fans: The Mirror of Consumption*, Cambridge: Polity.

Saporito, B. (2010), 'Yes, Soccer Is America's Game', *Time*, 3 June. Available at http://www.stumbleupon.com/su/337PB3/www.time.com/time/specials/packages/article/0,28804,1991933_1991952_1993757,00.html [accessed 6 June 2010].

Savage, M., Bagnall, G. and Longhurst, B. J. (2004), *Globalization and Belonging*, London: Sage.

Scambler, G. (2005), *Sport and Society: History, Power and Culture*, Maidenhead, UK: Open University Press.

Schechner, S. (2011), 'Super Bowl Draws Record Audience', *The Wall Street Journal*, 8 February. Available at http://online.wsj.com/article/SB10001424052748703507804576130502068719070.html [accessed 9 February 2011].

Schechner, S. and Ovide, S. (2010), 'Record Draw for Super Bowl: An Audience of 106.5 Million Bucks Trend of Declining Viewership for Networks', *The Wall Street Journal: Media and Marketing*, 7 February. Available at http://online.wsj.com/article/SB10001424052748703615904575053300315837616.html [accessed 6 December 2010].

Schell, M. J. (1999), *Baseball's All-Time Best Hitters: How Statistics Can Level the Playing Field*, Princeton, NJ: Princeton University Press.

Scherer, J. and Rowe, D. (eds) (2012), *Sport, Public Broadcasting, and Cultural Citizenship: Signal Lost?* New York: Routledge (forthcoming).

Scherer, J. and Whitson, D. (2009), 'Public Broadcasting, Sport, and Cultural Citizenship: The Future of Sport on the Canadian Broadcasting Corporation?', *International Review for the Sociology of Sport*, 44(2–3): 213–29.

Schneider, M. (2010a), '"Long-Term" Is Key for South African World Cup Investment', *Play the Game*. Available at http://www.playthegame.org/news/detailed/long-term-is-key-for-south-african-world-cup-investment-5031.html [accessed 24 December 2010].

Schneider, M. (2010b), 'World Cup Stadia: White Elephants or Golden Opportunities?' *Play the Game*. Available at http://www.playthegame.org/news/detailed/world-cup-stadia-white-elephants-or-golden-opportunities-4971.html [accessed 24 December 2010].

Schultz-Jorgensen, S. (2005), 'The World's Best Advertising Agency: The Sports Press', International Sports Press Survey 2005, Copenhagen: House of Monday Morning: Play the Game. Available at http://www.playthegame.org/upload/sport_press_survey_english.pdf [accessed 1 January 2011].

Scraton, S. and Flintoff, A. (eds) (2002), *Gender and Sport: A Reader*, London and New York: Routledge.

Seidman, R. (2011a), 'Super Bowl XLV on FOX Is Most-Watched Program in TV History', *Network TV Press Releases, TV Sports Ratings & News*, 7 February. Available at http://tvbythenumbers.zap2it.com/2011/02/07/super-bowl-xlv-on-fox-is-most-watched-program-in-tv-history/81751 [accessed 9 February 2011].

Seidman, R. (2011b), 'Super Bowl XLV Most-Watched Show in U.S. TV History Among Hispanic Viewers; Tops World Cup Final', *Network TV Press Releases, TV Sports Ratings & News*, 8 February. Available at http://tvbythenumbers.zap2it.com/2011/02/08/super-bowl-xlv-most-watched-show-in-u-s-tv-history-among-hispanic-viewers-tops-world-cup-final/81887 [accessed 9 February 2011].

Silkstone, D. (2010), 'Scandal Playing Out Far from the Realm of Sport', *The Age*, 22 December. Available at http://www.theage.com.au/afl/afl-news/scandal-playing-out-far-from-the-realm-of-sport-20101221-194eq.htmlb [accessed 22 December 2010].

Silverstone, R. (1994), *Television and Everyday Life*, New York: Routledge.

Simson, V. and Jennings, A. (1992), *The Lords of the Rings: Power, Money and Drugs in the Modern Olympics*, London: Simon and Schuster.

Singh, N. (2010), 'NBA Initiative Making Little Headway', *Hindustan Times*, 31 December 31. Available at http://www.hindustantimes.com/NBA-initiative-making-little-headway/Article1-644773.aspx# [accessed 21 January 2011].

Slater, M. (2007), 'English Football Under Threat', BBC Sport Football. Available at http://news.bbc.co.uk/sport2/hi/football/6975955.stm [accessed 13 January 2011].

Smart, B. (2005), *The Sport Star: Modern Sport and the Cultural Economy of Sporting Celebrity*, London: Sage.

Smith, B. (2008), 'Journalism and the Beijing Olympics: Liminality with Chinese Characteristics', in M. E. Price and D. Dayan (eds), *Owning the Olympics: Narratives of the New China*, Ann Arbor, MI: The University of Michigan Press, pp. 210–26.

Smith, D. (2010), 'World Cup Kicks Violent South African Crime into Touch', 9 July. *The Guardian*, Available at http://www.guardian.co.uk/football/2010/jul/09/world-cup-football-south-africa-crime-falls [accessed 24 December 2010].

Sociological Inquiry (2010), 'Toward a Sociology of Inequality in the Digital Century', Special Section, 80(1): 28–125.

Sparre, K. (2007), 'Prevention Programme Proposed to Stop Football Trafficking', *Play the Game*, 28 June. Available at http://www.playthegame.org/news/detailed/prevention-programme-proposed-to-stop-football-trafficking-1417.html [accessed 24 December 2010].

Spigel, L. and Olsson, J. (eds) (2004), *Television after TV: Essays on a Medium in Transition*, Durham, NC: Duke University Press.

Sport et Citoyenneté (Sport and Citizenship) (2010), Available at http://www.sportetcitoyennete.org/version3/page_anglais.php [accessed 1 January 2011].

Stevenson, N. (2003), *Cultural Citizenship: Cosmopolitan Questions*, Maidenhead, UK: Open University Press.

Stiglitz, J. (2007), *Making Globalization Work*, London: Penguin.

Stoddart, B. (1986), *Saturday Afternoon Fever: Sport in the Australian Culture*, North Ryde, NSW: Angus and Robertson.

Street, J. (2005), 'Showbusiness of a Serious Kind: The Cultural Politics of the Arts Prize', *Media, Culture and Society*, 27(6): 819–40.

Sugden, J. (2010), 'Critical Left-Realism and Sport Interventions in Divided Societies', *International Review for the Sociology of Sport*, 45(3): 258–72.

Sugden, J. and Tomlinson, A. (1998), *FIFA and the Contest for World Football: Who Rules the People's Game?* Cambridge: Polity.

Sugden, J. and Tomlinson, A. (1999a), *Great Balls of Fire: How Big Money Is Hijacking World Football*, Edinburgh: Mainstream.

Sugden, J. and Tomlinson, A. (1999b), 'Digging the Dirt and Staying Clean – Retrieving the Investigative Tradition for a Critical Sociology of Sport', *International Review for the Sociology of Sport*, 34(4): 385–97.

Sugden, J. and Tomlinson, A. (2003), *Badfellas: FIFA Family at War*, Edinburgh: Mainstream.

Supporters Direct (2010), 'Mission and History'. Available at http://www.supporters-direct.org/page.asp?p=3977 [accessed 20 December 2010].

Surowiecki, J. (2005), *The Wisdom of Crowds*, New York: Anchor.

Swanson, L. (2009), 'Complicating the "Soccer Mom": The Cultural Politics of Forming Class-Based Identity, Distinction, and Necessity', *Research Quarterly for Exercise and Sport*, 80(2): 345–54.

Sweney, M. (2011a), 'Jeremy Hunt Gives News Corp Green Light to Launch £8bn Bid for BSkyB', *The Guardian*, 3 March. Available at http://www.guardian.co.uk/media/2011/mar/03/hunt-bskyb-merger-murdoch?intcmp=239 [accessed 8 March 2011].

Sweney, M. (2011b), 'Super Bowl 2011 Draws Highest Ever Audience for US TV Show: Climax of American Football Season', *The Guardian*, 8 February. Available at http://www.guardian.co.uk/media/2011/feb/08/super-bowl-highest-ever-audience [accessed 11 March 2011].

Tagsold, C. (2009), 'The 1964 Tokyo Olympics as Political Games', *The Asia-Pacific Journal*, 23(3). Available at http://www.japanfocus.org/-Christian-Tagsold/3165 [accessed 15 June 2010].

Tay, J. and Turner, G. (2010), 'Not the Apocalypse: Television Futures in the Digital Age', *International Journal of Digital Television*, 1(1): 31–50.

Taylor, M. (2008), *The Association Game: A History of British Football*, Harlow: Pearson Education.

Thompson, J. B. (1995), *The Media and Modernity: A Social Theory of the Media*, Cambridge: Polity.

Thompson, J. B. (1997), 'Scandal and Social Theory', in J. Lull and S. Hinerman (eds), *Media Scandals: Morality and Desire in the Popular Culture Marketplace*, New York: Columbia University Press, pp. 34–64.

Thompson, J. B. (2000), *Political Scandal: Power and Visibility in the Media Age*, Cambridge: Polity.

Tierney, D. (2010), '"Say It Ain't So": The Historic Scandal Rocking World Cricket', *The Atlantic*, 31 August. Available at http://www.theatlantic.com/international/archive/2010/08/say-it-aint-so-the-historic-scandal-rocking-world-cricket/62301/# [accessed 3 January 2011].

Tomlinson, A. (1999), *The Game's Up: Essays in the Cultural Analysis of Sport, Leisure and Popular Culture*, Aldershot, UK: Ashgate.

Tomlinson, A. (2005), *Sport and Leisure Cultures*, Minneapolis, MN: University of Minnesota Press.

Tomlinson, J. (1999), *Globalization and Culture*, Cambridge: Polity.

Treagus, M. (2005), 'Playing Like Ladies: Basketball, Netball and Feminine Restraint', *The International Journal of the History of Sport*, 22(1): 88–105.

Turner, B. S. and Khonder, H. H. (2010), *Globalization East and West*, London: Sage.

Turner, G. and Tay, J. (eds) (2009), *Television Studies after TV: Understanding Television in the Post Broadcast Era*, London and New York: Routledge.

Union des Associations Européennes de Football (UEFA) (2010), 'The European Club Footballing Landscape: Club Licensing Benchmarking Report Financial Year 2008'. Available at http://www.uefa.com/MultimediaFiles/Download/Publications/uefaorg/Publications/01/45/30/45/1453045_DOWNLOAD.pdf [accessed 15 January 2010].

Urry, J. (2000), *Sociology Beyond Societies: Mobilities for the Twenty First Century*, New York: Routledge.

Urry, J. (2003), *Global Complexity*, Cambridge: Polity.

Urry, J. (2007), *Mobilities*, Oxford: Blackwell.

Vertinsky, P. and Bale, J. (eds) (2004), *Sites of Sport: Space, Place, Experience*, London and New York: Routledge.

Veseth, M. (2005), *Globaloney: Unravelling the Myths of Globalization*, Lanham, MD: Rowman and Littlefield.

Walters, C. (2010), 'Tune in to the Future', *The Guide: The Sydney Morning Herald*, November 8–14, pp. 4–5.

Wang, S. (2009), 'Taiwanese Baseball: A Story of Entangled Colonialism, Class, Ethnicity, and Nationalism', *Journal of Sport and Social Issues*, 33(4): 355–72.

Waters, M. (2001), *Globalization*, second edition, London: Routledge.

Weber, M. (2003[1905]), *The Protestant Ethic and the Spirit of Capitalism*, New York: Dover.

Weber, S. (1996), 'Television: Set and Screen', in A. Cholodenko (ed.), *Mass Mediauras: Form, Technics, Media*, Sydney: Power Publications, pp. 108–28.

Weed, M. and Bull, C. (2004), *Sports Tourism: Participants, Policy and Providers*, Oxford: Elsevier.

Wenner, L. A. (ed.) (1989), *Media, Sports, and Society*, Newbury Park, CA: Sage.

Wenner, L. A. (ed.) (1998), *MediaSport*, London: Routledge.

Whannel, G. (1992), *Fields in Vision: Television Sport and Cultural Transformation*, London: Routledge.

Whannel, G. (2001), *Media Sport Stars: Masculinities and Moralities*, London: Routledge.

Whannel, G. (2008), *Culture, Politics and Sport: Blowing the Whistle, Revisited*, London: Routledge.

Wheaton, B. (ed.) (2004), *Understanding Lifestyle Sports: Consumption, Identity and Difference*, London: Routledge.

White, J. (2010a), 'Wayne Rooney Deal: Manchester Madness, Mobs and the Jose Mourinho Mystery', *The Telegraph*, 22 October. Available at http://www.telegraph.co.uk/sport/football/teams/manchester-united/8082098/Wayne-Rooney-deal-Manchester-madness-mobs-and-the-Jose-Mourinho-mystery.html [accessed 24 October 2010].

White, J. (2010b), 'Homophobic Twitter Rant Costs Tearful Australian Olympic Swimmer Lucrative Sponsorship Contract', *The Daily Mail*, 8 September. Available at http://www.dailymail.co.uk/news/worldnews/article-1310063/Australian-swimmer-Stephanie-Rice-apologises-homophobic-Twitter-slur.html [accessed 3 January 2011].

Whitson, D. (1998), 'Circuits of Promotion: Media, Marketing and the Globalization of Sport', in L. Wenner (ed.), *MediaSport*, London: Routledge, pp. 57–72.

Williams, J. (2003), ' "Paki Cheats!" Postcolonial Tensions in England–Pakistan Cricket', in J. Bale and M. Cronin (ed.), *Sport and Postcolonialism*, Oxford, London and New York: Berg, pp. 91–105.

Williams, N. (2009), 'Priority on Global Outreach Expands NBA's appeal', *The Tampa Tribune*, June 10. Available at http://www2.tbo.com/content/2009/jun/10/priority-global-outreach-expands-nbas-appeal/sports/ [accessed 21 January 2011].

Williams, R. (1974), *Television: Technology and Cultural Form*, London: Fontana.

Williams, R. (1977), *Marxism and Literature*, Oxford: Oxford University Press.

Wilson, A. (2011), 'James Anderson and Seven Other England Ashes Heroes Ignored by IPL', *The Guardian*, 9 January. Available at http://www.guardian.co.uk/sport/2011/jan/09/james-anderson-ipl-england-ashes [accessed 28 February 2011].

Wilson, B. (2011), 'World Cup Games to Remain on Free-to-Air in the UK', BBC, 17 February. Available at http://www.bbc.co.uk/news/business-12482371 [accessed 9 March 2011].

Wilson, C. (2010), 'Fake Fans in Footy's Deadest Game', *The Age*. 29 May. Available at http://www.theage.com.au/afl/afl-news/fake-fans-in-footys-deadest-game-20100528-wllh.html [accessed 30 May 2010].

Wilson, J. (2011), 'Michel Platini Insists He Is Prepared to Ban Clubs from Champions League If They Do Not Comply with Regulations', *The Telegraph*, 11 January. Available at http://www.telegraph.co.uk/sport/football/european/8253566/Michel-Platini-insists-he-is-prepared-to-ban-clubs-from-Champions-League-if-they-do-not-comply-with-regulations.html [accessed 14 January 2011].

Wiseman, J. (1998), *Global Nation? Australia and the Politics of Globalisation*, Melbourne: Cambridge University Press.

Wouters, C. (1990), 'Social Stratification and Informalization in Global Perspective', *Theory, Culture & Society*, 7(4): 69–90.

Xu, G. (2008), *Olympic Dreams: China and Sports, 1895–2008*, Cambridge, MA: Harvard University Press.

Index